What a timely book! Being that the issue of spirituality is discussed and debated so often, Stephen Beck addresses this significant issue in a scholarly, theologically, and practical manner. In a day when spirituality goes in so many directions and according to personal preferences, this book takes us to the right foundation – the person of Jesus Christ. Stephen Beck clearly declares that Christian spirituality is about the person of Christ, and roots every aspect of spirituality into the soil of Christ. I like that. For this reason alone, I recommend this book.

Dr. Cecil Stalnaker
Chair and Professor of Intercultural Studies and Practical Ministries,
Tyndale Theological Seminary
JM Badhoevedorp, The Netherlands

This book is not sugar coated, yet another self-help handbook, but a direct appeal to the reader to explore spirituality that is not first of all self-improvement and self-actualization mantra, but one that requires the personal sacrifice of loving God and loving one's neighbor.

Dr. Kosta Milkov
President of the Balkan Institute for Faith and Culture
Skopje, Republic of Macedonia

In this book Dr. Beck addresses the question of the spiritual life from the vantage point of a theologian and a church planting practitioner. The result is a solid balance between in-depth thinking and down-to-the earth application, both being illustrated through inspiring story-telling. It is fascinating to me how Stephen shows God-centeredness to be the very fulfillment of every Me-centred longing. A very fine work indeed!

Raphael Anzenberger
General Secretary, France Evangelisation
Drulingen, France

Stephen Beck

Smart Builder

A God-centred Spirituality
in a Me-centred World

Stephen Beck

Smart Builder: A God-centred Spirituality in a Me-centred World

© 2011 pulsmedien GmbH, Worms, Germany

ISBN: 978-3-939577-06-5

Order-Number: 652.806

Scripture Quotations

Unless otherwise stated, Scripture quotations in this publication are from THE HOLY
BIBLE: THE NEW INTERNATIONAL VERSION® (NIV®), Copyright © 1973, 1978, 1984
by International Bible Society, www.ibs.org, all rights reserved worldwide.
Other quotations are from The New American Standard Bible (NAS), Copyright
1977 and 1995 by La Biblia de Las Americas; The New King James Version (NKJ),
Copyright © 1982, Thomas Nelson, Inc, all rights reserved; Holy Bible: New Living
Translation, second edition, Copyright © 2004 by Tyndale House Publishers, Inc,
all rights reserved; Today's New International Version (TNIV).
All Bible translations are used by permission.

Cover design: Patrick Mahoney

www.pulsmedien.de

To my students,
with whom I am learning the meaning and freedom
of a gospel-driven spirituality

Table of Contents

Forewords   11

Preface   19

SECTION 1

Maria's Journey #1:   30
An ordinary story with an extraordinary twist

   01   Foundation   39
   Getting the foundation right for your spiritual life

Maria's Journey #2:   48
Discovering God in an atheism course

   02   Building Material   59
   Finding the right mix in your foundation's cement

Maria's Journey #3:   82
Meeting with God in an Easter service

SECTION 2

   03   1st Cornerstone   89
   Building your life around the Sovereignty of God
   (I want to trust the most powerful good there is)

   04   2nd Cornerstone   99
   Fashioning yourself according to the Holiness of God
   (I want to become the most beautiful person there is)

   05   3rd Cornerstone   109
   Bathing yourself in the Love of God
   (I want to love the loveliest thing there is)

   06   4th Cornerstone   131
   Finding pleasure in the Pleasures of God
   (I want to be thrilled by the greatest enjoyment there is)

Maria's Journey #4   145
Discovering the costliness of unconditional love

SECTION 3

07   Floor   153
Running your life according to the Word of God
(Learning spirituality by the Book)

08   1st Wall   175
Connecting in 'No-Man's-Land' with the Heart of God
(Learning a spirituality of communion)

09   2nd Wall   195
Growing through others into Maturity in God
(Learning a spirituality of community)

10   3rd Wall   217
Deciding to live in the Will of God
(Learning a spirituality of obedience)

11   4th Wall   233
Carrying your cross through the Harshness of God
(Learning a spirituality of suffering)

SECTION 4

12   Ceiling   257
Doing the mission of the Smart Builder God
(the practice of a public spirituality)

13   Roof   289
Living your utmost for the Glory of God
(the fulfilment of a God-centred Me)

Maria's Journey #5   303
An extraordinary life in an ordinary world

Literature   313

Acknowledgements & Gratitude   315

Forewords

1   The author dedicated this book to his students. I am one of those students from all over the world. I had the privilege of reading and hearing the material of this book before it was published and I absolutely loved it. It expresses and illustrates so well many of the truths I have experienced in my own life. So how have I been impacted by the truths you are about to read?

Before beginning my theological education in Germany, I had been studying natural sciences in Zurich. It was a tough course stretching me beyond my limits in various ways. Failing several exams I quit the course after two-and-a-half years. That was devastating to me: I had been thought of as an intelligent man, but now was quietly thinking of myself as an intellectual failure. The whole experience uncovered layers of pride in my heart that I had not known existed there. I realized – as Stephen Beck has defined the Christian gospel to us over and over again – that "in and of myself I am more sinful than I ever dared to believe". For instance, I was avoiding people, so they wouldn't find out about my poor academic performance. What I was really doing, was clutching to an idol and holding it dear to my heart, namely the idol of preserving my image!

What set me free from all that image-stuff, with its carefully guarded secrets, inner conflicts, selfish motives, guilt, and the fear of being found out, was letting go of the image-idol and embracing my gospel-identity: that "in Christ I am more loved than I ever dared to hope." This is an identity based not on my academic or any other performance, but on Jesus' "performance" for me. Basing my identity on Jesus' righteousness and not my own, freed me from the pressure to conform to people's expectations of me.

Once I started into ministry, I realized that I was daily facing a big challenge: will I offer my self-image to the idols that promise me reputation, security or sweet comforts, or will I trust the gospel of Jesus? I was leading a cell group in my church and was constantly aware of the weighty spiritual responsibility of that task. I often struggled with my shortcomings. I would accuse myself of not taking enough time for people, of not praying for them like I should. The temptation was to "do ministry" out of a sense of duty, to simply ease my conscience, to tell myself that I am good enough for approval, whether it be from me, from others or from God. A gospel-driven spirituality allowed me to be honest with myself, to say to myself, "yes, Thony, you are falling short, but why be surprised: you are more sinful than you ever dared to believe", but then turn around and say, "yes, Thony, even as an average guy with many shortcomings and sins, you are in Christ more loved than you ever dared to hope." Putting my identity not in my accomplishments but in Jesus' settled opinion of and love for me, gave me the freedom to succeed without getting proud and the freedom to fail without condemning myself.

I soon realized that a gospel-driven spirituality was exactly what the people in my cell group needed, too! In fact, I started to wish this wonderful, inner liberation on everybody in the world. After quitting my course in Zurich, I decided to go to a different university. But this alternate plan didn't work out because the university I applied to had misinformed me about application procedures! I can still remember the shock I felt, the fear of having no viable plan left for my immediate future. In that moment, the Spirit of God turned me from clutching on to those promise-breaking idols in my soul and to trusting instead in God's promises to me in the gospel. A deep sense of God's sovereignty started to fill my heart. It comforted me, gave me peace, made me cheerful. When God pointed me to the seminary in Germany and the door for studying there opened to me, I could begin to see how my academic failure in Switzerland, and the bungling of my application to another university were all part of God's plan for my life.

It's not just experiences like these that have made this book resonate with me. It's the passion for God, His gospel, His church, and His mission which permeates this book, that have begun to permeate my life. I hope these passions grip your heart and shape your life, as you read, reflect, and apply these pages to your life. I tell you, it is a very liberating experience!

– *Anthony Fisher*

A German-Englishman near Frankfurt, Germany

2   I grew up in Africa. I can still remember the day I decided to acknowledge and follow Jesus Christ as my lord and savior. I was overwhelmed with joy and passion for him. Those feelings were founded upon the conviction that all my failures and the shameful things I had done in my life had been forgiven. I knew that I was no longer guilty before God but loved by him. I made an oath to God that I would never again hurt him or do anything that would make him sad about me. In that way I hoped to hang on to his love and smile on my life.

After some years of being a Christian and doing a lot of things for God, I noticed that the joy I had felt when I first gave my life to Jesus had started to die. The reason was simple: Every day I was tempted to think, watch, and do things that were wrong in the eyes of God. But instead of keeping my record perfect before God I was often overcome by those temptations. There also were expectations (either by other Christians or by me) of things I should be doing, reading or saying, yet not a week would go by without having to realize that I was falling short of my standard of spirituality. A "victorious Christian living" it was not! In order to help me keep my promises to God, I had made certain spiritual rules and habits. They were like my religion, and I sought to keep them religiously. I prayed religiously, went to church religiously, served others religiously, followed Jesus religiously. My rules and disciplines served as my security of God's acceptance of me.

That religious spirituality lasted until the day, when a professor of mine walked into class and in the course "Spiritual Life in Ministry" gave a lecture on the gospel-driven life and spirituality. He started that lecture off with the statement:

"Our biggest mistake in living the Christian life is thinking wrongly about the gospel. The gospel is not the A,B,Cs but the A to Z of Christianity. It is not the entrance into the Christian life, it is the whole house; not the diving board into living water but the whole swimming pool."

For my particular situation in life, those were the most powerful words I had ever heard. After that lesson on a Christ-centred and gospel-driven spirituality, I began a long process of repentance (turning away from idols of religiosity and turning to the gospel of liberty). I started to re-define my life and my identity not around my religious habits but around the person and the work of Christ.

The first joy came back to life again. In fact, my love and passion for Jesus Christ were re-awakened and grew to be stronger than they had been the first few months after my conversion. Why? Because I realised that I didn't need to keep keeping my oaths before God if I wanted to keep God's pleasure in me, nor to perform any extra holy deeds to make up for my failures and re-gain God's love. He wanted me to know that through his holy Son, Jesus Christ, he was already pleased with and satisfied in me, that regardless of how well I perform for God I am already loved by him beyond all measure and imagination. This good news (gospel) set me free. Not the kind of freedom that would let me rush into sin as if it did not matter anymore if I was obedient to God or not. Instead it is the freedom to love God without the fear of losing that love by anything I do or don't do. That, in turn, set me free to pray, to go to church, to do ministry, to tell others about the gospel as a way of expressing my love to God instead of needing to secure his love for me.

The professor who walked into class that blessed day was Stephen Beck. He even told us about how this gospel-driven spirituality changed his personal life, his motives, his relationships, his drive for significance, his marriage, and his way of dealing with personal failures. I, too, am on this journey.

What you read in this book is a description of that journey. If you go on this journey, you will get turned inside-out, from having to constantly worry about whether or not your 'Me' is okay to becoming motivated to live for God because he accepts you 'in Christ' as more than just okay. Bon voyage!

– Lionel Bendobal

A Cameroonian in Germany; Assistant Pastor in Church for all Nations, Frankfurt.

3 There is an odd little verse in John chapter 19, right at the end of the crucifixion of Jesus, that goes, "The man who saw it has given testimony, and his testimony is true. He knows that he tells the truth, and he testifies so that you also may believe" (v. 35).

There was a time in my life when I believed that I could invent my own life story, fashion myself as a work of art, as Nietzsche says. This was true freedom. I believed that God had abandoned me in my hour of greatest need, felt that he had deeply betrayed me and was untrustworthy. I raged against him like a wounded animal, believing he intended to do me harm. At times I wanted to reach out to him, but I felt too bad, too ashamed of everything I had done. Eventually, I came to believe that God did not exist at all, the arguments against God were too compelling, and that I was nothing more than a collection of cells, alone in the universe and without ultimate purpose. I had so lost my way that I believed I was beyond redemption, so I slipped into deep, suicidal despair. These were beliefs that made so much sense at the time, but, as you will soon find out, very nearly killed me. What we believe really matters. It can have life or death consequences.

Like a prisoner on death row, I got an eleventh-hour reprieve. When I least expected it, some mysterious force or power, or perhaps Someone, broke into my life. When I least deserved it, I was given grace and forgiveness. The chains of my addiction were broken by a power not my own, and I was set free to love a child I had not asked for but now would die for. I learned that I was not created to live for "me" but to be a blessing to others. And I learned that I could not save myself, I could not write my own story. I needed a Saviour, the Author of life himself.

As I began to meet God – or rather, as he began to meet me, for I could not find him on my own – I felt truly ALIVE for the first time in my life, the most "me" I had ever been! And I was most surprised to see that he was GOOD, that he loved me and had not abandoned me, but had pursued me for years. He had sat beside me in some very, very dark places, preserving my life despite my best efforts to destroy it. Though I had cursed him, he gave me hope and a future. It made no sense at all! But it brought me life, healing, and indeed, resurrection.

The Lord's Prayer says, "Forgive us our debts, as we forgive our debtors". There are some debts so huge they cannot be paid back and no amount of punishment can replace what was taken. In forgiving the man who hurt my family, it was like the power of God's forgiveness became really real to me. It got inside of me. It allowed a mountain of sadness, shame, and fear to melt away in light of the truth of God's burning love for me. It must be true what the Bible says about me, that God delights in me as a dad loves his little child, for him to pay the ultimate cost to forgive my debt. Knowing this deep in my heart, knowing the truth about who I am and who God is and that I can put my trust in him- this is the kind of freedom that actually sets you free!

I have just alluded here and there to details of my story. In the pages of this book Stephen Beck weaves 13 years of my experience with and without God. The author has known me for a long time and has walked through parts of my messy existence with me. I suppose it makes sense that my experience would illustrate for you how a gospel-driven spirituality challenges our deepest and dearest held beliefs and changes us inside-out. After all, mine is a normal and broken life to which God has broken through. I am a witness to the mighty power of God's deliverance.

My simple life continues to be a struggle. At the moment, my health prevents me from working and the disability checks have stopped coming. I'm not sure what the future holds. I believe in a God who came and lived among us, who healed people of their diseases and forgave their sins, who loved us to the point of dying for us though we hated and cursed him. I believe in a God who deeply knows our suffering, who went down into death and broke its power, securing for us an eternity with him. I believe in a God who is alive and active in the world today, who seeks out broken people and makes us whole, who knows all our ugliness and yet accepts us, who does not leave us in our filth but transforms us into his beautiful image.

If all this is really true, then this changes everything! If this God is for me, then nothing will destroy me. Since this God loves and accepts me as I am, I know I have become the recipient of over-the-top amazing, incredible, outrageous, and even scandalous love.

Enjoy my story, as you read this book and come to enjoy God. Your story could develop like mine as centering your life on God becomes the fulfillment of your Me.

– *Maria*
Toronto, Canada

Preface

We live in a complicated world. Many different waves are washing over us and into us all at once and from many different directions. There are moments in which I feel like my head is already under water. I am unable to catch my breath. I am drowning. You probably know what it's like.

Technology is an amazing thing. It has landed us on the moon, led us to discover the DNA, gets the news about far-away disasters into our living room within minutes, and allows us to be "friends" with people we don't even know. It has brought us an overload of daily information. We know more than we have ever known, and can gain new knowledge faster than we ever have before. We even know that there is more that we do not know than that we know. We also know that information we receive is tampered with or slanted according to what people want us to believe. What we know is only selective information, only part of the total picture. Is all our knowledge really correct? How many things that we know today as facts will be proven wrong tomorrow or will be known to have been based on completely erroneous assumptions by the next decade? Can we be sure about anything?

The worst of it is that although we have gained incredible amounts of self-knowledge in the past decades, it is precisely the self we have the hardest time understanding. We are complicated creatures. Why do we know that hatred, lust, unfaithfulness, greed, elitism, arrogance, denial, guilt, denial of guilt, addiction, and racist thoughts will ruin us, and still we give ourselves over to what we know will ruin us? Why are we so in love with ourselves yet unhappy with the selves we love? Why do we have so much available at our finger tips but still have unfulfilled longings in our hearts? All the technology and vast knowledge available to us today cannot make sense of our deepest selves, cannot stem the flood of torn, battered and unhappy people making their way to psychiatrists, therapists and counsellors. We need help. I need help. The more we know the more we know that we cannot figure ourselves out!

We live in a complicated world. We live inside a complicated self.

Postmodernism, the grandchild of the philosopher Friedrich Nietzsche, has sought to help us through our self-crisis. It has tried to simplify the mystery of the self by telling us that an objective understanding of self is completely impossible, anyway. After all, starting with the 18th century Enlightenment, humanistic modernism sought to put man and his scientific knowledge at the centre of the universe. Postmodernism has taken modernism to its logical conclusion. The pill we have had to swallow tastes bitter:

"Man at the centre? Which man is at what centre, by whose interpretation? Aren't we all just individuals with our own interpretations of reality? And since we are, who can even tell us where centre is? And since there is no centre anymore…

…there is no way to define truth except by your subjective experience,

…there is no meaning in life except the meaning you create for yourself.

…You are all you have, sucker! Bon voyage!

Do you get the point? Postmodernism has told us, that it's all about your self: All anyone has for himself is self-esteem, self-help, loving your self, pampering yourself, centring yourself on your self, being good to yourself, actualizing your self. Postmodernism is the attempt to legitimize our preoccupation with our selves.

But the philosophers who promoted postmodernism have become sceptical about their own philosophy. Recognizing the internal contradiction of their claims, they also realized that they had essentially obliterated any ability to define the self. How can we talk about the self when there is no objective definition of what the self even is? I am not saying that the discussion about postmodernism has become unnecessary. I am saying that while it did not reach most of the world it is virtually passé in Western Europe where I live, because it has failed to give Westerners answers to our identity crisis. What it did not fail to do is to confirm what we have already known for a long time: every human everywhere in the world is horribly me-centred! We are caught in a suction of self-consumption that pulls us deeper and deeper into our own prisons. All the self-help-books, seminars and programs have not helped set the self free. Postmodernism's attempt to legitimize our self-absorption has not liberated us; it has simply left millions of bankrupt souls in its wake.

What do vacuous souls have left for themselves? If nothing has meaning except the meaning you create for yourself, you have two options: either kill yourself because you are unable to create your own satisfactory meaning—which was Friedrich Nietzsche's choice—or create for yourself a culture of entertainment, fill your senses with what brings you pleasure in the moment and enjoy meaninglessness as much as you can before you go out in a meaningless whimper. Either way you choose, it's totally self-absorbed. Which is okay, as long as it is the authentic self being expressed. But how should you know what the authentic self is?

It's a very confusing world we live in!

Globalism has sought to give us meaning by bringing us all together into a united-we-are-the-world world. What this political movement has actually done is blow up the world into a million pieces. To create a uni-world we have had to become pluralistic. We have had to remove all divisions and distinctions, in order to unify the world. The result: there are distinctions, no neat categories anymore. Every mixture and blending and mainstreaming of everything has been granted the right to exist, except the voices that decry the mixing and mainstreaming of everything. Such people are labelled "fanatics" or "fundamentalists."

Personally, I think that globalism's mixing of cultures and

nationalities has afforded us wonderful opportunities. But at a great price! To keep everybody moving together in the same direction, everybody needs to be cloned into being politically correct. Pluralism tells us to march to the beat of the uni-drummer, all in a row, no exceptions allowed. Many feel the pressure of having to openly tolerate what we privately don't want and sanction what we secretly disagree with. For the sake of public harmony, personal faith is removed from the public square. Nobody should push their personal faith into the foreground or it will disrupt the uni-drummer's rhythm. Privatization of belief has become globalism's religious mantra. We are learning to be and say one thing on the outside, while feeling, sensing and believing something else on the inside.

It is a sad and lonely world we live in!

Religion has failed us! It has given the self no answer to his search for meaning. Christendom as a "folk culture" has come to an end. The religious moorings of the west have been uprooted. For many centuries Christendom has presented the Christian message simplistically. Some call it "liberalism", some call it "simplism." It is the reducing of the message of Jesus to an ethical lifestyle, to a set of moral values people are expected to live. You might say that Christianity is portrayed as the law of love, as the "you know what you have to do to love your neighbour, now go do it" commandment. Since this religious message fits the political push of globalism, many parts of the church have gotten in bed with the political scene. But wanting to have a voice in a political world, and accommodating its message to fit the political king, the church has by and large lost its prophetic voice and priestly role in the inner lives of searching people. The accommodating practices of the church with its compromised message and leaders have marked the institution with widespread hypocrisy. Even the irreligious sense at that point, that Jesus and the church are not on the same page.

A segment of the church has reacted to the liberal church and its simplistic message by going to the opposite extreme. It has withdrawn from world affairs and become its own (sub)culture. It points the finger at the world and judges it for its worldliness. The end effect is that the conservative and withdrawing church has become just as hypocritical as the liberal and accommodating church, because it ignores the reality, that every sin it judges in the world lies in seed-form in its own heart. This, too, the irreligious can sense and have written off the conservative option as arrogant, unloving and self-righteous.

The result has been, that while there is a 3rd way the church could go, an ever widening disillusionment with either expression of Christian religion has developed. Whether it be the liberal, world-accomodating church or the conservative, world-condemning church, most mainstream people are frustrated or hurt by either.

It is a hopeless world we live in.

This book is not about religion. It is about what one philosopher called true spirituality. It is about a spirituality that helps the self break out of its fragmentation and develop into a complete self; break loose from the pressures of keeping up the image and attain an authenticity you and others can respect; get free from self-absorption and live a life that leaves a meaningful legacy to others.

This book is about Christian spirituality. I have found that the key to developing my self to the ultimate self I can be is to not focus the self on the self but on the God who loves the self. This God has given me stability, calm and safety in this complicated, sad, confusing and hopeless world. He has helped me find my real self by telling me to centre my self on him instead of self. Centring on him is a practical process, touching every aspect of life, bringing every fragment together into a whole.

You will read about and learn the process throughout this book, in the true story of Maria that weaves its way through its pages, and in the many helpful and positive principles that come to us from Christian spirituality. You will learn the spiritual path of Jesus the Christ, what my friend Tim Keller has called the 3rd way, the middle road. It is not driven by the need to fit in with the political-cultural pressures of the day, nor by a desire to prove oneself better and purer than those who have accommodated the message. It is, instead, a gospel-driven spirituality, that means, it is driven by the good news about the righteousness of Jesus. What that means, and how that works itself out practically in your life, is what this book is about.

Frankly, Christian spirituality can be an uncomfortable path to walk on through life, so reading this book may not always feel like you are having a pleasant, postmodern experience. If I were creating a spirituality that stood a chance of getting a wide following, I would first create a divinity to fit my needs, and then I would put that divinity to work to satisfy all my needs. But true Christian spirituality does not work like that, nor does it begin with a divinity that serves as a spiritual butler. One reason why God does not exist to fill every need we feel is that God was not created by any needy person. He was not created at all. And precisely here is the rub. Before mankind was, and before mankind fell from the beautiful being it was, God was and had been for all eternity. This being true, it takes out of everybody's hands the opportunity to create a divinity according to his own pleasures and felt needs. It becomes a threat to the self that wishes to determine his own identity, ideology and destiny. The English scholar, Alister McGrath, put it like this in *Spirituality in an Age of Change:*

"We ought to attend to God as he actually is, rather than construct-ing ideas of what we would like him to be like... God has taken the ini-tiative away from us, pulling the rug from under our neat preconceptions of what a god ought to be like. In part, faith is a willingness to apprehend and respond to God as he has chosen to make himself known. It is a form of humility... in that it amounts to a willingness to submit to God, rather than to assert the validity of our own stereotypes of divinity... True spirituality is not a human invention, but a response to God. "[1]

---

[1] Alister McGrath, SPIRITUALITY IN AN AGE OF CHANGE: REDISCOVERING THE SPIRIT OF THE REFORMERS, Grand Rapids: Zondervan, 1994, pp. 78-79.

This makes Christianity at first encounter a bit unnatural, precisely because its origin is not natural but supernatural. Reading, hearing, and learning the content of God's revelation can be an uncomfortable experience because you don't get to create the content. You respond to it. The revealed content will include thoughts and ideas that will take you by surprise, challenge you, even frighten you. God's revelation can reveal truth to you that feels contrary to your nature and opposite from your inclination. It can hurt, dig deep into your wounds you never knew you had and call you to die humbly to your selfish self. This is terribly uncomfortable! But as Dietrich Bonhoeffer, the young Geman theologian and pastor who vigorously withstood the Nazi regime of his day and his church's compromise to the political pressures, used to point out: It is precisely because God does not correspond to our nature that he is able to move into our human nature and change it.[2]

That is what true Christian spirituality does: it changes us from the inside-out. In turn, that means that Christian spirituality is a lot more than just knowing certain things God revealed for us to know. It is like reading a story that has certain facts to its content, and then stepping into the content and becoming part of the story. It is an experience. It becomes an adventure of knowing God deeper and deeper every day, in the experiences of joy as well as in your encounters with the sorrows of life. But the deeper you come to know God, the more in touch with your longings you are. While you cannot create a god whose task it is to fill all your felt needs, God created us with certain longings that drive us to him. He desires to drive us to him precisely because he desires to satisfy our longings. He is that good, that generous! In your desire for the fulfilment of your longings, and in turning to God to have your longings filled, you become the fulfilled self, you become complete, free and authentic.

For this reason I include at the end of every chapter a section entitled, "What's in it for me?" One might criticise this as turning

---

[2] See for example Bonhoeffer's letter in 1936 to his brother-in-law, quoted in Metaxas, Eric, BONHOEFFER: PASTOR, MARTYR, PROPHET, Spy, Nashville: Thomas Nelson, 2010, p. 137.

Christian spirituality into nothing less than self-consumption. But here is the utterly astounding thing: in turning to God, the self ends up receiving tremendous personal gratification from God. You might be surprised at 'what's in it for me?' when you let your inner life be driven by the gospel of God to God instead of by religion to your inner self.

Here is the hope! Form a *God-centred spirituality in a me-centred world.* If developing toward the real self is like constructing a house, Christian spirituality is learning to be a smart builder! Let's proceed now to the construction site!

Yours sincerely and along for the lifelong project,

Stephen Beck
October 2011

As the Ruin Falls by C. S. Lewis

All this is flashy rhetoric about loving you.
I never had a selfless thought since I was born.
I am mercenary and self-seeking through and through:
I want God, you, all friends, merely to serve my turn.

Peace, re-assurance, pleasure, are the goals I seek,
I cannot crawl one inch outside my proper skin:
I talk of love --a scholar's parrot may talk Greek--
But, self-imprisoned, always end where I begin.

Only that now you have taught me (but how late) my lack.
I see the chasm. And everything you are was making
My heart into a bridge by which I might get back
From exile, and grow man. And now the bridge is breaking.

For this I bless you as the ruin falls. The pains
You give me are more precious than all other gains.

SECTION 1

In this first of four sections, we want to deal with the invisible part of a person's spirituality. If we were constructing a house, this would be the part that stays underground. Nobody sees it, but it provides the house with all-important stability to remain firm in life's heavy storms. It also gives structure to the visible parts. If we do not get this part of our spirituality right, we get everything else wrong. It demands deep soul-searching and a humble reflection on the facts.

Spirituality starts with a consideration of ideas. Alister McGrath, in Spirituality in an Age of Change, defines spirituality—specifically Christian spirituality—as "the way in which those ideas make themselves visible in the life of Christian individuals and communities." I have followed the scholarship of McGrath over the years and have immense respect for him. But I'd like to go a step deeper and further than McGrath's definition of ideas does: deeper than ideas, because behind those ideas are personal longings every human has, and spirituality is the human search for fulfilment of those longings; further than ideas, because Christian spirituality is about a person, and spirituality becomes an engagement with this most controversial person that ever existed. For that reason, Christian spirituality demands some hard decisions.

Perhaps that will make your journey as challenging as Maria's. It is with her that I begin and with her that I will end this book. In between you can follow how she came to deal with the foundations of Christian spirituality, how she put to use some of the spiritual ideas I will discuss in this book, and how her decisions about spirituality shaped her life.

Maria's Journey #1
An ordinary story with an extraordinary twist

*S*he was raised with devout religious principles by her
parents, Rob and Karina. Not to mention I was pastor of
the church that she and her family attended. With such good
influences in her life, what could possibly go wrong?!
Everything went wrong!
When Maria was 17, something happened that nobody
could have foreseen—at least not with her background. From
one day to the next she turned away from belief in God. She
had encountered so much wrong in her surroundings, had
witnessed so much suffering in the world, that a blackness
started to move in on her soul like an early morning fog. A
quiet rage took root in what had been a happy spirit. If God
really is good and all-powerful, how could he simply stand by,
hear the cries of millions of tormented and hurting people
and do nothing? God was neither good nor great.
Maria was disappointed with God. And the darker it got
in her soul, the more obvious it was to Maria that God had
abandoned her. She felt betrayed. There was nothing she
had done to deserve God turning his back on her. Just to the
opposite: she had always taken God very seriously and had
committed her life to living in a way that pleased him. But
he did not seem to care. Instead of making her happy, the
growing dark vacuum in her soul suggested he had gone far
away from her. In fact, all the suffering she was witnessing in
the world made it clear he had removed himself from all of
reality.
So one day she decided to call it quits on the religious

life. "Atheists must be right. This is my life, this is about me, because there is nobody else who can make me happy!" she started thinking to herself. Her anger at God turned into an inner rage toward anything and anybody who tried to place strictures around her. The speaker at her Toronto's high school graduation confirmed her suspicions when he encouraged the graduates to embrace the post-modern worldview. "We are the product of the Enlightenment," he declared with passion. "Today we know that every person is his own god, decides his own destiny, pursues his own path to happiness, while tolerating all paths. Here is your creed, the postmodern rule written over everybody's life: there is no rule over anybody's life! Nobody and nothing stands over you to dictate who you are, what you do, what you believe. Believe your own experience, no less and no more. It will be the most wonderful truth and reality to believe in and live for. Why? Because it is the authentic you, it is your very own faith!" It was an electrifying speech.

To Maria, the speaker's creed reflected the way the world seemed to be turning. People like Rob and Karina, who insisted there was only one true God (the God they worshiped) were 'fundamentalists.' They were power-hungry, dangerous, or psychologically so weak that they needed a make-believe god as a crutch. That was not the path for her. Not any more!

"This is my life. This is about me. This is about what I want!"

That is how Maria's mission to find herself got its start. It was an exciting adventure, shedding someone else's religious clothes that had been imposed on her and heading off down the pathway to her very own created self. The goal itself was not as important as the process. She was free to be completely free.

For every person it looks different. For Maria the buzz of happiness came through the party scene. That awful blackness was still enveloping her soul like a silk veil, so she needed the buzz. She filled her days with carefree and like-minded friends, alcohol, drugs, sex, and dancing the nights away.

And the more, the better! She was her own master, and she drove her search for fulfilment forward with reckless abandon. The party scene took on a maddening pace, though it was still important to keep up the look of 'having it all together,' especially in front of her parents. Eventually that created unwanted pressure, so she moved away from home into her own place, in order to flee the circle of authority and guilt-manipulation.

When she was 20 and in her second year of university the veil of darkness started to strangle her soul. Maria plummeted into a very deep depression. She visited a series of doctors and specialists, but no one was able to help her. Actually, she did not want help at the time. She had become dependent on the little idols she was bowing to – her friends, drugs, sex and alcohol - and she was determined to remain master of her destiny. She was going to prove that she could make it on her own, even if she had to drop out of university.

Then a big bomb dropped on her tightly built fortress of Me. She became pregnant. It was a horrible shock! Her drug-addicted boyfriend, who had regularly been sniffing cocaine and getting drunk with her, found the pregnancy a disruption to his drive for freedom and moved out. Maria, now 24, was left alone to deal with the pregnancy.

Quite unexpectedly, a light began to shine its rays through the cracks of Maria's broken soul. The first beams came in the form of thoughts that warmed her. Maria began to rub her stomach and feel love for the child in her. She knew she had turned her back on God. If he were to deal in fairness with Maria, he would make her pay the consequences for all her spiritual rebellion and moral wrongdoing. Instead, it seemed, he was giving her a very special gift: a baby. Many married couples try for years to have children and cannot. Unmarried Maria had had sex, not because she was trying to have a baby but because she felt desperately lonely. Yet she was being given a child to love. The way Maria perceived this turn in her life, it was over-the-top, scandalous, outrageous grace.

Perhaps God was loving and good, after all? Perhaps

he had never left her, even when she had wanted to leave him. Had he pursued her in grace? The more Maria thought about the turn in her life, the more she felt that the questions about suffering and evil in the world could not be answered by abandoning the existence and presence of God. Being pregnant suggested to Maria, that there were at least as many good things that people were undeservedly allowed to have and experience as there were bad things. If we are quick to blame God for bad things that happen, should we not in all fairness then also credit God for the many good things that come our way?

Maria felt the thrill of loving her own child. She had been utterly self-consumed, on a rampage to secure her own happiness and drown out the depression. Her feverish pursuit of the self had become a prison in which she was incarcerated. The thought of loving someone else, of giving up self-centred pursuits like drugs and nightly parties for the wellbeing of her little baby, was like following the rays of light out of the prison cell and realizing that beauty and freedom lay beyond selfish pursuits.

But Maria was scared to face the future alone, without an income and with a baby. This is where more light began to shine into Maria's soul. Her parents, Rob and Karina, offered to have Maria move into the house they had just built. Maria would have her own room, with a second room for her child. Everything would be hers to use freely, and Mom and Dad would help her raise the little one. It was hard for Maria to accept the offer. It meant giving in and surrendering to people whom she had wanted to prove wrong. Worst of all, it meant giving up. Her quest to prove she was self-sufficient had failed.

Grace has that effect on people. To experience the full benefit and generosity of grace, they have to admit humbly that they were unable to live without it. The other thing so disturbing about grace is that it does not act according to human nature, nor treat a wrongdoer on human terms. Grace is ready to give what is unexpected, to do what seems unfair, in order to extend what is undeserved. Grace is free; it demands no payment. Grace does not harbour bitterness for unjust treatment received. It forgives and lets go of the grudge, not because it must, but because that is its nature. God is filled to the brim with grace and his grace had deeply touched Rob and Karina a year earlier, in the midst of their brokenness over their daughter. It had transformed them so that now they could offer grace to the daughter who hated them. Greater than any rational argument, the grace her parents extended to Maria broke through to her hardened heart.

Maria moved home. That was not easy for anybody, not for her parents, not for her siblings, and not for Maria. Things went from bad to worse. In her sixth month of pregnancy, Maria had a check-up that added a whole new complication to an already confused life. The ultrasound showed that the child was not developing properly. The obstetrician said coldly, "If you bring this child into the world, it will be a child with 'special needs.'"

Sometimes life stinks when there is nothing in particular that you have done to cause the stench. Sometimes life stinks from the foulness of your own choices. If you are honest, really honest, you make decisions based only on what looks like a good experience at the moment. Then it comes back and bites you. What do you do with the mess you create, when all you have left is the self that created the mess? Is there a way out of this lonesome desert? When you have lost your way, can life be rebuilt on a solid foundation?

Smart Builder!

In the fall of 1928, 22-year-old Dietrich Bonhoeffer gave a lecture to German Christians. He noticed that in calling themselves 'Christians,' they had reduced the word to nothing more than a certain piety. He spelled out that the basis of all of Christian spirituality is the Person of Jesus. In this lecture, Bonhoeffer called those who wished to be known as 'Christians' to a clear and uncompromising commitment:

One admires Christ according to aesthetic categories as an aesthetic genius, calls him the greatest ethicist; one admires his going to his death as a heroic sacrifice for his ideas. Only one thing one doesn't do: one doesn't take him seriously. That is, one doesn't bring the center of his or her own life into contact with the claim of Christ to speak the revelation of God and to be that revelation. One maintains a distance between himself or herself and the word of Christ, and allows no serious encounter to take place. I can doubtless live with or without Jesus as a religious genius, as an ethicist, as a gentleman – just as, after all, I can also live without Plato and Kant…Should, however, there be something in Christ that claims my life entirely with the full seriousness that here God himself speaks and if the word of God once became present only in Christ, then Christ has not only relative but absolute, urgent significance for me…Understanding Christ means taking Christ seriously. Understanding this claim means taking seriously his absolute claim on our commitment. And it is now of importance for us to clarify the seriousness of this matter and to extricate Christ from the secularization process in which he has been incorporated since the Enlightenment.[1]

Bonhoeffer's call to an authentic Christian spirituality not only marked his entire ministry, it became the substance of his famous book NACHFOLGE (English: THE COST OF DISCIPLESHIP). It is an analysis of Jesus' Sermon on the Mount, which Jesus preached to an audience of a few disciples, a number of severe critics, and many curious folk. He ended the sermon by drawing a picture about spirituality. Jesus imagined life as a house, which must be carefully built and constructed with forethought.

---

[1] Eric Metaxas, BONHOEFFER: PASTOR, MARTYR, PROPHET, SPY. London: Thomas Nelson, 2010. p. 82.

Here is the climactic conclusion of Jesus' famous sermon: *"Everyone who hears these words of mine and puts them into practice is like a wise man who built his house on the rock. The rain came down, the streams rose, and the winds blew and beat against that house; yet it did not fall, because it had its foundation on the rock. But everyone who hears these words of mine and does not put them into practice is like a foolish man who built his house on sand. The rain came down, the streams rose, and the winds blew and beat against that house, and it fell with a great crash"* (Matthew 7:24-27).

Not exactly a positive ending to a world-famous sermon! It is almost as if the rabbi wanted to leave his audience all shaken up over the alternative to which everyone is headed, at least all those content to pat Jesus on the back and congratulate him for being a symbol of peace. But what they refuse to do is to smart_build their lives by studying and believing his truth *("Everyone who hears these words of mine")* and organizing every aspect of their lives around it ("and *puts them into practice"*).

Jesus was reaching back into the Jewish Bible, the Old Testament, and to the well-known Judaic concept of wisdom. In fact, part of the Jewish Bible was called 'Wisdom literature.' One book, Proverbs, begins with God personified as wisdom, making her way into the public domain and offering to guide the inhabitants through life, but wisdom is rejected by those who thought themselves too smart to need her. She enters the public square and authoritatively denounces those who chose the alternative to wisdom. She calls them "fools."

When he translated Proverbs from Hebrew into German, Martin Luther chose "klug" or "Klugheit" to cover such words as "understanding," "prudence," "discernment," and "wisdom." "Klug" means "smart." Being smart (or wise) is not just about knowing a lot. Many people know as much as the great philosophers and religious thinkers of Jesus' own day. Jesus nonetheless called them "fools," just like God-personified-as-Wisdom in the book of Proverbs had done. Being "smart" has to do with knowing what to do with the facts you know.

In the conclusion of the Sermon on the Mount Jesus presents himself as THE fact you need to know. You need to know what to do with this fact. Jesus presented himself as God-come-in-the-flesh (*incarnation*), going through the streets of our lives, calling us to build our lives on him. He who does so, Jesus claims, is "*a wise man.*" He who does not do so is a *"foolish man."*

Jesus' claim and mandate was as audacious in 1ˢᵗ century Judaism as it is in today's secularism. He is not just calling every person to build his life wisely by building it on the solid foundation of immovable, indestructible and unchanging truth. He is saying that he is that truth. This truth cannot be changed any more than Jesus can be changed. Not by evolving cultures, nor by opposing opinions. What makes this truth so appealing is that it is not cold, heartless, philosophical rambling. It is a person. Anyone who is really smart builds his lifehouse around a person who perfectly knows all there is to know, perfectly knows how to use all there is to know, and in grace moves into our construction to help us build the perfect lifehouse we long to have. Simply said, you build your lifehouse wisely if you build it on someone who is, and has proven to be, the perfect lifehouse.

When you build on this rock, your lifehouse becomes a lighthouse. It becomes a guide to people who need help. It impacts others. It leaves a legacy.

And it stands forever. The Bible refers to our dwelling in the afterlife as a house we have in heaven. It will be a house not made of bricks and mortar but built by God (2 Corinthians 5:1). Imagine your life built by God as an exhibit of his glory forever!

Who would want to choose the alternative?

Some wonderful books have been written in the last century on Christian spirituality. Here are a few:

- Dietrich Bonhoeffer, The Cost of Discipleship,
- Francis Schaeffer, True Spirituality,
- Richard Lovelace, Dynamics of Spiritual Life,
- Alister McGrath, Spirituality in an Age of Change,
- John Piper, Desiring God,
- Rick Warren, The Purpose-Driven Life,
- Glen Scorgie, A Little Guide to Christian Spirituality,
- Gregory Laughery, Living Spirituality.

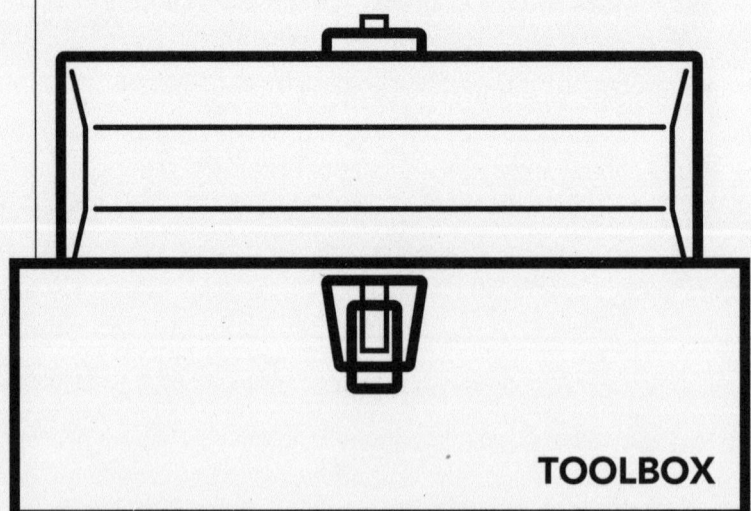

TOOLBOX

01
Foundation

The Right Foundation For
Your Spiritual Life

The foundation of Christian spirituality is Jesus. Not more, not less. Jesus was his earthly name, but he was and is referred to by his followers as 'Christ.' That is the Greek word for Messiah,' which means 'anointed one.' It is the picture of God laying his hands on Jesus and saying, "You are my chosen Saviour."

Followers of Jesus Messiah believe he is sent from God to make the way for us to God. Athol Dickson said it beautifully: *"To me, Jesus is the Creator of the universe on hands and knees, a proud Daddy talking baby talk to all humanity, a God who has become man so that I can better understand his answer."*[1]

Without the Person of Jesus, there is no Christianity and no Christian life. Everything comes from him, is through him, points toward him and leads to him. As John, one of his disciples and followers, called him in the Bible, Jesus is the Alpha and Omega, the beginning and the end. He was born in 4 B.C. and was crucified in 30 A.D. But he existed for all eternity before his birth, and he lives and reigns forever after his death. Why we can say that with certainty is spelled out next.

Christian spirituality is based on a historical fact

Most religions have no problem accepting the historical fact that Jesus died on a cross (Islam is the one major religion that denies

---

[1] Athol Dickson The Gospel According to Moses, Grand Rapids: Brazos Press, 2003, p. 28.

this). However, the crucial point, and therefore our starting point, is the resurrection of this crucified Jesus. The resurrection is that upon which the whole Christian faith stands! The first followers of Jesus were aware that this was the critical issue. One need only look at the four Gospels—Matthew, Mark, Luke, and John—and their focus on the empty tomb where the crucified Jesus had been buried (see especially John 20). Or note the Bible passages (Romans 1:4 or 1 Corinthians 15:15-20) in which Paul makes clear how much his entire faith in God depended on the resurrection of Jesus.

The resurrection of Jesus is the crux of all of Christian spirituality!

If Jesus did not rise from the dead three days after his crucifixion, the Christian faith is the greatest swindle there has ever been in the history of mankind. Then Jesus would be either a liar or a crazy man. He had claimed to be God (John 10:30), the only way to God (John 14:6), and the resurrection and the life (John 11:25). If Jesus did not rise from the dead, then none of the claims he made are true, and there would be no reason to believe that his death on the cross meant anything, that there is forgiveness of sins and absolution of any guilt you carry, that there is life after death.

However, if Jesus did rise from the dead, then it would be worth it for us to give up everything for him and serve him with total passion and devotion, because of the new, breathtaking future he offers us.

The only question is: how can we be sure that Jesus truly resurrected?

We were not there. We cannot go back into the grave and examine the grave cloths of Jesus, like Peter, John and Mary did (John 20:1-9). You and I were not there, like the heavily armed guards, who, standing in front of Jesus' grave to prevent an attempted grave robbery, reported with great fear to governor Pilate about an earthquake and angels and about how they had fled from the scene (Matt. 27:62-66). We were not there as Mary encountered Jesus in the cemetery, or when Jesus walked through a wall to show himself to the disciples, or when he stood in front of the doubting Thomas and showed him the scars in his hands and feet (John 20:24-31). You and I were not there to see with our own eyes how Jesus called from the beach to his disciples in their boat to come have breakfast with him (John 21.11ff). We were not there to experience how the disciples changed from cowards to courageous apostles and went all over the world to announce that Jesus of Nazareth had risen from the dead and is God.

But hundreds of people were there, and they saw, heard, and physically touched Jesus. Their reports have come down to us through people like Peter (Acts 2:32-36), John (1 John 1:1-3) and Paul (1 Corinthians 15:3-8). Thousands of scholars have studied the reports and have found them to be reliable down to the details. Millions have come to the historical evidence not believing that the resurrection could be true and have become as convinced as the over 500 people who, within weeks of Jesus' death, claimed that he had appeared to them bodily and personally.

Based on the standard of accuracy in oral tradition of 1st century Judaism, the number of eyewitnesses, and the tremendous amount of reliable manuscripts available to scholars today, the resurrection of Jesus is more believable as historical fact than most of ancient history we routinely accept as factual. Certainly, all alternative explanations for the empty grave have proven to be utter nonsense.

While I lived in Toronto, Canada, for many years I had a very enjoyable dentist. I know, that sounds like a contradiction— 'enjoyable' and 'dentist'—but this Jew with spiritual tentacles in Eastern mysticism, loved to discuss spiritual issues with me. Whenever I made an appointment he would schedule me for extra time, not just to pick at my teeth but to pick my brain on matters of spirituality.

At one appointment he introduced me to his new dental assistant, by telling her, "Talk to this man, maybe the questions you have been asking me about spirituality would interest him, too." As she cleaned my teeth, she talked about her background. She had grown up in Korea, where her grandfather had forced her to go to a Christian church with him every Sunday. But now that she was living on her own in Toronto, she had become a Buddhist. She asked me if I had ever examined the wonderful teachings of Buddha. I knew I had to keep my answers very short. Normally I have little trouble talking a lot (just ask my wife), but I have to admit that I do not speak very well when someone's hands are in my mouth.

"No," I gulped. "I stopped in my search for truth before I got to Buddha."

"What do you mean?" she probed.

"The resurrection of Jesus made everything else superfluous for me," I mumbled (I had a tube in my mouth at that moment... Try saying 'superfluous' with a tube halfway down your throat. It sounds a little like 'tuberculosis').

"The resurrection of Jesus?"

"Yes, the facts point to Jesus physically rising to life three days after his death."

"And therefore you are no longer interested in religion?"

"Oh no," I responded, my mouth now free from dental tools. "I'm more than ever interested in religion. I mean, religion is about our human need to have a vital relationship with our Creator. Jesus' resurrection confirmed to me that his claims must be true, that he is the only way to a relationship with God, that he reconciled us with God through his death, that only he can forgive sins, that he can give us eternal life here and now, and a life of completeness after death forever." At this point, she stuck her hands back in my mouth, so I said the rest sounding like a cow in heat.

"Since Jesus is risen from the dead and is reigning as Lord over all, Jesus is everything that I need for a relationship to God. The resurrection means my search for truth and meaning ended with Jesus."

Unfortunately, at this point the dentist came back into the room and wanted to discuss with me his latest spiritual insights. But here is the point:

If Jesus did not rise from the dead, the Christian faith is ultimately an illusion. But if Jesus did rise from the dead, everything outside of the Christian faith is ultimately an illusion.

Christian spirituality gives to the most controversial question the most wonderful answer

Recently I received an email from my 25-year old daughter, Elizabeth, who lives in London, England. She had offered a middle-aged man in a park a gift:

"Hi. I am really thankful for the Bible and how God has filled and changed my life through it. So I am giving away as a gift a small part of the Bible today, called 'John.' He was one of the disciples of Jesus, and wrote what he thought about Jesus, his life and stuff, in this book in the Bible. Would you like to have one?"

The man answered: "Would I like to have one what? A Bible or a John?"

Elizabeth almost burst into laughter, but was able to suppress it with a smile: "Eh, sir, the John thing. The Gospel of John. Most Christians just call it 'John'."

To her surprise the man responded: "Actually, I've had a bit of a notion to read the Bible some time, just never got around to it. Sure, I'll take one. Thank you."

When Elizabeth asked the Englishman why he had had the desire to read the Bible, the man spoke of a spiritual hunger that no church, no religious ritual, no feel-good-about-yourself power seminar had ever fulfilled in him. Elizabeth shared how God had met her own spiritual longings. Her natural way of relating to this intelligent man gave him the ease and comfort to admit: "I have a lot of respect for Jesus. But I have always struggled with the fact that the same guy who is ready to give you the shirt off his back, I mean, the guy will do anything for you, is still so arrogant and says all religions are wrong and that he is the only thing that's right. I mean, there were a lot of good people both before him and after him, who said good things about life and God.. Why did he ruin everything by saying he's the only way to God?"

I think we must first admit that Jesus' exclusivistic claim creates for many people a huge problem. It can bring with it emotional baggage. That could be memories of Christians bristling with rage as they pronounce judgment on other religions. It could be fear of uncomfortable implications for relationships with family or friends if one accepts this premise. So I zero in on the resurrection. That is the do-or-die point of Christianity, the point that pulls the question out of the subjective and private realm (the what-I-prefer-for-myself realm) and puts it into the objective, historic realm (the way-things-are-is-the-way-things-are realm). Then I work my way back:

- If Jesus really rose from the dead, then there is a God who is so great that he has the power over evil and death.

- If Jesus really rose from the dead, then all that he did at the cross must not only be true, but also effective (i.e. it has the power to go beyond the cross as a historic event to the cross as an existential experience: Jesus' words on the cross, 'It is finished' translate for the person who entrusts himself to the crucified Jesus into, 'For me personally, it was accomplished once and for all').

- If Jesus really rose from the dead, then he is who he said he is. But here is the problem: he said (and not the fundamentalists, not Christian bigots, not some television evangelist, but Jesus himself) he is the only way to God (John 14:6). For Jesus to say that and for his disciples to repeat it later (Acts 4:12) was as unpopular then as it is now. He and his disciples paid for such a claim with their lives. So why did they make such a costly claim?

  1) Because Jesus understood himself to be sent from God, to become the sacrifice for our sins. This is in complete contrast to other religions. Mankind always tries to make its way to the divine. In Jesus' teaching, God is the initiator. He decided to make his way to us. He came in the Person of Jesus. So Jesus virtually (and logically) *has* to say that he is the only way back to God.

  2) Because Jesus understood himself to be God (John 10:31; 14:7-11). No other religious leader before or after Jesus would dare to make such a claim: It was blasphemy in the eyes of the Jews (monotheists) and Romans and Greeks (polytheists).

  3) Because Jesus did something about our sins: he died on the cross. Nobody else—not Mohammed, Buddha, Krishna, or the Dalai Lama—did anything to conquer the sin issue. In fact, none of them made sin out to be a moral transgression against God. So none of them felt that there was even a need to do something about our sin, nor did any of them have the power to do something about it. Only

Jesus DID something about it and only Jesus COULD do something about it, because he was not only man (to take our place), but also GOD (who can forgive).

The problem—and this is part of the baggage that rolls along behind Jesus' claim—is the question, "but what about all the other religions or religious leaders? They can't all be wrong!" Actually, they aren't! When Jesus says he is the only way to God, he is not saying that all other religions are completely wrong. There is some truth in all religions. For example, other religions say that the supernatural exists, or that adultery is wrong, or that a human being has dignity, or that there is an ultimate to be reached and we are not there yet. These and many other truth statements are found within non-Christian religions. What Jesus claims is that though all religions have parts of the truth, he has and *is* all of the truth. Truth in its completeness is only found in him. The problem is that something that only has parts of the truth can only guide a person partly but not fully. Only that which is the absolutely complete expression of truth can guide someone straight and accurately into the truth. That is why Jesus made his exclusive claim in John 14:6. He did not see it as being controversial when he said, *"I am the way, the truth, and the life, no one comes to the Father [i.e. the true God] except through me."* He saw it as the only possible way to go at the question intelligently, since he alone is the perfect and complete embodiment of truth.

Many of us just write this off as arrogant, insensitive, and bigoted. But there is a great benefit to somebody saying that he is the only way to God: it makes the choice a lot clearer. If someone says, I am the only way to God, then either he is or he isn't. If the evidence supports "is," then it's clear and you can live with certainty that you are definitely on the right road. If the evidence points to "isn't," then it is clear again and you can live with certainty that you decided well by deciding against Jesus. But if the answer is, "There are a million different ways to God, and everyone has to define for themselves what that way is," you may end up doing a lot of searching over a long period of time and even then never be sure that what you decided is the correct answer. Maybe there is more, if only you look more.

Manuela taught me that. She was in a Discovery Group in Frankfurt in 2009. About 8 of us were seated in Jürgen and Margaret's living room, and the topic was what to do with religions that claim exclusive truth for themselves. The fact is, all religions do, not just Christianity, and the question should be, who makes that claim not only with logical consistency but as a motivation to serve others, especially people who disagree, in kindness, goodness, and humility. Manuela had come into the group a few weeks earlier, with a fairly negative view of Christianity. She had been quietly listening all evening, but at the end of the discussion said something astonishing:

"What became clear to me tonight is that it is really a good thing that Jesus claimed to be the only way!"

We were all startled. Then she explained: "If I decide, on the basis of the information I have, that I want to choose Jesus as my Saviour, and I come to him and say, 'Hi! I choose you as the Saviour and Lord I want to follow,' I would be very disappointed if he responded, 'okay, if that's how you would like it. There are a million good choices here, some of which may make life easier for you or may allow you to do pretty much what you would like to do—which I won't. But if you want to choose me, then I will do my best to make you happy.' No, if I come to Jesus, and say, 'I choose you,' I want him to break into an enthusiastic smile and respond 'Way to go, Manuela! You have chosen the best there is. In fact, Manuela, you have chosen the only one who has dealt completely and effectively with everything that lies between you and God, so that your sins are forgiven, your worries are now in God's hands, and your future is secured forever. I am so thrilled that you have chosen me. See, I decided that I wanted you to be like my bride, and I have been throwing little love hints at you for awhile, so that you some day might realize who I am and how much I want you and want you to marry me. And now that you have answered 'yes,' I am going to throw a big party.' Then he would yell, 'Hey, somebody, start hauling out of the wine cellar all that special wine I have been storing up for Manuela all these millennia. We have an engagement to celebrate!' That's how I would want Jesus to answer me. So maybe everybody else thinks his absolute claim about being the only way to God is bigoted, but for me personally it is a wonderful claim with a lot of good and security in it. It is a claim I want to trust!"

The Jewish scholar, Paul van Tarsus, for years viciously opposed Christians and the teachings of Jesus they followed. Once he came face to face with the facts about Jesus, he did a complete turn-around and wrote *"we have no other foundation to lay than the one that has already been laid, namely Christ Jesus"* (1 Corinthians 3:11). Sticking with the facts surrounding the resurrection of Jesus and the necessary implications that come with that historic event is the way to build a foundation for your lifehouse so that it cannot be shaken.

■ What's in it for me?

Jesus! Already in the Old Testament, in Isaiah 11:2, the awesome wonder of this Messiah is prophesied: *"The Spirit of the Lord will rest on him–the Spirit of wisdom and of understanding, the Spirit of counsel and of power, the Spirit of knowledge and of the fear of the Lord–with righteousness he will judge the needy, with justice he will give decisions for the poor of the earth, righteousness will be his belt and faithfulness the sash around his waist."*

This is a Person we can trust 100%. We can entrust the restoration of history, the earth, and our own lives to this One on whom God's Spirit rests and who will handle all things (even our personal lives) with righteousness.

Maria's Journey #2
Engaging with God in an Atheism Course

*T*he longer Maria was with her family, the more she felt the tension inside decrease. Her parents were not as threatening as they had once been, nor did they force their Christianity on her.

As the pregnancy developed and Maria began thinking about her responsibilities as a mother, a spiritual hunger resurfaced in her. She rediscovered her enjoyment of processing things intellectually. She had always been logical, even about the God-thing, at least until she was 17 and decided that the most logical thing was to live life without God.

But where to begin? What is the starting point of spiritual truth? Is it the non-existence of the supernatural, the evolution of the natural, Darwin's survival of the fittest? Where is it? Is it housed in Eastern Orthodox cathedrals and kissing icons? Is it at home in Roman Catholicism and lighting candles to release souls from purgatory, or is it in the Tibetan Buddhism of the Dalai Lama? Is it personified in the mystery of witchcraft or in the Confucian prayers to one's grandfather?

Maria found herself simply unable to say with certainty what could be the truth that would bring her strength and direction. But God took the matter into his own hands and showed up amidst her confusion. She did not know it was God, because he showed himself through the strangest means: a course on atheism.

Maria registered for the course at the University of Toronto and her mother decided to register too. Twice a week, mother and daughter went to the lectures. Karina wanted, with the permission of her daughter, to accompany Maria in her spiritual journey. And Maria wanted to get rid of God intellectually once and for all. No God would mean no need for guilt, no need to change, no need for forgiveness.

What developed in the next weeks was unique. The very course that was to deliver Maria of belief in the existence of God convinced her that God really exists. First, it dawned on Maria that the professor had to believe in certain presuppositions in order to try to prove the non-existence of God. For example, he spoke of evil in the world (and that the problem of evil apparently disproved God), but, Maria asked herself, if the professor believed in the existence of evil, where did he get the concept of good and the consequent distinction between good and evil? He spoke about the imperfect in our universe, but how he could do that without presupposing the existence of the perfect? He claimed that truth is relative, and no one can claim the existence of absolute truth, but wasn't such a statement a claim of absolute truth? Maria did not know it then, but her thinking began to reflect that of G.K. Chesterton, who stated, "If there were no God, there would be no atheists."

The clincher for Maria came in a lecture on "truth in post-modern thinking." The professor defined truth as "completely self-oriented." He stated, "Truth is the personal conclusion made by an existential being on the grounds of subjective experiences. This means truth becomes for every person something different, in that each person has different experiences and different subjective interpretations of those experiences. Therefore, no person has the right to transfer his or her personal, subjective definition of truth onto another person, for that is to impose what must remain within the boundaries of a subjective experience."

That was precisely what Maria had been claiming: her subjective experience is the only authority by which she would decide what is good and true for her. But somehow, now, hearing the professor say it the way he did, she felt that she could see right through his claim. On the way home that day,

Maria said to her mother, "It suddenly hit me; 'wait a second, didn't the professor, in making this claim, violate his own principle? After all, he fully expected the students to receive his subjective and personal interpretation of truth as an objective and absolute truth principle!'"

As far as reason was concerned, Maria concluded that one really can make great rational, philosophical and scientific arguments for atheism. It is possible to disbelieve in God for rational reasons. But the way we actually live points to a sort of intuition in us that God does in fact exist. Our experiences of truth, goodness, nobility, morality, beauty, and honour can be reduced to some sort of psychological/evolutionary phenomena, but that is not the best explanation of our behavior. For Maria, the fact that we live as if there were a God suggested to her that God exists. It did not give her absolute certainty, instead it left room for her to be aware that she was making a choice to believe in God. As she once wrote to me, "I could believe in the absolute truth of the existence of God, but without needing to be absolutely sure of the truth of that truth. In other words, it was ultimately a matter of faith, just like belief in atheism or evolution is no less than a matter of faith."

But it was really the way she was experiencing life that opened the door for Maria out of her dungeon: "Doesn't C.S. Lewis say something along the lines of, Christianity is like the sun: I know it is true not only because I can see it, but because by it, I can see everything else? For me, living apart from God actually made a lot of rational sense, but it led to death. Faith in God, on the other hand, didn't often make a lot of rational sense, in fact I frequently stepped out in faith before I understood rationally what it meant, but doing so always led to life and greater understanding."

Inch by inch God was taking Maria out of the captivity of her desert and into the presence of God. But that raised a big and frightening question for Maria: after all she had done wrong, would God want to love her?

...

Sorting through Spiritualities
without Discovering God

When I picked up the telephone on the third ring, I was surprised to hear Maria's voice on the other end. "Can we meet and talk about God and faith?" she asked. I was totally surprised. I had visited Maria several times at their previous house and tried to no avail to have meaningful conversations with the troubled girl. Now her voice sounded clear over the telephone.

We met on a sunny day at The Great Canadian Bagel at Bathurst and Lawrence in Toronto. She stirred her macchiato as we talked briefly about her pregnancy and the upcoming birth. Then Maria launched into a question:

"What is spirituality, anyway?" Maria was starting at the very beginning of the search for meaning.

"The common definition for spirituality is 'the internalizing of one's faith,'" I answered. "But to me, that definition is too impersonal. It does not take into account why people even feel the need for a faith, including the faith of atheism or the belief in Darwinian evolution. So, to get closer to the deep-seated longing we all have in common, I would prefer another definition."

"Like what?" she asked.

"I think spirituality is every person's attempt to attain righteousness. By that I mean an assurance that I am accepted, approved, and appreciated by the highest standard of goodness there is."

"You mean, we all want to know that the person we value the most thinks of us as being okay, or beautiful, or significant?"

"Exactly! I think it is innate to us humans to want to know that the person our identity and existence is tied to approves of us as good. On the one level, that would be children in relation to their parents. On the other level, that would be every human in relation to God. Not feeling approved, accepted, and appreciated on either level messes us up, creates a vacuum, makes us sad, restless, or rebellious."

51

"But what if the person is an atheist, like I have been trying to be. Does he have a spirituality?"

"He sure does! The atheist, too, has a spirit, a soul and a conscience. He also wants to have the assurance that he is accepted, approved, and appreciated by the highest standard of goodness there is. Whether he is a theoretical atheist or a functional atheist, he is a spiritual being and has the same longing for being deemed right and good as the theist."

Maria thought for a second. "What was that? Theoretical atheist and what?" I clarified: "A theoretical atheist is someone who concludes through cold, hard reasoning that there is nothing supernatural. The functional atheist is someone who does not deny the existence of God but lives as if there were no God. There are many people who call themselves 'Christians'—or Muslims, for that matter—who are in reality functional atheists."

"Now you are starting to confuse me," Maria smiled.

"Sorry," I responded, "but the fact that many people call themselves 'Christian' and mean by that no more than upholding a measure of goodness by which they can feel accepted, approved and appreciated makes them no more 'Christian' than an atheist with good behaviour. I think Christian spirituality is the character of God impressed on every aspect of a person's inner being and lived out in the world. In other words, it is an internalized faith that is lived out externally in such a way that it is consistent with the internal."

"Even though you come up with these convoluted sentences," Maria smiled, "I think what you just said makes sense. It also eliminates a lot of people who call themselves 'Christians' or go to church. Can I be honest with you? That's why I quit. There are many people who say they are Christian but gave me more of a reason to believe that God doesn't exist than to believe he does."

I remained quiet and let Maria vent. Then she asked another question: "You said in a sermon long ago that spiritualities flow in different directions. What about the claim that they flow in the same direction, that they all in the end say the same thing?"

I answered as best I knew how. "Maria, you can summarize all spiritualities in this world into four categories that start with the letter s:

The first is spiritism—like witchcraft, animism or new age thinking.

The second is saviourism—like Christianity and Judaism.

The third is sage-ism—like Islam or Buddhism.

The fourth is secularism—like atheism or religious liberalism.

The claim that all spiritualities lead in the same direction is made by secularism. It has been a massive attempt since the Enlightenment to reduce the whole sphere of spirituality to one common denominator under secularism's control. Spiritism, saviourism, and sage-ism hold to the existence of the supernatural, and secularism is the movement since Voltaire, Hume, Descartes, Kant, Darwin and today's atheists, like Dawkins and Hitchens, to reduce the universe to the natural. Secularism campaigns against any belief in the supernatural by saying, "Since you all (those from the other 3 streams) believe the same thing in the end, namely the existence of the supernatural, none of you really have anything extraordinary to say. Plus, the differences between you are inconsequential. So stop trying to convince each other, stop trying to convert the rest of us, and keep your spirituality private and out of the public arena. We all believe in something, whether the supernatural or the natural, and it is 'believing sincerely in something' that unites the whole human family. We are all swimming in the same stream in the same direction."

Maria came back at me: "Is that so bad?"

"Well," I answered, "it's simply not true. If you ask the other streams of spirituality—namely spiritism, saviourism, and sage-ism—they will tell you that secularism's claim that 'all religions basically say the same thing' is not only wrong, it is impossible."

"What? But the 3 streams all believe in the supernatural. They all have that in common!"

I responded, "Here is the basic flaw with that argument: secularism says that all spiritualities believe in some form of the supernatural. But what all spiritualities believe about that supernatural is vastly different from one spirituality to another. Religions even differ from one another in what they believe about the natural—like the creation of the universe, the origin of evil, sin, and the need for salvation. Secularism says it's offensive to try to prove your religion as the correct one because all religions basically say the same thing. But for a Buddhist or a Muslim, the secularist claim that all religions basically say the same thing is highly offensive."

"But why should it be offensive? Can't two opposing claims both be true?"

I had to smile. Two weeks earlier I had read a book by the postmodern philosopher, Foucault, in which he made that exact claim, one that has made its path deep into western thinking in the past decades. "It doesn't mean that I have any less respect for you, Maria, if you choose to believe that. I was trained in rational thinking by German, Austrian, American, and Scottish professors, and everyone of them still cannot believe—and neither can I—that if 1+1=2, 1+1 can also =3."

Maria understood and smiled back. "So despite all the profound thinking of philosophers and theologians, you still believe in absolute truth?"

"Absolutely! So does everybody, even those who say they don't."

I expected Maria to blow like a volcano. Instead, she took a sip of her macchiato, in deep thought. Then she said, "My friends keep saying that spirituality is like a piece of clothing. You wear whatever fits. I thought so too when I was 17 and went on a wild search for the clothing that fit me. But now I wonder if the question of spirituality is deeper and more serious than the 'what works for me' approach. It seems to me to be a very self-centred, even self-absorbed approach to the question of God. 'What works for me?' I mean, how can you answer a question about something greater than yourself by circling around yourself? Anybody with a bit of logic should recognize that turning circles inside yourself to find something greater than yourself leads to no more than self-deception."

I was frankly surprised at this sudden turn in the conversation. We sat for a long time in the cafe, drifting from one topic to another. I did not have answers to all her questions, but that was okay. What Maria wanted was for me to be honest. She wanted to know how I had gone about finding the answers that had given my life so much joy and direction, stability and freedom. How could I have a strong faith in God when there were aspects of God that remained incomprehensible to me?

Two months later Monica was born. The first few moments on the delivery table were pure joy for Maria. But they quickly turned into fear and deep disappointment. The baby could hardly breathe. Monica was born with a handicap that would require several surgeries in the future. With the help of good medical intervention the little infant's life was spared. But in the next few days, questions abounded as to whether this little girl would ever be able to communicate with any kind of normalcy.

That is when Maria experienced God in a profound way. It was like a vision: He appeared to her, he made himself felt, he flooded her soul with peace. These highly personal meetings with the Almighty are very difficult to explain. It happened one day after her daughter's birth and the confirmation of Monica's special needs, as Maria was crying to God for help in her despair. He answered her. God met with her and assured her, that she belonged to him, that he loved her very much, and that she and Monica were safe in his arms. It was a personal encounter of the spiritual dimension.

Shortly after that, Maria had her newborn daughter baptized in the church her parents were part of. It was Maria's way of committing herself and her most precious possession to the God who still held much mystery for her but without a doubt had taken hold of her heart and filled it with faith.

1. Memorize Acts 20:28 and John 3:16.

2. Read Hebrews 1:1–3:6. The author compares Jesus to several important and highly spiritual figures. List all the ways Jesus is unique and "better" than all these figures.

3. The Apostolic Creed was first coined in the 5th century, which Christians around the world use to regularly profess and summarize their faith. You are invited to memorize it. I will give it to you line by line with explanations:

I believe in God the Father almighty, Maker of heaven and earth,
The first person of the Trinity. He called everything into being. Not 'survival of the fittest' but the 'fit sovereignty of God to uphold all things' (otherwise referred to as 'providence') is what guides creation and history forward.

And in Jesus Christ, his only Son, our Lord,
The second person of the Trinity. 'Son' does not mean that God created Jesus, but is simply the term the Bible uses to show that Jesus stands in a unique relationship to God. In a creed known as the Nicene Creed, Jesus is referred to as 'very God of very God.' In relation to the Father he is the Son, in relation to our lives he is the Lord.

Who was conceived by the Holy Spirit,
The third person of the Trinity. 'Conception' here refers to Jesus having divine origin. The phrase also emphasizes, that Jesus did not become anointed as Messiah and empowered by the Holy Spirit later in life; he was in union with the Spirit from the first moment of his earthly existence onward.

Born of the virgin Mary,
In contrast with the foregoing phrase, this emphasizes that Jesus was human. Mary had remained a 'virgin,' though she became pregnant with Jesus. This was to emphasize that Jesus came to us, not from a human father but from God the Father.

TOOLBOX

Suffered under Pontius Pilate,
Governor at the time Jesus was crucified. This reference places Jesus' crucifixion in history. It also emphasizes the place of suffering in the life of every follower of Jesus.

Was crucified, dead, and buried.
Islam denies that Jesus ever died on a cross. He did die not merely to die a martyr's death, but rather to be the sacrifice for our sins.

He descended into hell,
It is difficult to know precisely what the author had in mind here. Some think it might be intended as a reference to the fullness of his sufferings at the cross. There does appear, though, in Scripture to be a reference to Jesus appearing before the whole host of Satan and his demons to declare his victory as once and for all secured.

The third day He rose again from the dead,
There are many historical indicators showing that this really happened. The entire teaching and preaching of the apostles was based on this event, and most New Testament books make reference to it as the basis of Christian spirituality.

He ascended into heaven,
The Bible teaches that in heaven Jesus sat down at the Father's right hand. This indicates that his work as a priest was finished once and for all. Our salvation was secured.

From thence he will come to judge the quick and the dead.
This is a reference to the climactic point of history: the triumphant return of Jesus to earth. 'Quick' is an old English word for 'those alive'

I believe in the Holy Spirit,
The third person of the Trinity. He makes all of Christian spirituality possible. Without the Holy Spirit in our lives, we cannot be followers of Jesus.

The holy, catholic church,
'Catholic' originally meant 'universal' and is used that way here, not as a reference to the Roman Catholic Church. To prevent confusion, some modern versions of the Apostles' Creed use 'Christian' at this point. But 'catholic' is intended to say more: God has a people from every tongue, tribe, and nation, whom Jesus reclaimed for God through his death and resurrection, and for whom Jesus will return.

The communion of saints,
This clarifies that the church is not an organization but the gathering of people whom God has set apart for himself. This 'setting apart for himself' is the actual meaning of 'saints.' It is not a reference to dead people a long time ago, who were such good servants of God that they hold some special place in heaven.

The forgiveness of sins,
The work of the Holy Spirit is to apply to us the blood of Jesus he shed on the cross. The perfect blood of Jesus washes away anything and everything we have ever done wrong.

The resurrection of the body,
Our great hope! We will rise again, in body and soul, with the identity we have here on earth, but in a completed and perfected state.

And the life everlasting.
Our completed and perfected condition will go on forever. We will be forever without pain and bad memories, filled to the brim with joy and satisfaction, with pleasure and peace.

Amen!

02
Building Material

The Right Mix of Cement
in Your Foundation

I remember a terrible day at work. I don't know how often I had the Monkeys' song going through my head that day: *"I wish I would have stayed in bed, my pillow wrapped around my head,"* because I felt like either everything was going wrong or the brick layers found wrong in everything I was doing right. I was standing on the ground looking up at one of the brick layers. I had mixed some cement and carried it up the scaffold to him. It was far too watery for him to be able to lay the bricks in a straight line. Disgusted, he scooped some of the watery cement on his trowel and flung it down at me with the words, "I can't use this disgusting sh*#!" The reason I remember this moment so vividly is that I happened to have my mouth open as the watery cement came flying down at me. Before I could react, it flew into my mouth. I just remember vomiting everywhere.

One of the great lessons I have learned over the years is that if you are going to have a solid foundation for your life, you have to have the right mix of cement in the foundation for it to be solid. Anything other than the right mix will make you sick!

Christian spirituality is about having perfect righteousness

Remember the conversation I had with Maria about 'spirituality'? I defined spirituality according to the human longing we have in common: Spirituality is the attempt to attain righteousness; seeking to fill the longing for assurance that we are accepted, approved, and appreciated by the highest standard of goodness there is.

In terms of true Christian spirituality (that is, the way Jesus Christ taught it), it ends up looking like this:

Being a Christian is not about being moral,
it's about being intimate,
and
being a Christian is not about being good,
it's about being perfect.

A Scottish theologian, John Murray, once wrote that the heart and soul of Christian spirituality is union with Christ.[1] With that, he pointed to a remarkable truth: while many religious streams are essentially about moral conduct (e.g. Islam) or spiritual enlightenment (e.g. Buddhism), the Christian faith has at its centre an intimate union with Jesus. This intimacy is so...well, intimate that the biblical writer, Paul, uses "in" throughout his writings to describe it. In 2 Corinthians 5:17 he says, *"If anyone is IN Christ,"* and in Galatians 2:20, *"Christ lives IN me."* [P] Christian spirituality is one-in-another-ness! It is not a losing of oneself in another, not a blending of two selves into an indistinguishable oneness, but a one-in-another-ness-without-losing-the-other-ness.

At its centre, Christian spirituality is about an intimate relationship to God. Yet because of our human nature, we love to reduce spirituality to a level of DOING, instead of a state of BEING. We want to reduce it to our own goodness or our own attained enlightenment or our own accomplishments. But being a Christian is not about being good; it is about being intimate with God.

However, the pride and stubbornness of our human nature has many of us trying to remain on the moralistic track. We continue to measure our personal goodness by the standard of morality we have set. So we say things like, "I don't need God; I live a pretty good life as is, thank you," or "If what I see in Christians is sup-

---

[1]   John Murray, REDEMPTION ACCOMPLISHED AND APPLIED, Grand Rapids: Wm. B. Eerdmans, 1955, p. 161.

posed to be Christianity, no thanks." When we do that, we need to hear that Christianity is not about being good; it is about being perfect!

"But," most people argue at this point, "nobody is perfect!" That is exactly the point! I say *most people,* because there are a few people on this globe who profess to have never done anything wrong. They are also very proud of their perfection!

My friends, Dave and Joyce, have been attending the local symphony for a number of years. They frequently sit beside a man about Dave's age, a retired teacher and practicing Roman Catholic. He goes to mass every day. One evening, Dave and the man were having a discussion about sin and forgiveness when the man announced that he is not a sinner. Period. Never sinned! He doesn't lie, doesn't steal, has never done anything wrong. The man was dead serious.

David asked him, "Then why do you feel the need to go to mass every day?"

The man answered, "Just in case!"

Nobody is perfect! Even if you claim you are, you cannot be completely sure. That's not perfect! *"Who can say, 'I have kept my heart pure; I am clean and without sin'?"* (Proverbs 20:9).

Self-righteousness is the act of justifying yourself, declaring yourself 'not guilty' before your highest standard of goodness. If you make the level of badness in others your standard of goodness, you will always find a way to feel okay about yourself. There is always someone you can compare yourself to and reach the verdict, "I'm glad I'm not like that one!" With that kind of self-justification, you have good reason to feel proud of yourself, smug, indifferent toward others and apathetic toward religion.

There are three problems with self-righteousness:

- One, it is the root cause of every wrong and evil in the history of humanity.

- Two, it dwells in every human heart, including yours, mine and the person who thinks he's perfect.

- Three, God does not grade on a curve. Righteousness is not about your life being compared to another's level of goodness and getting a passing grade from God. In reality, the only one you are being compared to is God. His righteous standard is no lower than God himself: perfection.

We are all terribly guilty and every attempt to justify ourselves only makes us guiltier!

Several years ago, in a small group meeting for sceptics and spiritual seekers, an irritated 72-year-old man named Dennis blurted out in exasperation, "That is nonsense! I don't need Jesus. I have lived a civilized life, served my community well as a school principal, have been a good husband and father, raised my kids to be the good people they are today, and continue to do lots of good things for other people."

I really like this man Dennis. He *had* done a lot of good for his community and he *had* raised his children well. His daughter, a mother of 6 children, had begun to attend our church in Toronto, had committed her life to Jesus, had decided to host the Discovery Group I was leading, and had invited her parents. Only, she had not told her parents what the group was about!

"I understand what you mean," I said to Dennis. The man obviously was shocked to find himself in a group discussing spiritual things. "If all that it means to be a Christian is to live a moral and ethical life, then you are absolutely right: you don't need Jesus. You just need to try hard. But Jesus taught us that being a Christian is not about being good, but about being perfect. In his first recorded sermon, the Sermon on the Mount, he even said, *'Be perfect'*" (Matt. 5:48).

Now Dennis was really irritated and scoffed, "Nobody is perfect!"

"That's exactly the point," I responded. "No one is perfect. Even worse, God, who is perfect, has a perfect standard of righteousness. I mean, a perfect God cannot possibly have an imperfect standard for us, or he is not perfect in all his ways. And if God is not perfect in all his ways, then God is not God." The man looked at me with glazed eyes, but I went on anyway: "That means, of course, that no good thing that you do, no matter how good you or others think it to be, is good enough for God, because it is not perfect. The Bible expressed this divine logic long before any of us ever thought of it. Romans 3:23 says, *'All have sinned, and fall short of the glory of God.'* Worse, every attempt to win God's favour by doing good, is an imperfect work. That means that with every good work you actually increase your debt to God."

Now the man's eyes had gotten so huge, I thought they were going to pop out of his head.

"That is so ridiculous," he blurted. "Then everybody, including the pope, the Dalai Lama, Mohammed, and Mother Theresa are completely hopeless!"

"Exactly!" I said. "That's why a man by the name of Martin Luther once reflected on all his attempts to get right with God by admitting, *'The more I tried* [to pay my debt to God by doing good deeds], *the worse it became!'"*

It took Dennis several weeks of attending this Discovery Group to understand: None of us are good enough for God, but Jesus was perfect for us. God himself solved what no human being can solve. In fact, there are actually two things that have to be solved.

First, Jesus came into the world to stand in your place to live the perfect life before God that you and I fail to live. That is why Jesus had to combine in his one person two natures: human and divine. He had to be a human being, which is why he was born of Mary. And he had to be God, which is why he was conceived by the Holy Spirit (and not Joseph). Jesus came as the God-Man with a sinless nature. His sinlessness was essential to his ability to save us out of our hopelessness.

Jesus was tempted and confronted with extremely difficult life situations, just as we are. But in every situation he remained perfectly obedient to God in our place. He achieved for us the impossible perfect standard of God. It is, therefore, not our attempt at a good life that saves us, but a spiritual union with the one who lived the perfect life for us, Jesus Christ. *Being a Christian is not about being moral, it's about being intimate.*

The second problem to be solved is that no matter how good you are, we each have to pay for our transgression against God with death! A criminal who comes before the judge is not acquitted just because he stops committing crimes. He has to pay for his crimes. That is how justice works. Parents of a murdered child do not come to peace about their child's death simply because the murderer promises to never again murder. They feel that justice is done when the murderer of their child is arrested, judged and punished for his crime.

God's demand for righteousness requires that the penalty for the wrongdoing be paid. But even here, we see the ingenuity and incomprehensible grace of God. Before Adam committed the first sin, God had warned him that one sin against the perfectly holy God would result in horrific death—death for Adam, death for his descendants, death for the whole world. This would be death in all its dimensions: death in a physical sense (every person's body deteriorates and comes to an end), death in the creative sense (the image of God in us is terribly disfigured), death in a spiritual sense (man's spirit is dead and without relationship to his creator) and death in a relational sense (every relationship experiences tension, disharmony and sometimes alienation). Through the original human being, who Paul called the First Adam, death in every sense spread to us all and to every facet of life.

But Jesus, who Paul called the Second Adam, came as the representative of the new man and conquered death in all its dimensions: physically (he died on the cross and rose again), creatively (on the cross, he, the perfect image of God, became totally disfigured for us), spiritually (he took our rebellion against God into himself) and relationally (he experienced the animosity of enemies, betrayal by friends, even abandonment by God). Through his death, Jesus died our death (in all its dimensions), and thereby paid our death penalty. In this way he satisfied the perfectly righteous requirement of the Father.

That puts spirituality on a completely different level than morality. Christianity is not about what I should do for God, but about what God has done for me. Being a Christian is primarily not a matter of your activity for Christ, but of your union with Christ. All your attempts to make yourself right before God, every form of religiosity you use to demonstrate to others that you are a good Christian, every activity by which you attempt to earn God's love, every form of striving to be perfect before God...it all becomes a moot point. *Being a Christian is not about being good, it's about being perfect.* Jesus was perfect for you. He accomplished God's standard of righteousness perfectly for you.

The only thing left to do is explained in the Bible like this: *"The name of the LORD is a strong tower; the righteous run to it and are safe"* (Proverbs 18:10). Union with Jesus is the essential core of Christian spirituality.

Being a Christian is not about being moral,
it's about being intimate,
and
being a Christian is not about being good,
it's about being perfect.

Christian Spirituality is about living out of the gospel

In and of myself I am more sinful than I ever dared to believe
but
in Christ I am more loved than I ever dared to hope.

One of the reasons I love being back in the country in which I grew up is the cars. The German design of cars is unique. Simply masterful! BMW, Mercedes, Audi—Wunderbar! Even hand the German a VW, and he will design out of such a simple car a super one. Give him a few decades of tediously working through every possibility of something going wrong before daring to manufacture it right (I kid you not, that is the German way!), and he will turn a Volkswagen into Fahrvergnügen.

My VW, for example, is a simple Golf station wagon. But it has a Turbo Diesel engine with Direkteinspritzung (direct injection). I don't know the deep meaning of this but I know the results: my VW can fly like the wind and can accelerate like a man fleeing from an irritated wife. It is a pleasure driving my VW with that Turbo Diesel engine and Direkteinspritzung. My wife used to growl at me, "Slow down!" But the disease of Fahrvergnügen got a hold of her, as well, and now we both fahren with Vergnügen.

One of the things my mechanic always tells me is, "Be sure to put the right oil into your car!" He says that because the Dühsepumpe requires very special and expensive oil. If I were to put ordinary car oil into my Turbo engine, it would not be able to withstand the heat and would grind to an awful halt. No more Fahrvergnügen!

That special and expensive oil reminds me of our spiritual lives. It takes a very special oil to lubricate the engine of our spirituality. This special oil for your spiritual life is called the 'gospel.'

Romans 1:17 says, *"For in the gospel a righteousness from God is revealed, a righteousness that is by faith from first to last, just as it is written: 'The righteous will live by faith.'"* This Bible verse is the Christian life in a nutshell. It is the magnificent peak of the mountain from which you ski down the slopes of Christian spirituality. It is also a historic verse, because it is the verse that sparked the Reformation in Europe in 1517. A Catholic monk and professor at Wittenberg University, Martin Luther, had agonized for several years about this most basic of questions: how does a person become righteous enough in order to be fully accepted by his perfectly righteous Maker and God? In one of his most famous writings, THE BONDAGE OF THE WILL (1525), Luther described every person's moral dilemma as follows:

"If I lived and worked to all eternity, my conscience would never reach comfortable certainty as to how much it must do to satisfy God. Whatever work I have done, there would still be a nagging doubt as to whether it pleased God, or whether He required something more."[2]

In the midst of despair over his inability to ever make peace with God who is perfectly righteous and has a perfect standard for our righteousness, Romans 1:17 was the lightning bolt that struck his heart and set fire to his soul, so that he ended up writing years later, *"It was as if I had been born anew."*

What Luther discovered in Romans 1:17, and what became the Reformation flame that engulfed many parts of Europe, was the gospel. He discovered that the gospel is not the ABC of the Christian life but the A-Z. He realized that the gospel is not merely that which enters us into a relationship to God, but that which defines our relationship to God for our entire life. It is the special oil that is needed to make the spiritual life of any and every person run the way it was built to run.

One reason that is true is because the gospel communicates God's perfect righteousness to us. My friend, Tim Keller, who has written a fabulous book called THE PRODIGAL GOD, has defined the

---

[2] John Dillenberger, ed., MARTIN LUTHER: SELECTIONS FROM HIS WRITINGS. New York: Anchor Books, 1961. p. 199.

gospel for years in two catchy sentences. The first sentence goes: "In and of myself I am more sinful than I ever dared to believe." Not very flattering! But it is a realistic picture of our innermost being according to Isaiah 64:6: *"All of us have become like one who is unclean, and all our righteous acts are like filthy rags."* As I described previously, even our best, most charitable deeds are so far from perfect that while we are performing them we look like dirty, smelly people, dressed in worn out clothes before God. No living person can be righteous before God (Psalm 143:2). Our condition before God is far worse than we "ever dared to believe."

But here is the gospel: God washes us and dresses us in perfectly clean clothes. Isaiah 61:10 states, *"I delight greatly in the Lord; my soul rejoices in my God. For he has clothed me with garments of salvation and arrayed me in a robe of righteousness, as a bridegroom adorns his head like a priest, and as a bride adorns herself with her jewels."* This verse reminds me of my 34th wedding anniversary. On that occasion I pulled out our wedding album, blew the dust off the cover, and started looking through it. I want you to know that my wife was an absolutely beautiful sight in 1976. I turned a page, looked at her standing there in her wedding dress with her brown hair hanging down over her shoulders and thought of how I went ga-ga the first time I laid eyes on her 3 years before our wedding. I turned another page and saw a picture of me standing in the front of the church sanctuary, looking at Susan walking down the aisle. My eyes were big, a smile covered my face, and I remember how a river of delight flooded my whole being: "This beautiful girl will be my wife, she is all mine!"

Isaiah describes in similar terms what happens when God takes us, washes us, and puts a bridal dress on us. The God who demands perfect righteousness becomes totally enthralled with you. He finds you to be the most beautiful thing in the universe. You! The most beautiful thing in the universe! How does this happen?

It is the "great exchange," as many have come to call it. On the one hand, God took the sins of the world, every single transgression, flaw, shortcoming and shame, and placed the incomprehensibly enormous death-deserving load on his most holy Son. I never thought about the magnanimity of that act until I read Luther's COMMENTARY ON GALATIANS:

"And this, no doubt, all the prophets did foresee in spirit, that Christ should become the greatest transgressor, murderer, adulterer, thief, rebel, blasphemer, etc. that ever was or could be in all the world. (Hold it! Stop the wagons! Honestly, at this point, my reaction was, 'Luther, now you are blaspheming against holy Jesus. Probably had too much beer at this point!') *For he, being made a sacrifice for the sins of the whole world, is not now an innocent person and without sins, is not now the Son of God born of the Virgin Mary; but a sinner, which has and carries the sin of Paul, who was a blasphemer, an oppressor and a persecutor; of Peter, which denied Christ; of David, which was an adulterer, a murderer, and caused the Gentiles to blaspheme the name of the Lord: in short, which has and bears the sins of all men in his body, that he might make satisfaction for them with his own blood."*[3]

Honestly, I was totally shocked by this description! But Luther must be right. If all the sins of the world went over on Jesus, including all the ugly thoughts and deeds of my own life and yours, Jesus must have turned into the ugliest, morally most abominable and most disfigured sight imaginable. No wonder the Father turned his face!

On the other hand, God dressed you in the righteousness of Jesus. *"For in the gospel a righteousness from God is revealed"* (Romans 1:17). This righteousness is totally foreign to you, but when it encloses you it feels like it was made for you. It fits you perfectly. In the moment you entrust yourself to Jesus—to his perfect life, death and resurrection—God dresses you in the righteousness that is not your own. He dresses you in Jesus' righteousness.

The result of that is absolutely stunning. It is expressed in the Heidelberg Catechism from 1563, in question/answer #60:

Q: "How are you right with God?"

A: "Only by true faith in Jesus Christ. Even though my conscience accuses me of having grievously sinned against all God's commandments, and of never having kept any of them, and even though I am still inclined toward all evil, nevertheless, without my deserving it at all, out of sheer grace, God grants and credits to me the perfect satisfaction, righteousness, and holiness of Christ, as if I had never sinned nor been a sinner, as if I had been as perfectly obedient as Christ was obedient for me. All I need to do is to accept this gift of God with a believing heart."

---

[3] Dillenberger, p. 135.

Imagine! God looks upon you as if you had never sinned nor ever been a sinner. It is a perfect position to be in, because now God the Father looks on you the way I looked at my Susan in 1976 as she walked down the aisle. He is completely attracted to your beauty. Actually, it is his own beauty, the righteousness of the second Person of the Trinity. You could say: God is attracted to your beauty as much as he is attracted to his own beauty, because it *is* his beauty. He dressed you in it. The label on the back of that pearly dress says: "Made in Jesus'-righteousness."

That is how you became the most beautiful thing in the universe!

The gospel is the A-Z of the Christian life. You do not wear the dress of Jesus' righteousness only on the day of your conversion to Jesus. It is your dress as his bride from that moment on. You wear it every day. Always! Forever! Wherever you go, whatever you do. This means that there is no time or moment in which God loves you less than he did the moment before. It also means that there is no thought or action you can do that would lessen God's delight in you.

That is why the second sentence which Tim Keller has used for years to describe the gospel is "In Christ I am more loved than I ever dared to hope."

So there you have the special oil that makes the engine of Christian spirituality run smoothly, the oil that is so costly, it cost God his Son and cost his Son his life:

In and of myself I am more sinful than I ever dared to believe,
but
in Christ I am more loved than I ever dared to hope.

The gospel-driven Christian:
learning to live like a child instead of an orphan

Another key phrase in Romans 1:17 is *"from faith to faith."* With this Paul means that the entire Christian life is lived, from one moment to the next, by faith in that very righteousness of Christ that has been credited to you. In every situation, you can either trust in your own righteousness or in the righteousness with which

God has dressed you, Christ's righteousness. You either put your faith in how good you are or look, or you put your faith in how perfect Jesus is for you. Christian spirituality is a daily, moment-by-moment decision: in which righteousness will I trust this time?

Jesus called our trust in our self-righteousness an orphan mentality. He said, *"I will not leave you as orphans; I will come to you"* (John 14:18). The person with an orphan mentality is the Christian who has been adopted by God into God's family, who stands in a warm, intimate relationship to God as his Daddy (Romans 8:16, *Abba*), who has his name written in the Father's will as co-recipient of the entire inheritance that has been promised to Jesus, in whom and in whose righteousness the Christian lives; yet despite having all these things, he thinks and lives as if none of this were true, as if none of it were reality. He interprets what people say to him or reacts to situations as if there were no Heavenly Daddy, who has dressed him in that most beautiful bridal gown of Jesus' righteousness. No, in any given moment or difficult situation he thinks of himself as a poor orphan who has no Daddy at all.

The difference between an orphan Christian and a child-of-God Christian is the difference between a moralistic Christian and a gospel-driven Christian.

The moralistic Christian tries as hard as he can to keep his own righteousness intact, as if it were the only righteousness he has. Consequently, he is driven by the need for others to think well of him and to approve of him. His quest is to do those things that make him look good, especially that make him look like a good Christian. It is about image—his own image in front of others. And so he is always trying harder, doing more, performing better. His goal is to prove himself, to prove his own righteousness. Keller is right in claiming, "To most people in our society, Christianity *is* religion and moralism."[4] One reason people view Christianity as moralism is because many Christians live as if moralistic Christianity is true Christian spirituality.

The gospel-driven Christian, on the other hand, trusts moment-by-moment in Christ's righteousness to give him full acceptance with God. Therefore he feels no need to prove himself. Having

---

[4] Tim Keller, THE PRODIGAL GOD, New York: Dutton, 2008, p. 14.

Christ's perfect righteousness as his garment means (to paraphrase an old song): "I need no other argument; I need no other plea, what's good enough for righteous God is good enough for me!"

What is good enough for righteous God? The perfect righteousness of Jesus. No matter what the person dressed in Christ's righteousness does or does not do, one thing is constant: "In Christ I am more loved than I ever dared to hope."

The gospel-driven Christian does not start with the need to prove himself, but with the delight of being approved. As Helmut Thielicke wrote, *"God doesn't love us because we are so worthy; rather, it's precisely the opposite: we are worthy because God loves us."*[5]

Due to his already and permanently established approval by God, the gospel-driven Christian is free to honestly face the first fact of the gospel: "In and of myself I am more sinful than I ever dared to believe."

Whatever sins in his life make him more sinful than he ever dared to believe, they do not change the fact that in Christ he remains more loved than he ever dared to hope. This allows the gospel-driven Christian to get to the heart of his sin. Since he does not need to wear a mask to preserve his good image, he does not merely look at his outward actions (in hope that they look good enough to get God's approval), but at the heart behind the actions. He bores deep into the sin behind the sin. He asks, "What is driving me, what is motivating me? Is it a desire to prove my own righteousness or is it a delight in the righteousness of Christ?"

That is the reason why Paul says in Romans 1:17, *"The righteous* (i.e., those who have been declared righteous because they are dressed in Christ's righteousness) *shall live by faith* (i.e., by trusting in that righteousness)." *(NAS)*

Living out of the gospel

Let's look at 3 examples of how living out of the gospel works in day-to-day situations.

Take two Christians, one driven by moralism and one driven by the gospel. Both strive to do their best at something. It may be a

---

[5] Helmut Thielicke, Das Schweigen Gottes, Giessen: Brunnen, 2008, p. 73: "Gott liebt uns nicht, weil wir so wertvoll wären, sondern es ist genau umgekehrt: wir sind so wertvoll, weil Gott uns liebt".

particular school course, it may be something athletic, it may be work-related or it may be a ministry in the church. Both Christians do the same thing, and both give their absolute best. The moralistic Christian does his best so that he looks like a stellar saint to others or so that God will think him worthy to be God's child. The gospel-driven Christian does his best out of gratitude for the righteousness of Christ that makes him worthy to be called God's child. He knows that when he does a particular activity, his identity and personal value remain intact with the Father, regardless of success or failure. That freedom fills him with such thanksgiving for the liberating gospel that he enthusiastically gives his best. Though the two Christians perform the same action, the heart behind the action is radically different. One is motivated by the desire to prove himself (his own righteousness), the other by the desire to express his joy in being approved by God (due to Christ's righteousness). The action of the moralistic Christian may actually bring a better result than that of the gospel-driven Christian, but in God's eyes, only the latter could be considered "good."

Another example is two Christians who are both criticized for having done something poorly. The moralistic Christian finds the criticism a shock to his system, a threat to his self-righteousness. He thinks like an orphan; he thinks that his very own righteousness is the only righteousness he has. Consequently, he has to run to the rescue of his righteousness. How does he do that? Some of this may sound familiar:

He may try self-pity, thinking to himself, "Poor victim that I am. I always get the brunt of people's false interpretation! Nobody understands me!"

He may try giving the cold shoulder, the silent treatment or some kind of reaction by which the critic is punished for his criticism. "Maybe next time he will think twice about finding wrong in my performance."

He may defend himself: "Hey, I'm sorry, I couldn't help it! It's not my fault—the circumstances simply didn't allow me to do better."

He may go over onto the offensive, picking up the hand grenade that was lobbed at him and hurling it right back at the critic: "Look at you, you're no better!" or "Hey, you did the same thing!"

The gospel-driven Christian, on the other hand, hears the criticism and is not surprised. When someone finds a flaw in the gospel-driven Christian's life, it simply confirms what he has known all along: he is indeed more sinful than he ever dared to believe. He knows this sometimes translates into doing some things not quite right; he also knows that acknowledging this will not change anything about his personal identity or value—he is still loved in Christ more than he ever dared to hope.

The gospel-driven Christian also knows that not only he, but everyone else as well, is more sinful than anybody ever dared to believe. This means that others can misinterpret or misjudge the value of his actions. Just as it is possible that the gospel-driven Christian has done something poorly, it is possible that another person thinks this action was wrong, when, in fact, it is not.

Therefore, he is able to respond to the criticism with something like this: "Thank you for observing that. I'm not surprised, quite frankly, that someone would see that flaw in me. I'll tell you what I'm going to do. I will take this matter to God in prayer daily, and ask him to show me the truth of what you are saying about me."

Two Christians are criticised. One tries desperately to hold on to his orphan righteousness, resulting in a strained relationship. The other who knows his identity and value is protected by Christ's righteousness and allows the criticism to become an opportunity for the Holy Spirit to bring about positive change and growth in his life.

A third example of living out the gospel comes from my private life and my marriage to the girl I went ga-ga about when I first laid eyes on her in 1973, the girl who put the sun in my eyes when she came down the aisle in her wedding dress in 1976. Following that blissful day, Susan and I had a good marriage for 29 years. All that changed in 2006 when our marriage turned to some kind of wonderful!

Good marriages have times of crisis. Our marriage is no different. We have had long-standing cold wars; we have had atomic-like explosions when one of us (usually me) has dropped a bomb on the other. But the worst crisis we have ever had was a feud that lasted 3 whole years. It was no cold war; it was more a heated battle, in which we repeatedly took aim at each other. I felt deeply hurt by Susan; she felt deeply disappointed in me. I felt under-appreciated by Susan; she felt falsely accused by me. I felt rejected by Susan; she felt abandoned by me. Our relationship spiralled downward. Our anger would boil over into accusations: "Why can't you...!" "How is it that after all these years you still don't understand what I need in a wife?" "How is it that you aren't the man I married? Why do I feel like I am married to a stranger?"

One morning, 3 years into "the war," I came home from an 8 o'clock lecture to get my second cup of coffee. As I dragged myself into the house, Susan met me there, kissed me and smiled. Something in my spirit began to realize that the anger had lifted from her shoulders.

As the day wore on, I became more aware of what was happening around me. Whatever it was, it was different than the past 3 years. By the evening, I realized that my wife had been sweet to me the entire day. I went to bed that night thinking, "Probably just a few rays of sunshine before the next big storm." But the next day the sun was still shining, at least between Susan and me. The day after that it was too, and the day after that. I don't mean to suggest that my wife had turned into some sweet-smiling mush, with daggers hidden behind her back. It was more like the daggers were gone. The kindness was genuine. She even communicated respect toward me, which touched my masculine soul deeply. I got the feeling that she was suddenly content to have me as her husband; in fact, it felt like she cherished me and was glad to be around me (even though I had hurt her very badly). It became hard to be angry with her, especially when this new disposition of hers went on for a whole week. I kept waiting for it to stop. It didn't. It went on for two weeks, then three.

Finally, I had to know what had happened. Why, after 29½ years of marriage, had the last 3 weeks been to me as if I was married to the woman of my dreams? It was, after all, the same woman: the same Susan who had walked down the aisle in 1976, the Susan who had given birth to our four daughters, the Susan who had stood by me through thick and thin. But she wasn't the same.

"Honey, what happened 3 weeks ago that you have become so sweet toward me?" I asked, as I stuck my fork into my piece of cake.

"The gospel!"

"The gospel?"

"Yep, the gospel," she said, as she took another sip of her coffee.

"Honey, you have believed the Christian gospel since you were a child 200 years ago. What do you mean, 'the gospel'?"

Then she began to explain, "You know that I have been doing that Sonship course with Karina in Toronto over Skype, right?"

"You mean Maria's mom?"

"Yes. Well, I had just worked through another chapter with her. One night, three weeks ago, when I was feeling so mad at you, it suddenly hit me that I had not really let the gospel do its work of liberation in me. I had believed in the gospel with my head, but I had never really let it get to the core of my being and drive my whole sense of identity from inside out. That night, sitting in the kitchen and thinking about how bad things had become, I found my entire self, with all my longings for security and significance, being submerged into the pool of God's love for me. You know how Tim Keller has always said, 'In Christ I am more loved and valued and accepted by God than I ever dared to hope'?"

"Yeah, but what does that have to do with the fact that you don't seem to be angry at me anymore, and you have been so kind toward me, as if you were content being married to me, after all the hurt I have caused you?"

"What the Holy Spirit laid on my heart that night was that, dressed in the righteousness of Jesus, I am secure in God's love. For 29½ years of marriage I have been trying to find my security in your love for me. If I felt you were loyal to me, I felt secure in myself. If I felt your eyes or your heart looking upon other women as being better than me, I felt deep insecurity and would say, 'What is wrong with me that I am not enough for him?' But the gospel has pointed me to the Father's unchanging love for me, because the righteousness of Jesus is like a huge magnet that pulls the Father's love uninterruptedly toward me. My mistake has been to believe in the gospel with my head, but to never bathe my innermost longing for security in it."

"That's heavy!" is all I knew to say.

"But that's not all," Susan explained further. "I thought about the things that you have done that have made me angry. I realized that I have been acting like a spiritual orphan. I wanted you to act in a way that would give me security from you. I hung my image as a Christian on the appearance of a marriage that looked like it had it all together. When you did or said things that threatened that image, I felt the threat to my own image. But three weeks ago, it hit me: I had made our marriage into an idol that I worshipped and sought approval from. I had made you into a golden calf that I danced around, in the hope that you would feed me with the security I want. The gospel showed me how I have been guilty of idolatry and that I need to turn to Christ and trust his righteousness, which secures the Father's love to me, and in which my longing for security finds rest."

"Wow!"

She continued, "As I realized that my sense of well-being depended on the state of our relationship, I ended up saying to God, 'How he behaves is actually his problem, not mine. What he does or does not do has no bearing on who I am.' So I gave you over to God. I no longer need to bear responsibility for your behaviour, only for my own. That frees me to love you just as you are. And I can forgive you the way God has forgiven me, since I myself am more sinful than I ever dared to believe."

Susan had changed! And what she said to me that day in the café penetrated my own heart. It revolutionized my life. How had I been so blind? For all of my marriage, I had measured my personal significance by how much Susan displayed affection toward me, by how much she complimented me for being a nice guy and doing great things for God. Every silence from her when I hoped for a good word, any show of disinterest when I wanted to have her affection, every criticism toward my way of leading when I really had wanted her recognition—it all cut like a knife at my longing for significance.

But the gospel that set my wife free to love me as I am set me free too. Life, love, and marriage driven by the gospel—it has become better than what I ever dreamed. She no longer feels a need to keep my actions under her control, to keep everything looking good and appearing perfect. She has become patient with me and my rough edges. I have stopped trying to inflict guilt on her when she does not respond the way I had hoped or when she doesn't pour great words of affirmation on me. For me, that has translated into no longer being manipulative toward her, trying to get her to do or say what I want her to do or say.

■ What's in it for me?

- The gospel sets you free to feel secure. You place your trust in Christ's righteousness, in which God's approval of you truly rests and God accepts you forever as his dearly beloved son or daughter.

- The gospel sets you free to feel significant. You place your trust in Christ's righteousness, in which God's appreciation of you as *"the apple of his eye"* rests (Zechariah 2:8).

- The gospel sets you free to succeed in what you do without being proud, because you no longer do great things simply to elevate your self-righteousness.

- The gospel sets you free to fail at things without falling apart due to your failure, because your value no longer depends on great achievements. It depends on what Christ's righteousness has achieved for you before God.

- The gospel sets you free because it takes the pressure off of you to perform, to prove your worth, to be better than others. Nothing can rob you of being highly valued and deeply loved by the Father. Nothing—not being neglected or abused by others, not being ridiculed, not being worse than others, not having less than others. Not when the gospel defines who you truly are.

And who are you?

In and of myself I am more sinful than I ever dared to believe,
but
in Christ I am more loved than I ever dared to hope.

Let your spirituality be driven by the gospel; let it saturate your entire being! It is the special oil that Jesus paid for with his life; let it flow into the engine of your life. It is the right mix of cement you need to build the foundation of your spiritual house.

If your spiritual house is not built on the gospel, it will have the same result as the badly mixed cement that ended up in my mouth in 1975: It will make you sick!

1. In your own words, why is "union with Christ" the heart and soul of Christian spirituality?

2. Read and meditate on Galatians 2:16-17 and on Philippians 3:7-9.

3. Christian spirituality – actually the life, death and resurrection of Jesus –assures you that your personal identity is not dependent on how much you accomplish for God or for others or how good you appear to be. Your identity is anchored in Christ, who was perfectly obedient for you and paid the perfect penalty on the cross for your disobedience.
Evaluate: In what situations or with what people do you tend to define your identity? When do you measure your value by your deeds, accomplishments or acceptance, instead of by what the Creator accomplished for you or has defined you to be?

4. For the purpose of explaining Christian spirituality to others, memorize:

Being a Christian is not about being moral, it is about being intimate,
and
Being a Christian is not about being good, it is about being perfect.

5. For the purpose of putting into perspective who and what the gospel of God declares you to be, memorize:

In and of myself I am more sinful than I ever dared to believe,
but in Christ I am more loved than I ever dared to hope.

Start the habit of reciting this definition of the gospel to yourself every morning before you get started into the day, as well as in every moment you feel worthless, and on every occasion you fail at something. In your own words, explain to a friend what this 2-statement definition of the gospel has come to mean to you.

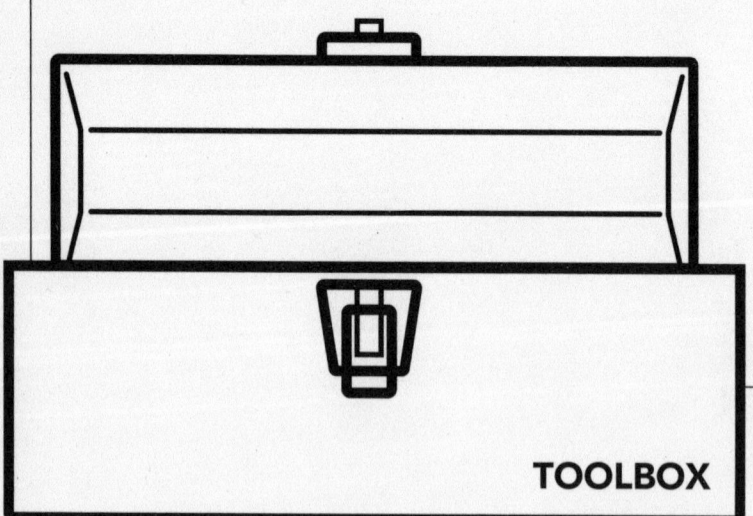

TOOLBOX

6. Give yourself a "Susan moment":

- In what areas of your life are you dancing around an idol in the hope of having security or significance communicated to you?
- Talk to God about the idols in your life and ask him for grace to repent (turn) from believing them to trusting God and his value statements for you.

7. We presented Christian spirituality as the process of learning a new relationship: no longer an orphan but a son/daughter of the Heavenly Father. Is it difficult for you to associate God with 'Father'? If 'father figure' brings with it negative associations, you are not alone. Many in this world can identify with you. May I suggest that you:

- Start all over through "the renewal of your mind" (Romans 12: 2). Instead of moving from below to above, associating your negative image of a father with God, move from above to below, covering over the concept of earthly fatherhood with all that you learn about God the Heavenly Father. God, not your dad, is the archetype of fatherhood (Ephesians 3:14-15). As you read in the Bible how God is a father to those who have come into a relationship with him, begin to see his character traits and manner of dealing with his children as the model of all fathering.
- Meditate daily on the reality that the Heavenly Father is a daddy who will always receive you and always has time for you: Psalm 27:10 says: "My mother and father may have forsaken me, but the Lord will receive me." Even if you have forsaken God or have sinned against him, he does not turn his back on you, nor does he passively wait for you; he pursues you with kindness (Romans 4:2; 2 Timothy 2:13; see the father's movement toward the son in Luke 15:20).
- Read a best-seller of our time, a narrative on spirituality written by a man who sought to work through the deep wounds caused by his father. The book has not gone without criticism, and many would consider the Christian spirituality of this book superficial. I find certain parts of the book profound, and think it offers therapeutic effects for those wounded by their fathers. I therefore recommend a careful read of Wm. Paul Young, THE SHACK (London: Hodder & Stoughton Ltd., 2007).

Maria's Journey #3
Meeting with God in
an Easter Service

The same church in which Monica had been baptized and Maria had committed herself to orienting her life around God was the place of worship she attended on Easter Sunday morning.

The preacher did not look trendy to Maria in his black robe, but he spoke enthusiastically about the resurrection of Jesus from the dead. Maria noticed—and here she thought about the university professor—that for the preacher, the resurrection of Jesus was a real and objective event that translated into his own personal, subjective experience. He spoke as if he had personally encountered Jesus. In his introduction he made a startling statement:

"Precisely because Jesus' resurrection is an objective and historic event, it crashes in on our subjective experience with all its truthfulness, threatens to steal us away from our closely guarded autonomy by demanding our lives, and offers us the way into the freedom of having a clear orientation and meaning in life."

In that moment, it became crystal clear to Maria that if Jesus really rose from the dead, if he really conquered the powerful force of death, then he must really be the incarnation of God. God in the flesh! Then there must be absolute truth, embodied in Jesus. Then there is one absolute and objective authority that stands over her life, reaches into her subjective experience, and demands that she put to death her self-orientation and her it's-all-about-me-centredness, and offer herself up to Jesus.

The preacher went on: the implication of the resurrection must be that Jesus' teaching is completely true. In every detail! What Jesus said about God, about the Bible (at Jesus' time that was the Old Testament), about the creation of the world, about heaven and hell, about sex, about money, about children and the value of life, in fact, everything he said about everything must be—on the basis of the resurrection of Jesus—completely true and trustworthy.

Now the pastor directed his thoughts at the personal level of those who made up the Easter crowd that morning:

"Our lives receive purpose and are infused with meaning when we align ourselves completely with Jesus, when we make him the centre of our selves, when we follow him. And then the question of purpose in life resolves itself," he said, "because to step into the path of Jesus is to walk in the only real reality."

Maria wondered if the congregation could follow the preacher at this point. She certainly was having some difficulty. The pastor tried to explain by referring to a German theologian, Dietrich Bonhoeffer, who was executed by the Nazis in 1945 for his stand against Hitler. Bonhoeffer once said to his students at the seminary in Finkenwalde that there is only one reality—the reality in which God exists—and that anything outside that reality is an illusion, which means that life is being lived in an unreal way. Bonhoeffer called this reality the "Christuswirklichkeit" (Christ-reality), because reality as it really is includes the historic event of the resurrection of Jesus. Therefore, life is only life within reality (the way things really are) if it is lived and centred on the fact that Jesus rose from the dead.

Some of the listeners in the cathedral glanced bewildered at their neighbour, not understanding the preacher's philosophizing. Others did understand and felt the preacher had gone too far because his statements sounded dangerously exclusivist.

For Maria, though, it became another moment of God breaking through to her. It felt like with the resurrection of Jesus, God was moving a rational foundation underneath her

83

existential experiences, both the vision of God appearing to her personally and the committal of her life to God at Monica's baptism. She looked down at her 6-month-old baby in her arms, and began to silently cry. 'Christuswirklichkeit!' Maria knew she had tried to frame a reality for herself without Christ. She knew she had sinned against God by wanting to get rid of him and pursue her own selfish way of life. Her rebellion against God, her hatred toward her parents, the way she had wasted many good things in life because of selfishness, the prostitution of her beauty for the sake of gaining the approval of men; all this and more lay like a mountain of human dung in front of the crucified and resurrected Jesus. This is what she had presented to the true and real Lord. She felt the guilt of what she had to offer him. She started to doubt again: how could God love and accept her?

As the Lordship of Jesus came crashing in on Maria, so did another ray of hope. The preacher said, "Because Jesus has risen from the dead, everything about Jesus must be true. That means that what he accomplished on the cross must also be true. It means—get this!—he really took the guilt and shame of our rebellion against God on himself, and he really paid for all our wrong. Love's greatest expression of love was made in the moment Jesus offered up to God through the cross his perfect righteousness, laying it over the dung heap of your sins, and thereby burning away the putrid sight and smell of your shortcomings. The resurrection confirms once and for all that through Jesus, God's face has turned toward you with a look of pleasure and affection, that he is ready to forgive every wrong in your life and to let it go, as if it had never been committed. This is freedom indeed! But you must place your faith in this resurrected Jesus!"

Suddenly a new feeling flowed into Maria's soul. She did not feel guilty about her heap of dung; she felt thankful for God's amazing grace. She realized that if she had never become so vile and selfish and confused, she would not have made such a mess of her life, but then she never would have awakened to God's grace. Had it not been for the birth of Monica, Maria would never have gone on the spiritual journey she was on, a journey that brought her to meeting and experiencing God in his holiness and mercy.

She could feel like she had completely stepped out of the prison cell of self. It was like walking out of a desert into a luscious garden. Maria felt like she was drinking satisfaction deeply into her soul.

SECTION 2

The 4 Cornerstones
that Give Your Spirituality Shape:

The Sovereignty, Holiness,
Love and Pleasures of God

Every building has to have cornerstones. They determine the shape of the structure yet to be built. The shape of your spiritual life is equally determined by its spiritual cornerstones. You need to get these solidly in place, and you need to place them right! They determine if the spiritual house of your life is sturdy, straight, and able to withstand the storms that pound you. Cornerstones have to do not only with the beliefs you develop and out of which you operate, but also with the motivations behind your actions and reactions. What motivates you to live for God? What drives you? We will state the four cornerstones of Christian spirituality in terms of 4 motivations that drive every human being:

1) I want to trust the most powerful good there is.
2) I want to become the most beautiful person there is.
3) I want to love the loveliest thing there is.
4) I want to take pleasure in the most enjoyable thing there is.

Over the next few chapters, we will look at what the cornerstones are and how you build them solidly into your life.

03
1st Cornerstone
Trusting the Sovereignty of God

Driving motivation:
I want to trust the most powerful good there is

When William Barclay's child fell overboard and drowned, he wrote, "I believe that pain and suffering are never the will of God for his children. To call a fatal accident an act of God is blasphemous."[1]

When Sarah Edwards received news that her husband, Jonathan, who had just arrived at Princeton as the new president, had suddenly died as a result of a freak accident, she wrote to her daughter, "What shall we say? A holy and good God has covered us with a dark cloud. O that we may kiss the rod and lay our hands on our mouths! The Lord has done it. He has made me adore His goodness, that we had him so long...We are all given to God; and there I am and love to be."[2]

The difference between the reactions of William Barclay and Sarah Edwards to personal tragedy is based on the difference in their beliefs regarding the sovereignty of God.

Everybody wants someone he can rely on all the time, in every moment, for every situation. God is that someone for you, because God is sovereign.

The sovereignty of God is the bedrock of Christian faith. Basically, "sovereignty" means that God is free to do as he pleases. He is the absolute authority over all things; He controls all things and is controlled by nothing. The Bible states it this way: *"The Lord has*

---

[1] William Barclay, A SPIRITUAL AUTOBIOGRAPHY, Grand Rapids: Wm. B. Eerdmans Publishing Co., 1975, p. 44.

[2] Ian H. Murray, JONATHAN EDWARDS: A NEW BIOGRAPHY, Edinburgh: Banner of Truth Trust, 1988, p. 442.

established his throne in the heavens, and his sovereignty rules over all" (Psalm 103:19).

Or again: *"Who has directed the Spirit of the Lord, or as his counsellor has informed him? With whom did he consult and who gave him understanding? And who taught him in the path of justice and taught him knowledge, and informed him of the way of understanding?"* (Isaiah 40:13,14 *NAS*). God is not dependent on anyone, nor swayed or manipulated by anything. God is perfectly free in all his thinking and doing. He is sovereign.

Does that sound scary? If God is free to do all that he pleases, what if he pleases to do something bad? What if he pleases to do something that is bad for you? This is where a second meaning of God's sovereignty is helpful. While God is free to do all that he pleases, God is able to do all that he desires. And since God is holy, his desires are pure; since his desires are pure, he desires only that which is good. That is why, if you are in a relationship to God as his dearly beloved child, God's sovereignty need not threaten you. It is full of mystery and has many inexplicable elements, but it should comfort you in every circumstance of life.

Sovereign in all things

How sovereign is God? The answer can be found in the word "sovereign" itself. Either God is completely sovereign or he is not sovereign at all.

The Scriptures portray God as sovereign in all affairs of men. Isaiah 46:10 states that God is sovereign over the general flow of history. Then, in verse 11, the mind of the Spirit applies that sovereignty to the smallest and seemingly insignificant details of every-day events: *"I make known the end from the beginning, from ancient times, what is still to come. I say: My purpose will stand, and I will do all that I please. From the east I summon a bird of prey; from a far-off land, a man to fulfil my purpose."*

Proverbs 16:1, 9 says, *"To man belong the plans of the heart, but from the Lord comes the reply of the tongue...In his heart a man plans his course, but the Lord determines his steps."*

Isaiah 45:5-7 teaches that God controls light and darkness, abundance and poverty, good times and disaster: *"I am the Lord, and there is no other; apart from me there is no God...from the rising of the sun to the place of its setting men may know there is none besides me. I am the Lord, and there is no other. I form the light, and create darkness, I bring prosperity and create disaster; I, the Lord, do all these things."*

This has caused lively discussion and vigorous debates, because this leaves us with a lot of mystery and unanswered questions, yet the Bible teaches that God sovereignly controls evil actions. Amos 3:6 says, *"When disaster comes to a city, has not the Lord caused it?"* In 1 Samuel 18:10 and 19:9 we have two incidents in which the *"evil spirit* (demon) *from the Lord"* was directed by God to enter King Saul, prompting Saul to such rage that he hurled his spear at young David, who was playing the harp to bring tranquillity into the king's troubled life.

Yet God controls the evil actions of people to his desired goal. Proverbs 16:4 tells us *"the Lord works out everything for his own ends—even the wicked for a day of disaster."* The evil that is done to his servants, God uses as a means to bring about the accomplishment of His purposes and the forward motion of His plan. Joseph (Genesis 37-50) was repeatedly victimized, first by his brothers, then by slave owners, by his boss, Potiphar, then by the unfair circumstance of jail time, and finally by a cupbearer who forgot him. Years later, when Joseph's brothers—those scoundrels who had started the whole chain of evil—stood in front of him, and Joseph, now as prime minister of Egypt, revealed to them his true identity, they shook in fear because of the evil they had done to their brother. Joseph was able to respond in grace, because his perspective was shaped by his understanding of God's sovereignty: "*You intended to harm me, but God intended it all for good.* " (Genesis 50:20 *NLT*).

God taught Paul the same perspective, when Paul suffered from what the apostle called *"a thorn in the flesh"* (2 Corinthians 12:7-10). Whatever it was—some think it was a physical ailment; I personally think it was all the harsh experiences he endured and referred to in v. 10—Paul recognized that the thorn in the flesh *was "a messenger from Satan to torment me."* He says that this messenger *"was given to me,"* probably referring to God as its giver. The "thorn experience" was so painful to him that he pleaded with God on three separate occasions to remove it. God's sovereign answer was that Paul should continue experiencing the agony in order to learn how God's daily grace can carry him through life. Paul was to learn the hard lesson that only God's sovereignty, and not our own strength and ability, can be trusted, especially at times when we feel weak and helpless. How good to be able to trust the most powerful good there is!

Sovereign in the pain of life

Later we will look at the role of suffering in your Christian spirituality. For now, let's look at how God's sovereignty in people's suffering has redemptive value.

My friend Elaine decided to commit her life to Jesus when she learned that God had everything to do with the deep pain in her life. Elaine was pregnant and her husband was having an affair. By the time she gave birth to their son, her husband had moved out. Caught up in a dizzying whirlwind she was unable to control, Elaine was left alone with her little infant. Her loneliness was accompanied with the awful sting of rejection and a yawning hole of hopelessness. One week, a fellow teacher at the high school invited Elaine to come with his family to our church's worship service. Her first experience with church became her first encounter with God.

When I called her a few days later to thank her for her visit, I encountered a woman who had been intrigued by the sermon, but especially by the acceptance of the people toward her, a woman who was anything but a pious church-going person. As the young mother told me the details of her unhappy story, I felt I needed to quote to her Romans 8:28: *"We know that God causes all things to work together for good to those who love God, to those who are called according to his purpose."*(NAS) I had never used that verse in a conversation with a non-Christian before or since. But in the moment I quoted that verse, something in Elaine came to life. Minutes later, as I was explaining to her how bad experiences in life can be God in his grace "hunting people down" in order to help them see how wonderful he is (the "pursuing grace" of God), Elaine interrupted me and asked, "Wait! What was that thing you quoted from the Bible, from Rome or something?" I quoted Romans 8:28 a second time. "That's it", she called excitedly into the receiver, "that promise becomes true for me if I start to love God, right?"

I explained to her that she needed to turn her life from its self-directedness to God. As if it were a prayer to God, she said, "I want that. I want that kind of a God to have my life." Elaine felt God's love for her, the love he had so clearly expressed through Jesus' life, death, and resurrection for her, and she placed her entire self, with her nightmares of the present and her dreams for the future, into God's hands. She wanted to belong to the God who is not only sacrificially and unconditionally in love with her, but also sovereignly able to direct all the details of life for her good.

The following years were not easy for Elaine, but God was good. He surrounded Elaine with many people who helped her get through those challenging years. Years after her conversion, she married a dear widowed elder in our church. God directed the evil of Elaine's first husband so that Elaine would find Christ, marry a man who has loved her deeply and faithfully, and have a home in which her son grew up knowing who Jesus is and what a sovereign God we have.

What Elaine came to experience is a truth about God that instils confidence and hope: When you know that God is sovereign in everything, then everything – even the bad in our lives – has a purpose. You may not always understand what that purpose is, but you may believe that there is a good purpose. It's what Joni Eareckson Tada, who has endured severe handicaps for decades, wrote about our sovereign God: "God permits what he hates, to accomplish what he loves."[3]

■ What's in it for me?

1. Contentment

Jeremiah Burroughs (1599–1646) preached a sermon series in London, England, based on Philippians 4:11 *("I have learned to be content in whatever circumstances I am"*[NAS]*)*, called *"The Rare Jewel of Christian Contentment"*. The following highlights of that series are still helpful to us today:

---

[3] From Nancy Guthrie, BE STILL MY SOUL. Wheaton: Crossway, 2010, p. 35.

93

"Christian contentment is that sweet, inward, quiet, gracious frame of spirit, which freely submits to and delights in God's wise and fatherly disposal in every direction."[4]

Christian contentment does not mean that

- ... you are without affliction and suffering in life.
- ... you cannot complain to God and to your friends: Certainly the Psalms are a suffering person's unburdening of heart to God ("Likewise he may communicate his sad condition to his Christian friends, showing them how God has dealt with him, and how heavy the affliction is upon him")[5].
- ... you do not seek help nor that you do not want to be delivered out of your afflictions.

Christian contentment does mean that

- ... you will not murmur about God's ways with you, like the Israelites did in the desert, and brought God's punishment upon themselves.
- ... you will not allow yourself to grow bitter from the oppression or affliction you have experienced under God's sovereign will.
- ... you will not be distracted from your present responsibility that God requires of you in your relationship towards God, yourself, and others.
- ... you will not allow anything to choke your deep commitment to Jesus Christ.
- ... you will not seek relief from your affliction by doing anything that is sinful, unholy, or contrary to integrity.

When you go through hard times in life, quote Philippians 4:11 to yourself and pray for God to give you contentment.

---

[4] Jeremiah Burroughs, THE RARE JEWEL OF CHRISTIAN CONTENTMENT, Edinburgh: Banner of Truth Trust, 1987, p. 19.

[5] Ibid., p.. 21-22.

2. Thankfulness

On the basis of God's sovereignty, you can acknowledge the presence of God's goodness, compassion and mercy in every situation you experience, even the bad and the sad ones (1 Thessalonians 5:16-18).

Somewhere years ago, I read how the theologian, Matthew Henry, reacted after he was robbed on his way home from a university lecture. He wrote in his journal:

"Thank you, Lord, that I was robbed, not that I did the robbing.

Thank you that in taking my belongings, they did not take everything I own.

Thank you that they took what I had but they did not take my life.

Thank you that they took earthly possessions but they could not take you from me."[6]

Every time something "goes wrong", you can thank God for his sovereign intervention that not more went wrong.

3. A Realistic but Positive Outlook on Life

Knowing the triumphal end toward which God is moving all of history as well as your personal life, you can face life with optimism.

a) You can look at your life from the perspective that your cup is not half empty but half full. Why? The world is in the hands of a sovereign God, who made it and before whom the nations are a mere drop in a bucket (Isaiah 40:15). History is in the hands of a sovereign God who turns it according to his predetermination and promises. Your life is in the hands of a sovereign God, who promised to turn to your good whatever happens to you (Romans 8:28). The actions of every enemy are in the hands of a sovereign God, whose purposes and plans will not be thwarted (Daniel 4:35). You may look at your life positively and at your future optimistically regardless of what evil has happened to you, because God is sovereignly moving all things to a victorious finish line. Your cup is not only half full, it is getting fuller all the time, even if you do not notice.

---

[6] Cited in Chris Craig, Becoming a Person of Prayer, Salem: Xulon Press, p. 49.

b) This means also, that there is no room in a Christian's life for a victim mentality. You may indeed be the victim of abuse, misunderstanding, lack of love, or neglect. In one way or the other, we all are. To define yourself as a victim of evil is to wallow in unbelief. A victim-mentality is the attitude of self-pity, self-defeat, and cowardice. With a victim-mentality we begin to manipulate others into orienting themselves around our needs. We begin to define good relationships according to how well others, including family members, care for us and our needs. It is the pathway into total me-centredness.

Furthermore, having a victim mentality is wallowing in unbelief, because it is a denial of the sovereignty of God. It is saying things can happen, where God is absent, where God is surprised and where God must necessarily react in hindsight: "Oops, I just let an accident occur in his life that I had not counted on." With God there are no accidents. Your parents are not an accident, your spouse is not an accident, your children are not an accident and difficult people in your life are not an accident.

If God is sovereign—and he is—then he has only a Plan A, and what happens to you is according to his Plan A with which he purposes to challenge you to grow and know him more deeply, personally and intimately. Spiritual maturity is a constant and determined ability to define yourself according to the gospel independent of the harshness of circumstances or people's opinions or treatment of you (see chapter 2). The sovereignty of God calls you, when victimized, to be gospel-driven, not victim-driven. This leads to the next point of application:

4. Endurance and Resilience

Resilience is the ability to bounce back after a setback. Because God is sovereign in all things, there is never a reason to quit just because the going gets tough. And just because you feel like you took 2 steps backward, does not mean the day is not coming when you take 3 steps forward. In fact, the way God works is that you may take 3 steps forward *because* you took 2 steps backward.

I used to enjoy playing the game 'Sorry' with my wife and daughters. Once Elizabeth, Rachel and I were at it and I was close to winning. So was Elizabeth. And both of us are competitive. She had 3 of her 4 pieces 'home' already, and one piece moving swiftly around the board. On my turn, when I picked up the next card, it was a 'Sorry'. Nasty daddy took his piece that was still at 'start' and sent my four year old Elizabeth's lone remaining piece back to her 'start' (all over again). She started to cry and wanted to run from the room. I had to almost force her to take her next turn. When she turned over the next card, it was a 2. That meant she could bring her last piece back out on the board and take an additional turn. The next card was a 4. In 'Sorry', a 4 means you go 4 steps back. But in Elizabeth's case, 4 steps back brought the piece she had just placed outside of "start" close to the finish, just 8 steps to 'home'. On her next turn, she picked up an 8 and won which was quicker than if she had continued moving swiftly around the board without getting sent back to 'start'.

Life with a sovereign God is like that: every setback is actually a quicker way home. That is why Paul could write 2 Corinthians 4:8: " *we are afflicted in every way, but not crushed; perplexed, but not despairing*" [NAS]

Motivation #1:
I want to trust in the most powerful good there is:
the sovereign God

---

1. Look up the following groups of Bible passages, and after each group, summarize what these passages say about the sovereignty of God:
(1) Proverbs 16:1-3; 19:21; 20:24; Isaiah 46:10.11 (2) Proverbs 16:4; Isaiah 45:5-7; Amos 3:6 (3) Ecclesiastes 8:17 (4) Job 1:6-12; 1 Samuel 18:10; 19:9; 2 Corinthians 12:7-10 (5) Luke 21:12-19 (6) Romans 9:10-18; John 1:11-13.

2. If God is sovereign, what role does planning have in the Christian life?
Look up the following passages and write a one sentence answer for each one: Proverbs 16:1-3; 20:18; 21:5; James 4:13-16.

3. Memorize the following verses: Romans 8:28; 8:31-32, Genesis 50:20.

4. Memorize the Heidelberg Catechism, 1563, Question 1
Question: "What is your only comfort in life and in death?"
Answer: "That I am not my own, but belong—with body and soul, in life and in death—to my faithful Saviour Jesus Christ, who with his precious blood has fully satisfied for all my sins, and has freed me from the tyranny of the devil, and so watches over me, that not a hair can fall from my head without the knowledge of my Father in heaven. By his Holy Spirit, He also assures me of eternal life, and makes me willing and ready from now on to live for him."

5. Take the 3 points of character application ("what God's sovereignty will do for you"—2nd paragraph), and ask yourself: on a scale of 1 to 10, with 1 being very low and 10 being very high, how you would rate your current spiritual maturity as far as .

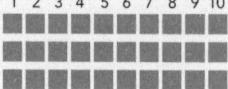

...contentment in life
...thankfulness in all things of life
...a positive spirit and attitude about life

6. Begin the habit of asking God daily to form in you the 4 character traits listed and described under "What's in it for me":
1. Contentment in life, 2. Thankfulness in everything in life, 3. A realistic and positive outlook on life, 4. Endurance and resilience.

TOOLBOX

04
2nd Cornerstone
Fashioning Yourself according to the Holiness of God

Driving motivation:
I want to become the most beautiful thing there is

Being a Christian has to do with holiness. That may not sound very exciting. It could have overtones of boredom, prudishness, or living on earth like something from outer space. Actually, it is anything but boring! And prudishness is unfortunately what moralism turns Christianity into. Holiness has to do with a beauty, purity and completeness yet to be attained. Christian spirituality is the exciting invitation into the experience of becoming everything you were meant to be!

The apostle Peter writes: *"Like the Holy One who called you, be holy yourselves also in your behaviour; because it is written (in the Old Testament, in Leviticus 11:44), YOU SHALL BE HOLY, FOR I AM HOLY."* (1 Peter 1:15-16 *NAS*).

The invitation to become all you were meant to be is nothing short of becoming what God is: holy!

God's holiness is breathtakingly beautiful

There are a lot of people who think that God's love is the main and defining characteristic of God. Thankfully, that is not true. The most fundamental attribute of God is his holiness. That God is holy means that every aspect of his being (including his love) is perfect. Every part of God's character and personality, as well as the resultant deeds—everything about him is beautiful, brilliant, blameless, without the slightest touch of wrong or hint of imperfection.

This certainly applies to God's sovereignty, the attribute of God we looked at previously. The fact that God is holy in his sovereignty means that while God is almighty in all he does, he will never abuse his might, but only use it to good and beneficial ends even if our lives are so clouded by sorrow that we cannot yet see the good end). While the sovereign God is free to do and choose according to his own pleasure, he will never do something that deserves to be 'called into court' and questioned by our own hearts.

Or take God's righteousness as an example. Holiness means that God doesn't have a single speck of anything unrighteous. He cannot do anything that is not perfectly right. Not even the slightest little error or the tiniest aberration in his steps will ever, in all of time and eternity, be found in his ways.

In his faithfulness he is also always holy, meaning that he can never break a promise he has made to you or anyone else; he will always be true to his own character. 2 Timothy 2:13 says that even if we should be unfaithful to God, he will never be unfaithful toward us, because he is unable in his holy character to be unfaithful to himself and the promises he has made, and he has promised never to leave us or forsake us. For every confession of sin we bring to him, he is bound to forgive us completely; not to forgive us would be unfaithfulness toward his promise in the cross and resurrection of Jesus. *"If we confess our sin, he is faithful and just to forgive us our sins and to cleanse us from all unrighteousness"* (1 John 1:9 *NAS*).

His love is perfectly holy. That means that he can never love you less than one hundred percent, one hundred percent of the time. Since his love is completely holy, it is never dependent on our actions toward God. It is independent of who we are and what we do, because it is completely rooted in the character of God. That means that his holy love is based on Christ's actions toward us, not on our actions toward Christ. God's holiness defines his love, not the other way around.

Or take his justice. Holiness means that God can never have a single touch of error in his justice. He can never be unfair with anybody. Think about that! He can never punish wrongly, and he can never give anyone less reward than they deserve.

Do you see why holiness is God's fundamental attribute? It is what makes him so utterly beautiful! God's holiness is what causes spiritually-opened eyes to view him with adoration as the most glorious being in the universe.

What holiness is not

Only God has an absolutely sinless holiness. A person who has invited God into his life, and has thereby come into union with Christ, has the new and holy nature of Christ existing in him by the indwelling presence of the Holy Spirit. But while we live in this sinful world, we still have our sinful nature within, and it is at constant war with our new nature. So for us to live holy lives does not mean we become sinless.

I believe Martin Luther was correct when he explained our condition with the now famous words *"simul justus et peccator"*, simultaneously justified (declared completely righteous) and sinful. With this phrase, the German reformer summarized what Paul wrote in Romans 7: *"Oh wretched man that I am, who will deliver me from this body of sin!"* (Romans 7:24 *NKJ*). Luther, following Augustine, understood this as the expression of a Christian who realized that even if his spirituality had matured to the point at which he could tell others to follow his example, he still keenly felt the gravity of the sin nature within, pulling him into sinful and selfish motives, thoughts, attitudes and actions. He was always having to battle against his me-centredness. It certainly kept him humble and seeking to grow in holiness, but he was not sinless.

Being holy also does not mean to be constantly on a spiritual high, moving from one dramatic experience with God to another. To be sure, experiencing God, who involves himself in our lives, will include dramatic moments and miraculous occurrences. But, as we will see later, Christian spirituality also includes the experience of being identified with the sufferings of Christ (Philippians 3:10). These sufferings can involve deep anguish and pain, the loss of someone very special, or illness, even illness unto death. God does not always step into our sufferings and remove the thorn that hurts (see 2 Corinthians 12:7-10); he does not always heal the sick. Actually, the normal Christian life is usually a quiet constancy of going about the ordinary tasks to which God has called us. The real sign of a Christian growing in holiness is obedience to God, not great experiences with God.

Being holy does not mean being stern, boring or removed from the world. People who think holiness means not being allowed to wear jewellery, yell and cheer in a stadium and have a lot of fun, have forgotten that as his first miracle—at a wedding reception while everybody was dancing—Jesus turned water into wine, not tea.

Running from the God who is holy

Holiness is "being wholly different". Karl Barth, professor at the University of Basel, Switzerland, used to refer to God as the "eternally other". You might say that if we are to be holy as God is holy (1 Peter 1:15, 16), then we first have to recognize that God is wholly other than we are. That means God is the moral complete opposite of our sinful nature. When God gave Moses the 10 commandments, the Israelites were told not to go near the mountain because the perfectly pure otherness of God, which contrasted sharply with their moral impurity, would immediately kill them. *"For no one may see me and live,"* God says (Exodus 33:20). This is why Isaiah, in his vision of God, the Holy One, seated on his throne, reacted with the outburst, *"Woe to me! I am ruined!"* (Isaiah 6:5). In the same way, Peter, when he recognized that the one standing in front of him was the incarnate God, reacted to Jesus by blurting out, *"Go away from me, Lord; I am a sinful man!"* (Luke 5:8).

While God's holiness is what makes him so utterly and indescribably beautiful, it is also, at first sight, the most threatening thing a human heart could lay eyes on. Standing in all your unholiness before His holiness makes you feel so vulnerable that the most natural reaction is to recoil in shame and fear and run the other way. While your soul bolts panic-stricken out of his presence, God's word calls after you, *"You shall be holy, for I am holy"*.

When a person runs from God, he usually does it in one of two ways: He may deny that there is a holy God. This is an ingenious move, quite frankly, because without God in the picture, he can basically ignore the whole issue of holiness, instead of having it defined for him by some high and holy Being.

The second way to run from God's holiness is to re-define it. This is also ingenious, because according to the people who have done just that, they can do this but still call themselves Christians. Here is the procedure:

- Step 1: Look at your sinful and unholy nature.

- Step 2: Define God's highest attribute as love.

- Step 3: Say that love is never judgmental and always unconditional.

- Step 4: Conclude that whatever you prefer morally as your lifestyle is acceptable to God, whose love is never judgmental and always unconditional.

- Step 5: Make it your cause to justify yourself by interpreting all calls to holiness in the Bible in the light of the morality you prefer for yourself. This way you are not only a "Christian", but one who has oriented his Christian spirituality around the Bible.

Both of these alternatives—denying the existence of a holy God or re-defining the holiness of God—are 'below-to-above' approaches. They fit into our postmodern world-view and way of thinking, because they allow the self to begin with the self and end with the self, leaving the self as the defining centre of all things.

The reason why Jesus, who is neither pre-modern, modern nor post-modern, but trans-modern, stated that you can only be his disciple if you 'deny yourself' (Matthew 16:24), is because he understood himself as 'sent from God', meaning that he is and represents a spirituality that is 'above-to-below'. I know this means we are left with our unholy selves standing before this terribly holy God, unable to justify ourselves any longer. But it is only when we let God's holiness stand in its own right as the central attribute of God that we can gain a proper estimation of God's grace.

God in his holiness will not stand for any sinfulness in his presence. Yet God in his love desires a relationship to us. His plan to make that relationship happen is nothing less than the most amazing grace. It is also *truly* ingenious. He came as Jesus, the second Person of the Trinity, into the world. The completely holy came to the utterly unholy. On the cross, the Holy One transacted the "great exchange": he took the sins of his (unholy) people on himself and placed his (holy) righteousness on his people (see chapter

2; 2 Corinthians 5:21). Now the (marriage) union happens: *"You have been raised with Christ...where Christ is, seated at the right hand of God...For you died and your life is now hidden with Christ in God"* (Colossians 3:1-3).

Nikolaus von Zinzendorf (18th century) wrote a hymn to this effect, translated by John Wesley (18th century): "Jesus your blood and righteousness, my beauty are, my glorious dress; midst flaming worlds in these arrayed, with joy shall I lift up my head. Bold shall I stand in your great day, for who ought to my charge shall lay? Fully absolved through these I am, from sin and fear, from guilt and shame."

What holiness is – The PROCESS of becoming what in POSITION you are

At the moment of faith in Christ, God takes you as his bride into the yet unseen heavenly chambers, not that your body and soul leave earth. It is a spiritual mystery, but it is real. You begin to live in two places at once. Your life in Christ means you have a new POSITION with God: Irrespective of your moral condition, you are viewed as if you had never sinned nor been a sinner (remember Heidelberg Catechism #64?); you are accepted as his beloved bride, perfectly beautiful in the perfect righteousness of Jesus, flawless and without any speck of shame or guilt.

What at the outset had you standing in terror before the All-Holy and causing you to bolt from his presence, now—protected by Jesus' righteousness—has turned into a safe standing before and healthy reverence toward the Almighty.

In his work, TRUE SPIRITUALITY, Francis Schaeffer wrote that every day the Christian ought to mystically rise into heaven, see what he is like there in his completed and perfect state, then mystically return to earth and live his life accordingly.[7] Why? Because holiness is becoming in our earthly reality, what we already are in our heavenly reality.

On the one hand, holiness is a position we have with God. On the other hand, it is a lifelong process. It means you become less and less what you were, and more and more what Jesus is. Or to

---

[7] Francis Schaeffer, THE COMPLETE WORKS OF FRANCIS A. SCHAEFFER, Westchester, IL: Crossway Books, 1988, Volume 3, p. 193ff.

pick up on the language of the previous section, holiness is the *process* of becoming in practice what you already are in *position*. I know that some people in the church refer to exemplary people who are long-gone dead as "saints", and have made statues to remind us who our examples of morality and charity are. But the Bible calls people who have a sinful nature and who have turned to Jesus for grace, forgiveness and a relationship with God 'saints'. 'Saint' means something like 'having been set apart so that God can work something very special'. It is along the lines of what Karl Barth called God: The 'eternal other' or the 'wholly other'. Having become a saint, you now must be sanctified, you must become "wholly other" than what you have been. You must become what God is—holy! The biblical word for growing in holiness is "sanctification". So Paul wrote, *"this is the will of God, your sanctification"* (1 Thessalonians 4:3 *NAS*)

■ What's in it for me?

The real me! A beautiful me!

In 1994, Susan and I bought a house in Toronto, Canada. We had 4 daughters, a dog and 2 guinea pigs, and needed a house that was big enough for the nine of us, but still affordable. The house we purchased was certainly big enough for nine lives. The reason it was affordable for us was that it was in terrible condition!

Every time we looked at the house before buying it, we saw more things wrong with it. But with every visit, we also saw more potential. We could imagine what original beauty this house must have had, and see the potential to restore it to something beautiful. We decided to buy the house and to invest in its restoration (we must have been delusional that day!).

Some friends were excited that we had bought a house and wanted to see our new treasure. Their smiles quickly faded to looks of disbelief when they walked in. One said, "Beck, have you lost your mind? Why did you buy such a piece of work?!"

Everything in this house had to be removed, replaced, rewired and redone. The more we did, the more we realized how much more needed to be done. New plumbing, new electric, new walls, new windows, new floors, and new paint. It took years, lots of perspiration and back pain, many tears, and at one point almost cost me my life.

This house cost us almost everything.

But it was worth it! A few years after purchasing the house, the same friends came by. This time they said, "Wow! What a great house!" We had turned it into something beautiful. Then, after 9 years, two of our daughters had moved out, the guinea pigs had died, and the house was too big, so we sold it for a nice profit. The process of restoration had paid off.

Your life is like that house. By his death on the cross, Jesus purchased your house (the Bible word "redeem" means "purchase with a price" and is used to describe what Jesus did for you at the cross). It is a house which through sin had lost its original beauty and had become marred. I can hear Satan looking at your 'house' and mocking, "Jesus, have you lost your mind? Why would you buy such a piece of work?!" But Jesus, in covenant with God the Father, had decided to invest his life in you. His answer to the mockery was, "I recognize the value in this piece of work—it is the value of my own life, and I see the potential of what it can become—holy. Wholly other!"

After Jesus purchased your 'house', and upon your asking him into your life (John 1:12), he moves into your 'house' and makes it his home. That means that ever since your conversion to Christ, you are 'under construction'. Your old self is being completely torn apart, reworked, rewired and refashioned. The reconstruction project is painful, because the hammer and chisel of the Holy Spirit plunge deep into each moral part, each emotional corner, every attitudinal floorboard, every fibre of your thinking. Nothing is left as is. Everything must be changed. With every step forward there is protest from the sin nature within, as well as setbacks and surprises in life you had not counted on. Sometimes you wonder if the pain is worth it all. It is!

Christian spirituality is the process of *"being renewed day by day"* (2 Corinthians 4:16). Over the years your house looks more like the blueprint which the holy architect had designed for you. That blueprint is the perfect and holy image of Jesus. Through all that drilling and cutting and hammering and forming emerges a beauty: you—a stunning beauty, a likeness to Jesus. When you die

106

or when Jesus returns (whichever happens first) you will reach the goal of your existence.

Here is how one of Jesus' closest disciples, John, described it: *"Beloved, now we are children of God, and it has not appeared as yet what we shall be. We know that, when He appears, we shall be like him, because we shall see Him just as He is."* (1 John 3:2 *NAS*)

That is what growing in holiness is all about. In "sanctification", the holiness of God is no longer a threat to your self. Instead, the beauty of God becomes the goal of your existence. God's call to *"be holy, because I am holy!"* is then no longer reason to hide or deny or re-define, but an invitation to run your life like a race toward the finish line—the perfectly holy image of Jesus.

Breathtakingly beautiful!

Motivation #2: I want to become the most beautiful thing there is: like God in Christ

---

1. What in this chapter especially spoke to you at an emotional level? Why?

2. Read 1 Peter 1:14-16. How does God's holiness become a motivation to become holier, when in fact God's holiness hates that which is unholy in us?

3. More on the word „saint": In the Roman Catholic Church, a saint is someone who has died, and who lived such an exemplary life that the church makes him a saint.
In the Bible, however, a saint is someone who is still living, who has a relationship to God through Jesus, and is a sinner. This is why the apostle Paul spoke of the sinful Corinthian Christians as „saints". They were saints in their position with God. United to Christ, God views you as perfectly righteous in Christ and calls you a „saint".

Read 1 Corinthians 1:2; 2 Corinthians 1:1; Romans 1:7; Ephesians 1:1; 1 Thessalonians 4:3; Colossians 3:1-15.

What aspects of holiness are emphasized in these passages?

4. What false understanding of the Christian life can result from:
- seeing holiness as our POSITION, but forgetting that we are in **process**?
- seeing holiness as our PROCESS, but forgetting that we are in **position**?

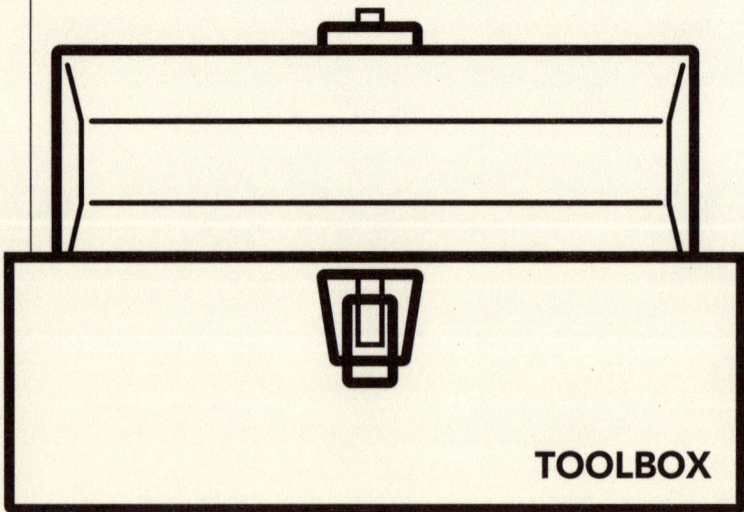

TOOLBOX

05
3rd Cornerstone

Bathing Yourself in the Love of God

Driving motivation:
I want to love the loveliest thing there is

Sorry, what is a parasite…or whatever that word was he just used?" I leaned over to the lady who had just whispered in my ear, and answered, "The word is Pharisee, but it might as well be parasite."

Evelyn turned to me. "Pharisee? What is a Pharisee?"

I had just met Evelyn half an hour earlier. It's a long story. Evelyn had arrived at a point in life at which she felt a desperate hunger for a relationship with God, heard an announcement on the radio that piqued her curiosity, called an organization, where a guy listened to Evelyn's question, and called a guy…Now that we were seated in the large auditorium where Don Carson was talking about „what is truth?" it did not take the pagan lady beside me long to get tripped up by biblical concepts and words.

"The Pharisees were a religious movement within Judaism at the time of Jesus, like a right-wing political party," I whispered. "Pharisees were really strict Jews, who had life all together or appeared to have it all together. They knew the Old Testament inside and out, knew all the laws prescribed there, knew the rules and regulations of Jewish civil and ceremonial procedure to the minute detail, had them organized into 613 different obligations to be kept, and believed that if the Jewish nation would follow them all, the Messiah would come back sooner."

Evelyn leaned over to my ear again, "What exactly is a 'Messiah'?"

Don Carson was talking about a Pharisee, whose concept of spirituality was turned upside-down by Jesus one blissful day in the history of religions.

This particular Pharisee was so proud to know so much, that he approached Jesus with a question designed to show Jesus how much he knew. "What is the highest law?" he asked. But Jesus did not point to some ritualistic behaviour, nor to one of the 613 regulations. He pointed to wholehearted love. Quoting from the Old Testament, Deuteronomy 6:5 and Leviticus 19:18, Jesus answered, *"'Love the Lord your God with all your heart and with all your soul and with all your mind.' This is the first and greatest commandment. And the second is like it: 'Love your neighbor as yourself.' All the Law and the Prophets hang on these two commandments."* (Matthew 22:37-40).

With this answer, Jesus threw a stick of dynamite at any and every religion's idea that doing something good, like keeping a rule or observing a ritual, will win God's favour. It also explains how the followers of Jesus, unwilling to reduce spirituality to religious observances, monastic lifestyles, or admiration of stone buildings, were quickly branded a sect—and still are by the many religionists who have not comprehended the enormity of Jesus' response.

False love: Loving God for what loving God gets me

Let me begin mid-stream! Jesus' exhortation to love God and neighbour is like open-heart surgery: it cuts right through the breastbone, rips the chest cavity apart, lifts the barely-alive heart out with his hand, and starts a life-giving procedure.

In the 18th century, in a little town in Massachusetts, USA, a spiritual revival swept over its inhabitants. Through the preaching of the pastor, Jonathan Edwards, hundreds of people in Northampton were convicted and believed in Jesus Christ. But Edwards, one of the most brilliant pastors and theologians in the history of America, became concerned about what he saw in this mass conversion. Edwards was not swayed by the dramatic, nor convinced by a mere profession a person made. He knew from the Bible that there can be apparent (not real) conversion, and temporary (not saving) faith: faith that does not result from a deep, inner, spiritual rebirth. He knew the Bible's teaching that people can have faith without a divine root, without divine substance and without the divine result of eternal life. Such faith, Edwards knew, does not last. Consequently, he warned his hearers to examine their hearts, to test whether their faith, over which they were understandably exuberant, was real. He summarized his warning in the famous treatise called, *On Religious Affections*.

"Those affections for God or Jesus Christ, that result from self-love, cannot be a spiritual love, which has its source in the grace of God… Self-love is a natural affection and can be discovered even in the hearts of demons. Therefore, nothing that results from self-love can be supernatural and of God…People who have affections for God, because they find him helpful for themselves, start at the wrong end of things. They view God as an unending stream of divine good, and want to know that his goodness profits them. They do not have an awe of the glory of His nature, even though it is this glory that is the source and only fountain of all good, the true fountain of all that is lovely."[8]

Honestly, as much as Jesus' words to the Pharisee cut me, so Edwards' exhortation unsettles me. It nags me. It digs around inside my heart like a quadruple-bypass, probing deeply into my motives, into the unstated thoughts behind my actions, into the sin behind the sin. It puts us on the spot, and makes us get honest with ourselves. It lays us bare with the question: "When I say 'I love God', do I really love God or do I simply love what loving him gets me?"

Think about it:

- **You can love the good things that go with believing in God…**your church, your denomination, the comfortable religious circle in which you and others like you mingle and keep religious traditions that give everyone a sense of belonging in that circle; you can like the music that is played in your worship services; the good, moral upbringing your Christian parents have given you; the morally upstanding lifestyle that has resulted from the good values ingrained in you…**and still not love God.**

---

[8]   Edward Hickman, ed., The Works of Jonathan Edwards, Edinburgh: Banner of Truth, 1979, Vol. 1, p.275.

- **You can be involved in Christian ministry and do ministry with passion**...you can look forward to every sermon you preach; you can enjoy telling others about Jesus and feel a deep thrill in your soul when people convert to your faith; you can practice a strict form of discipleship and get others to be just as strict as you are; you can be thrilled about the vision of a world transformed for God; you can change a whole neighbourhood by helping the poor, the homeless and the unemployed; you can live in the squalid part of the city and feed the hungry in Jesus' name or drive out demons by the power of his Spirit...**and still not love God**.

- **You can love good, solid theology...**you can be persuaded that you have all the right doctrines; you can quote passages from the Bible, refer to excellent books that state the faith well and defend your view with intelligence; you can love listening to good preaching; you can be deeply moved by dramatic testimonies of amazing experiences with God; even love the experiences you yourself have had with God...**and still not love God**.

It is easy to love a god you have created in your own image, a god fashioned to fit your wishes, your sexual preference, your political orientation; a god who supports your pursuit of happiness however you shape your path to it. The reason why Jesus' statement to the Pharisee hits me hard is because it does not begin and end with the self. It starts with a God who was there long before the self ever was.

When Jesus said, "Love the Lord, your God", he meant by "God" (Hebrew original: Elohim) the God who created us in his image, not a god we create in our own image. He meant "the Lord" (Hebrew original: Yahweh), that is the Sovereign Authority who initiates relationship with us on his own holy terms, not a kind of holiness shaped to fit our pursuit of happiness.

False love loves God for all you wish God to give you.

False love starts with expectations of God, but when God disappoints, when God makes your life harder than you expected life with God to be, when he does not give you that for which you gave God your life, your love for God comes to an end.

False love shapes the spiritual experience into an idol. It bows down to it in joyful adoration of how the emotion or the sense of power or the amazement of onlookers fill your longing for significance. But when the so-called 'experience of God' does not happen anymore, you feel disappointed in your spirituality.

False love will—to use Jesus' words in Matthew 13:22— get *"choked"* by the *"cares of the world"*. (NKJ)

True Love: Loving God because he is altogether lovely

What a contrast: While false love loves God for all you wish God to give you, true love loves God because even if he gives you nothing, he is completely lovely, because of his holy grace, holy mercy, holy compassion, holy faithfulness, holy justice, holy humility, holy patience, holy joy, holy kindness and holy gentleness.

False love starts with great expectations of God, and yet when God disappoints, it comes to an end; true love loves God for who he is, and that does not change even when we find God hard to understand or disappointing.

While false love loves God as an experience and vanishes like smoke when there is no more experience, true love loves God for what you know about him: he is a God whose ways are sometimes bathed in mystery and incomprehensibility. Even when he appears to have abandoned you, and you find it impossible to see him in the terrible experience you are going through, you hang on to the bare hope that he is hanging on to you.

False love loves God as long as its dreams come true; when it involves personal cost or surrendering its dreams to his will, it prefers to look to the world's quick fixes to make you happy. True love loves God at any cost, because you can never quite get over how great the cost of God's love was in giving you his eternal life.

There is the contrast. But here is the great dilemma: in and of myself I cannot love God with a true love. Neither can you. We are too selfish, too self-consumed to come out of our self-orientation and orient ourselves around God. There is only one thing that can save us from our prison and free us to love God with true love: His love.

I said earlier that I started mid-stream. The reason I started there, is that that is where Jesus started with the Pharisee. The command to love God and neighbour is, in fact, downstream. It makes us ask: "if I cannot love God with all my heart and my neighbour as much as myself from within this self that is so wrapped around itself, then where will such love come from?" It moves us to paddle our canoe upstream and seek the origin of such self-denying love there. We find it in the love of God for us: 1 John 4:19 says, *"We love because he first loved us."*

Jonathan Edwards made a very helpful distinction within God's love. There is God's *general love*. This is the love with which God loves everybody. *"God is love"* (1 John 4:16). All love begins here, at this point of the fountain. That "God is love" means that God cannot do anything that is not characterized by love. It is his nature to love, to extend himself to his creation, to mix in with our unlovely situation and, out of love, to give us what is good, what we need, what makes our lives in a sinful world tolerable and sometimes even enjoyable. In this general way, God loves everybody.

Then there is God's *special love*. Edwards called it God's 'decreetal love' (from "decree": God's decision to run the world the way he does); I would prefer to call it his *"familial love"*. This is likely that aspect of God's love that those theologians overlook who cannot believe in predestination because they feel it is inconsistent with God's love. While God loves everybody generally, he loves those who belong to him with a special love. It is what 1 John 3 and 4 describe as the love of God the Father for those who have been "born of God" and have become God's children. *"How great is the love the Father has lavished on us, that we should be called children of God!"* (1 John 3:1)

You might ask: "Does God love his children more than he loves those who are not his children?" I don't think so. Because God is holy, God is perfect, and because God is perfect, He can only do things 100%. God loves everybody—children of God or not—with 100% of his love. But it is fair to say that God loves his children differently than he loves everybody else. Every good parent loves his children in a much more intimate, familial way than he loves the rest of the world. If you do not think such special, familial love to be appropriate, be glad you do not live on my block. In all my years as a dad, I did not run through the neighbourhood even once and kiss all my neighbours good-night. That special affection was reserved for my four children. Likewise, my wife didn't fix a meal daily for everybody in our city of 4 million, though she showed many people how much she loved them, sometimes by fixing them meals. But for her children, she showed her special love by putting a delicious meal on our family table every evening. We did not expect our four children to have to sleep somewhere in the neighbourhood, nor did we open our door every night to allow all the neighbourhood children to sleep under our roof. That did not mean that our children were better than other children; it meant that our children were, well, our children, whom we loved with a parental love. The same goes for God's family. God loves his children with a special love, a "perfect kind of dad" kind of love.

The point is that this perfect kind of daddy love came looking for you.

Another question people ask about God's love is how wrath and anger fit in with it, if they fit in at all. Any Bible reader will notice quickly that God's anger and wrath are mentioned often. Several times he is characterized as being "slow to anger," while in numerous instances his anger is described as "burning" towards people or nations. Even hell and hate are linked with God (who is love). Many see this as a contradiction in the character of God and feel they can only come to terms with the 'harsher side' of God by soft-pedalling it or erasing it from their theology altogether.

I think we can only understand God's wrath if we first understand God's love, though I could equally say that God's love cannot be comprehended in its magnitude if we do not first understand God's wrath. Here is what I mean:

God loves; that is established. But God also loves his glory; that means God loves all his own characteristics in their purity and splendour. If God loves his glory, then he loves righteousness. If God loves righteousness, then he does not love unrighteousness. In fact, he hates unrighteousness. Before anybody wishes to judge God for hating anything, it is good to remember that unrighteousness includes the little girl being raped and murdered; the drunk, 300 pound husband beating up his 95 pound wife; the chief sacrificing 30 children to the demons in order to appease them; and the homeless man starving and found frozen to death one morning. God hates these situations of unrighteousness no less than you do. It is so contrary to his nature that his anger burns against unrighteousness and those who insist on persisting in it.

God judges unrighteousness. In itself, that is good news! Since he is sovereign, and hates unrighteousness, we can believe his promise that he will judge all unrighteousness that has ever been committed or occurred, and he will restore the earth to a place of complete righteousness.

But God has gone even a step further. He does not simply stand by and watch while those atrocities are committed. Instead, he took all of your unrighteousness and loaded it onto his perfectly righteous Son, whom he nailed to the lowest point of humiliation—a cross—and poured out on Jesus the burning wrath that he felt toward all your unrighteousness.

This perfect kind of Daddy came looking for you, because his anger and wrath cleared an insurmountable roadblock, so that his love could draw you to himself.

Reflexive love:
1. Loving God because he first loved us
This is the story of how it happened. It is not the same encounter you had when you were terrified the first time you were confronted with God's holiness. This is a later encounter, one that happened after you had been running from God for awhile.

Once you were an orphan in a cold, dark neighbourhood. You had never known anything other than orphan life. For you it was normal. When someone told you the best thing in life is to have parents who love, protect and provide for you, you sneered, "There is nothing better than to love, protect and provide for myself."

Then you met God. Or actually, he put himself on the road to meet you. You saw him from a distance. You did not know exactly what he was, and immediately turned away from him. You sensed that a threat to your autonomy was moving in on you. You felt fear. With your back turned to this distant Presence, you began to notice something strange: it was getting lighter around you. In fact, you had not even noticed how dark it was until this moment, when it started getting lighter.

It started getting warmer, too. Again, you had not even noticed how cold it was until this warm breeze wafted through the air. You turned a little to see if you could make out where these new sensations were coming from. Out of the corner of your eye you saw that the object you had turned away from was a warm Brilliance. It was still far off, but getting closer. You were not sure if it was safe to face this Brilliance—maybe it would blind you or kill you with its light or set you on fire with its heat. But you noticed that the more you turned toward it, the more beautiful things around you started to look, because you could begin to see things in colour instead of black and white. Strange but wonderful feelings coursed through you; terror was turning into healthy respect, as you felt your resistance to the Brilliance washing away. You felt in complete control of yourself, like it was your will, your decision, your choice that you were making to turn toward the Light; yet you also felt like you had no choice because there was nothing you would like more than to experience more of this Brilliance. The closer it got, the more irresistible you felt its pull. You never were coerced to turn toward it; still you felt like you were made for this moment, for this encounter. It was not as if you were not free to run—you were!

Then the Brilliance stood face to face with you. He was the most beautiful Being you had ever seen, more beautiful than anything you could imagine. The desire that surged through your nerves was the longing to do nothing but admire the beauty of this Being—more beautiful than all the beautiful pieces of art put into one museum, all the sweetest tunes of music into one song, all the most breathtaking landscapes on the globe in one place, all the most brilliant red sunsets over one lake.

When the Brilliance reached out its arms toward you, you suddenly understood: all the beauty you had ever known was just a pale reflection of this stunning Beauty. It was Beauty in its perfection, pure and pristine. There was something else you suddenly realized: the most beautiful thing that could ever happen to you was happening right now: You were being embraced by this beautiful Being.

Then he spoke. The voice was low and gentle and soothing.

"I am God and I am your dad. I have adopted you to be my child, and in me and in my love you will experience the beauty of family. You are no longer an orphan. Your home is no longer here in the cold and the dark, but in my warmth and light."

There was a pause. Obviously he expected you to respond. But how? How do you respond to someone so indescribably brilliant that has made you an offer? No, you cannot say it is an offer, because he spoke as if it was already a done deal. Of course, you are free to say, "No way!" but who would want to be so foolish as to refuse the most generous gift a beggar could ever imagine. So you began to stutter:

"Uh...s-s-orry. I-I-I p-p-ic-c-tured y-you d-d-d-if-f-f-erent. Uh...w-w-why would you w-w-want me as your child? I am s-s-so disfigured compared t-t-to your beauty. And...and...God, how c-c-can I be sure y-you really a-a-a-adopt-t-ed m-me?"

God smiled broadly at you, took out a piece of paper and unfolded it. It was an adoption certificate. You viewed it more closely. It had your name on it. Then he pointed to the name of the person who signed it: Jesus. "You see this? He signed this paper with his blood, as he hung on the cross for you and paid the price for your adoption."

This is the best news you had ever heard! Someone wants you? Someone loves you so much that he offered himself up to death for you? You could see how someone might lay down his life for a friend, but to lay down his life for an enemy?

Like out of nowhere, a song was released in your soul, and as if you were the music bars, the melody danced through all your senses:

"What wondrous love is this, oh my soul, oh my soul, what wondrous love is this! What wondrous love is this that caused the Lord of bliss, to bear the dreadful curse for my soul? When I was sinking down, sinking down, sinking down, when I was sinking down beneath God's righteous frown, Christ laid aside his crown for my soul."[9]

Suddenly a new realization broke in on you like the sun breaks through after days of dreary weather. You asked, "D-D-Dad, w-why am I n-not af-f-fraid of you, anym-m-m-ore?" He smiled and simply said, "Son, *"perfect love casts out fear"* (1 John 4:18). I am never again your condemning judge (Romans 8:1), I am your

---

[9] "What Wondrous Love is This," American folk hymn, TRINITY HYMNAL, Suwanee, GA: Great Commission Publications, 1995, p. 261.

daddy. This brilliance that you see and feel all around you is the reflection of my glory. It is Christ. You are now living 'in Christ' and he in you. The brilliance of his glory resides in your heart like a bright floodlight in a house: *'For God, who said, 'Let light shine out of darkness,' made his light to shine in our hearts to give us the light of the knowledge of glory of God in the face of Christ'* (2 Corinthians 4:6). Those living in my natural Son are my adopted sons and daughters. I have come to you (John 14:18) and you are no longer an orphan."

As you looked at the loveliness of your adoptive Dad, you felt a tear rolling down your cheek. This amazing love he so clearly has for you, is the very same love that sent Jesus into the world and to the cross for you. It is the same love that kept Jesus on the cross during those excruciating hours in which all of your sins were placed as a crushing mountain on top of him. The extended arms of Jesus on the cross were like the embrace of Dad you were feeling and by which he was saying to you, *"You are mine"* – *"I have called you by name"* (Isaiah 43:1 ^NAS^).

Some other things became clearer to you in the light of God's loveliness: how lovely and pure his sense of right and wrong is... how lovely his actions in history begin to appear to you, as you see how he turned disasters and disappointments in people's lives into something beautiful...how lovely your surroundings have begun to appear in God's light, as the beauty emanating from God is making the red flowers look redder and the green bushes greener...how you yourself have taken on a loveliness that somehow strangely looks like a tiny version of God's loveliness, as if he had made you to be a miniature version of himself that would remind a world—if only it had not gone blind—that the Mega-original is unbelievably gorgeous.

Everything about God is altogether lovely!

A new sensation made itself felt in you. Something in the deepest core of your being began to bubble up. Then it started to flow like water. It felt warm, like a stream running through an ice-covered landscape inside your thawing soul. You felt dead parts coming alive, frozen parts breaking up. You felt the sun shining inside of you and thawing your once frozen heart. Everything inside you wanted to respond, wanted to come out of yourself, like a lover wanting to throw himself on the one he loves and embrace her with passion.

As if he knew what question was burning in your mind, your Dad explained, *"The love of God has been poured out within your heart through the Holy Spirit who was given to you"* (Romans 5:5 ^NAS^). So that's it! The love of God was lavished on you with incredible force. It felt like a waterfall in your soul, running down over everything inside of you. 'That's my sweet Holy Spirit' (John 7:38), God explained.

His love filled you so much that you needed to open the barricaded gates of your fortress, and let it pour out of you. Bathed in his love, you wanted nothing more but to love Him back.

Love is reciprocal. It desires to respond.

God loved us first. Because he knows that He is the loveliest being, he lovingly attracted you to him, in order to do the loveliest thing anyone could do. He knew, as John Piper stated, "Loving God is not our highest duty, but our greatest delight."

Your desire is to love God back with everything you've got. Jesus knew the motivation behind the Old Testament commandment is: it was to push us upstream, where we take our stand under the waterfall of God's love. God did not give the Law to beat us into submission, nor to turn religion into joyless or boring ritual, but to drive us to those things that fill our innermost longings. That is why Jesus said, *"Love the Lord, your God, with all your heart, with all your soul and with all your mind."* The commandment leaves us—as Jonathan Edwards' analysis of love did--standing helpless in front of its demand, asking, "But how? How? How can I, when I am imprisoned by self-love?!" Such honest agony turns us into seekers who are desperate for a solution. When The Seeker has come after us, and poured his love over us, we recognize how the Law drove us to Grace, how the commandment drove us to Christ and how God's love itself has filled and enabled us to love God back, *with all our heart, with all our soul and with all our mind.*

2. Loving your neighbour as yourself
It is the love of God which fills us and flows from us. Not only does it flow vertically into a love for God, but it also flows horizontally into love for the next person. That is what Jesus meant when

he said to the Pharisee, *"And the second is like it: you shall love your neighbour as yourself."*

In contrast to the way some have understood Jesus' words, our Master is not saying that we are to learn to love ourselves in order to love others. Quite the opposite: self-love is naturally the drive in every person, by which he bows to the idols in himself instead of to God. Self-love holds us in its clutches and keeps us from reaching out to the person in front of us. It blinds us from seeing the needs of others; it rationalizes why it is too much trouble and too costly to intervene in someone's pain; it bloats itself into self-righteous pride about how good we are when we do intervene. It is from this self-righteous, self-consumed self-love that we need to be freed.

When a person encounters the God of love and is filled with the love of God, he begins to love what God loves. God loves the self, and so your self starts loving itself with a healthy, self-respecting love. I know people who, once they encountered the love of God, started taking much better care of their bodies and taking up disciplines of the soul for which they had felt no motivation before. But you also begin to love all those God loves with his *general love*. That means those who do unlovely things, or have fallen to unlovely depths, or are unloving in return—these he loves by blessing them, honouring them as his creatures, and providing for them generously. Even when they reject God, deny his existence and live in disobedience toward him, he gives them air to breathe, food to eat and other expressions of his *general love*.

When you are filled with the love of God, you start loving these people the way God loves them. You might say, you love them in the way God loved you before you started to experience his *familial love*. That is precisely the point Jesus is making when he says, *"And your neighbour as yourself."* While God's love becomes the love with which you love others, the self becomes the standard for how much you love others. "Love your neighbour as much as you already love yourself," Jesus is saying here.

"Who is my neighbour?" a Jewish scholar once asked Jesus. So, Jesus told the story of the Good Samaritan. There was a Jewish business man on his way from Jerusalem to Jericho, when some bad guys attacked him, beat him to a pulp, stole everything he had, and left him to die in a ditch. Throughout that day, several religious

Jews, including a priest, walked by the man, but felt their religious task too urgent to take care of the badly injured man, whose life was ebbing away. It was a Samaritan, someone who did not even like Jews, who saw the broken man in the ditch, turned his donkey into an ambulance, took the man to a place where his wounds could be nursed, and paid the guy's entire hospital bill.

By 'neighbour', Jesus meant the next person you come across who has a particular need. You are to love him as much as you love yourself, serve him as much as you would like to be served and bless him as much as you would like to be blessed, even if you do not like him.

That's right even if you do not like him! You can love people you do not like!

Actually, I think it is more difficult to like someone than to love him. "Liking" is a positive feeling you have toward someone, a certain empathy that stirs within you for a person. To have that positive "liking" feeling, you have to feel some chemistry with a person; you have to feel respect from that person. He has to be "likeable" to you. I doubt that if a person walks into the room, spits into your face, kicks you in the shin and tells you that your face is so ugly it looks like your throat threw up, that you will stroke that person's arm and say softly, "Honestly, I like you very much."

But you *can* say, "Honestly, I love you."

God has called us to love one another. This does not mean we always have to like each other, nor are we unspiritual if we don't like each other. You can have a healthy church in which some people do not like each other but everybody loves each other. You can work with people you don't like and still be an effective team, because you are led by principles of love. The distinction between 'loving' and 'liking' is absolutely essential for healthy parenting. When your child refuses to obey you, you discipline your child out of love, even though you do not like disciplining and even though you know your child will not like you for it. Love, not 'like', drives the parent-child relationship. You can have a great marriage that is filled with love, but have moments in which you do not feel romantic, or do not even like each other. You can be respectful, honouring, and self-sacrificing toward your spouse—which is what love is—even when you are irritated at him for snoring like a chain saw, or when he has reacted toward you in a way that reminds you of your mother-in-law.

How so? Because the love that now flows through your being is God's love. The quality of His love toward you, while you were God's enemy, while you essentially spit in his face and told him to leave you alone (Romans 8:5), was to go to the cross and die the death you had coming to you. This crucifixion-love has now filled your soul (Romans 5:5), and continues to fill your soul daily through the Holy Spirit. The more God's love fills you, the more it overflows onto people around you ('neighbours'), including people you don't like.

■ What's in it for me?

1. The power to live for more than me

Jonathan Edwards was right: love for God that is motivated out of a desire to get from God is not love for God. It is nothing more than selfishness, so it does not translate into love that serves people you don't like, because your disposition is still your self-absorption and the need for others to fill *your* needs. But love for God that springs up out of wonder for the loveliness of God and his work in/through Jesus, is love that is motivated by gratitude for God, love that is willing to go to the cross for others, love that will sacrifice itself and invest in others. There is no greater power than that which will sacrifice itself for others. It can change history. In fact, it already has!

2. The power to forgive

God wants you to feel freedom by forgiving those who have wronged you. His love for you, with which he forgives you of all wrongs committed against him, gives you the power to get free from the deep hurts others have inflicted upon you.

The word "forgive" in the New Testament literally means "to loose" or "to let go." It is crucial to understand that forgiving someone does not mean you sweep the injustice done against you under the rug or that you now relate to the person as if he had never inflicted wrong on you. What it really means is that you are going to "let go" of the matter and not allow it to have a hold on you any longer. You are releasing its grip on you. The person and his misdeed have no more power in your life, no more control over your emotions.

Wm. Paul Young, in THE SHACK, echoes a conversation between God and Mack, the father who is seeking revenge against the man who killed his daughter.

"I'm stuck, Papa. I just can't forget what he did, can I?" Mack implored.

"Forgiveness is not about forgetting, Mack. It is about letting go of another person's throat."

"But I thought you forget our sins?"

"Mack, I am God. I forget nothing. I know everything. So forgetting for me is the choice to limit myself...because of Jesus, there is now no law demanding that I bring your sins back to mind. They are gone when it comes to you and me, and they run no interference in our relationship."

"But this man..."

"Mackenzie, don't you see that forgiveness is an incredible power—a power you share with us, a power Jesus gives to all whom he indwells so that reconciliation can grow? When Jesus forgave those who nailed him to the cross they were no longer in his debt, nor mine. In my relationship with those men, I will never bring up what they did, or shame them, or embarrass them."

"I don't think I can do this," Mack answered softly.

"I want you to. Forgiveness is first for you, the forgiver," answered Papa, "to release you from something that will eat you alive; that will destroy your joy and your ability to love fully and openly...When you choose to forgive another, you love him well."[10]

When you forgive someone—be it for something they said to you; or the rape committed against you or marital unfaithfulness or the spreading of lies about you or emotional, physical, or sexual abuse, whatever it is—you are saying four things to the guilty one and to yourself:

> 1) I will no longer think about the sin you committed against me; instead, in my mind I will bless you.

---

[10] Wm. Paul Young, THE SHACK, London: Hodder & Stoughton, 2007, pp. 224-225.

2) I will not bring up to you the sin committed against me; instead, I will do good to you.
3) I will not talk to anyone about your sin against me; instead, I will speak well of you publicly.
4) I will not judge you in my heart anymore for the sin you committed against me; instead, I will leave the judgment or vindication or making-right of the matter to God.

When you do this in the power of God's love, you are truly liberated.

But forgiving is the hardest thing on earth to do, because it is as if you were swallowing into yourself the injustice done against you, instead of being able to spew it back in just and equal punishment on the wrong-doer. Only the gospel has the power to forgive and set the wronged free of the nagging desire for vengeance and justice. When Jesus died on the cross, he was punished for our injustices, not for his own—he was sinless. Instead of judging us for the wrong we have done and will do against God and neighbour, instead of spewing out on us all the fire of his wrath for the wrong inflicted, he was like a sheep led to the slaughter. Only he was silent!

Why? Because he swallowed into himself all the injustices we committed against God and one another, and—in the moment he cried out, "My God, my God, why have you forsaken me!"—was severely judged and condemned to hell by the fire of God's wrath for those injustices we committed.

Furthermore, at the cross he swallowed into himself every injustice anyone has done against you. It was something that happened in the mysterious realm of the heavenlies: while on the cross he went to every incident of injustice committed against you. He was there! He experienced the injustice with you! He felt its shame and he felt your pain. Then he took the injustice into himself and was punished and damned by God in place of him who committed the injustice against you.

When you "let go" of the wrong done against you, you are handing it over to Him who said, "Vengeance is mine." When you forgive someone, you enter that particular part of the atonement of Jesus and say, "Thank you, Jesus, that you took this wrongdoing into your soul, so that it does not have to plague my soul. Thank you that you made the justice of this matter your issue, so that it no longer needs to be mine."

You get free!

There were three years in my life, during which I experienced something of abuse, at least by today's standards. I attended a school in Wiener Neustadt, Austria, known for academic excellence and rigour. What was missing with me was the excellence part, so that what certain teachers enjoyed practicing on me was the rigour part. In grades 6-8, I learned to fear my teachers. I cowered before them when I did not know the answer to a question, knowing that the next moment, a barrage of humiliating words would descend upon me in front of the class. At any point a teacher could find cause to slap me across the cheek. It was a bit like having the Gestapo as teachers. In fact, Professor Holzbein had served in some decorated capacity in World War II. He was the fiercest them all. He was rigour, discipline, and the old German concept of "Ordnung, Achtung, and Jawohl, Herr Kommandant" all wrapped up in one red-faced screaming teacher. And because I was one of the all-time worst students in those days (and had been born in one of the allied countries!), I had the privilege of experiencing Professor Holzbein's rigour-methods often.

Those years left more of an imprint on my life than I was conscious of at the time. I am not sure when it started, but a number of years after I married Susan, I started having nightmares. Not about Susan, mind you, but about Professor Holzbein. The dream came at least once a month and was always the same. It was the day before a math test, and I realized how unprepared I was and what that meant in terms of having to feel the humiliating effects of his forehand in front of my classmates gathered at the court of justice. In each of my nightmares, I felt deep fear at the thought of what awaited me. I would long for release from the clutches of the dream, and when I would wake up I could feel the cold sweat on my forehead.

This went on for years.

Sometime in 2007, I had a totally different dream about Professor Holzbein. In this dream I was in a bus, making a trip to Wiener Neustadt to tell Herr Holzbein that I forgave him for the abusive treatment. I was sitting on the left side of the bus as we pulled into a parking lot that had flower beds on both sides, directly across from the school (Gymnasium) where I had spent my three years of terror. There was no parking lot with flower beds across from the Gymnasium 40 years ago. In this dream, I walked out of the bus with a sense of confidence and joy, knowing that I was going to finally get free from the past. The school was locked, so I began to walk through the city. I came upon a house with a yellow door on which was imprinted the name "Holzbein". I had arrived at the moment of liberation from my fear!

Then I woke up. I didn't give the dream much thought, except to be amazed at its vividness and my feeling of relief in the dream. But the monthly nightmares continued.

In the summer of 2008, Susan and I attended a conference just an hour's drive away from Wiener Neustadt, and I was eager to show her the place where I had lived for 6 years as a boy. I had not been to my "second home" since 1970. We borrowed a car and drove to the town. I wanted Susan to see the three main stations of my life then. First stop was the soccer stadium, where I showed my unimpressed wife the goal posts where I, in my glory days, made some of the most incredible saves in the history of Austrian soccer. That was on the youth team, of course.

Then we drove down the street to our former house. I knocked on the door and introduced myself to the lady. She remembered my family name, and told me excitedly that she had been a little girl when her parents rented the house to us. Happily she let us in, so I could see the rooms, including my old bedroom, where I spent hours studying for my math exams, to which my monthly nightmares had taken me back so often. In the course of our conversation, I mentioned Professor Holzbein, and that I still dream about his math tests. Our hostess enthusiastically revealed to me some stunning facts: for his academic contributions to numerous generations of students, Holzbein was a celebrated man in Wiener Neustadt.

"Actually," she went on, "his daughter and I are best friends and our children play a lot together."

I was dumbfounded, "Do you mean to say the man is still alive?"

"Oh yes, he's doing well."

I asked how I might be able to contact the old professor. She gave me the telephone number of Professor Holzbein. I could not believe my eyes! In my hands, 40 years later, I had the phone number of the feared Kommandant. I thanked her, and we left to go to the third station of my past life.

We pulled up in front of the Gymnasium and I pointed to certain windows in the building, describing to Susan what classes I had where. "There, 3rd floor, 3rd window from the left, is where I experienced most of my verbal humiliations and beatings from the professor," I explained to her. It was early August; all the doors I tried were locked. So I pulled out my cell phone and called Professor Holzbein. I could hardly believe this was happening!

An answering machine kicked in. "His daughter probably called him to tell him that the menace from yesteryear would be trying to contact him," I said to my wife. Then there was a beep, and I was suddenly expected to say something.

What? What do I say after 40 years and 400 nightmares about this man?

"U-h-h-h, hello, Professor Holzbein," I said in German. "This is Stephan Beck. You may not remember me—I was your student 40 years ago. Remember, the American kid who caused you a lot of frustration because I wasn't good in math or physics, and I wasn't particularly good in behaviour either. Well, Professor Holzbein, I just wanted to say, 'Thank you.' You see, something decent did become of me. You may find this hard to believe, but I improved academically, got my Ph.D., and today teach at a university in Germany. I know I have you to thank, because you taught me discipline. [At this point my wife bent over double, trying to stifle her laughter.] You instilled in me the concept of working hard, and I just want to thank you. I hope you are doing well and that God has blessed you richly. Good-bye, Professor Holzbein."

Peace flooded my soul. It was as if I had made closure with a dragon from my past. I reached for the car door, and suddenly noticed, on the other side of the Gymnasium, a parking lot with flower beds on either side, exactly like the dream in 2007. I noticed a plaque in one of the flower beds, so I went over to read the inscription. It told me that the landscaping of this parking lot had been done a few years earlier, in honour of some noted citizen.

There is no way I could have known or seen this parking lot and these gardens before.

That was two years ago. And I have not had a single nightmare of Professor Holzbein since that August day. Forgiveness sets you free!

The alternative to bathing yourself in God's love and forgiveness is the pharisaic approach to spirituality, trying harder, doing your spiritual duty, performing better, keeping score, comparing yourself with others, judging others and holding grudges against them. While that is the pharisaic way, Evelyn may have had it right the first time: it is the parasitical way, because it will eat you alive.

Motivation #3:
I want to love the loveliest thing there is:
God

---

1. Ask yourself the following questions and answer honestly:

- Do you love God? Do you love God because he is altogether lovely in his being and actions?
- Do you love God with your entire being?
- Do you love him with your mind? How does one love God with his mind?
- Do you love him with your heart, the place of commitment, priorities, values?
- Do you love him with your soul, the place of adoration, of hopes and dreams for life, of personal identity, of sense of significance and security? With your obedience to his marriage vows (commandments)?
- Do you love God so much that his love fills you daily and you are loving people who are unlovely toward you?
- Do you love God so much that it breaks your heart that so many people have never opened their lives to Jesus in order to experience the greatest love?
- Have you stopped doing things you would love to continue doing because you have come to love Jesus more?
- Have you started to do things you find personally difficult to yourself because you love Jesus more than yourself?

2. Read John 14:21-24: What turns God's love in your direction as 'Father love'? What, according to verses 21-24, are the results of the Father-child love in your life?

3. Look up the following verses and write down the various ways God has expressed his love for you: 1 John 3:14-18; 4:7-21; Ephesians 1:3-14.

4. Meditate on Ephesians 3:18-19.

5. Memorize 1 John 3:1 and 1 John 4:19.

TOOLBOX

06
4th Cornerstone

Finding Pleasure in the
Pleasures of God

Driving motivation:
I want to be thrilled by the greatest enjoyment there is

Christian spirituality is about finding pleasure in the most delightful thing there is.

Are you surprised? Then you are not the first! When I made that statement at a conference, a dear lady raised her hand and kindly suggested that using the word 'pleasure' to describe a cornerstone of personal faith was a poor choice of words. Being a good German, she indicated that 'pleasure' describes the feeling from a sip of cold beer on a hot summer day, but you would not use that word to describe God.

Perhaps you agree. Not necessarily with the beer thing, but with the use of the word 'pleasure' in relation to the sacred. Maybe you would use the word 'pleasure' for the enjoyment of lying out on a sandy beach, or the thrill of having just won the championship, or the moment of breathing in pure, cool forest air. But not for God.

Is it not true, however, that when you love somebody, you take pleasure in that person? Imagine I suggest to my wife: "Let's head to Heidelberg for the weekend. I know you love that place. Let's spend the night in an old, romantic hotel near the beautiful, romantic square in the old city, just below that big, romantic castle. Then we'll enjoy a comfortable breakfast together, and after that we'll walk hand in hand down the Hauptstrasse and spend time together. You could even do some shopping and I will not be the usual old grouch every time you want to walk into a store."

Now imagine that my wife responds, "Why would you want to spend your weekend that way? You hate shopping, and the last time you visited a castle you said something like, 'one more castle and I will throw up'." Imagine her disappointment, even anger, when I answer, "To be honest with you, I had a chat with my dear Cuban buddy, Alberto Herminio Carzola Santa Maria, and he said I need to spend more time with you. To be honest with you, I don't have time for that this weekend because I have piles of work waiting for me in the office and I would like to have my desk cleared for Monday, but I will do this so that I stay on your good side and look like a good husband to Alberto Herminio Carzola Santa Maria."

That is the answer that would definitely keep us home from Heidelberg all weekend. Worse, I might as well take my sleeping bag out to the shed for the night. It is not what my lover wants to hear. The answer Susan would enjoy sounds a bit more like this: "Alberto Herminio Carzola Santa Maria sent me $300 for my birthday, and told me to spend it on something that would mean a lot to me. Well, to be honest with you, I cannot think of anything or anyone more meaningful to me than you."

My wife's eyes would be glowing at this point. She enjoys Heidelberg. But more than that, she enjoys it when I enjoy her. She would wrap her arms around me, and a glorious and romantic weekend would begin. When you love somebody, you take pleasure in that person.

Glorifying God by enjoying him

The Bible says in 1 Corinthians 10:31, *"Whether you eat or drink, or whatever you do, do all to the glory of God."* That sounds a little bit like something that came out of England many years later. In 1643, a large group of pastors and theologians came together in the Westminster Abbey in London. Parliament called them together with the commission to rewrite the 15 Articles of Faith of the Anglican Church. These men spent the next 4 years together talking theology! I can imagine sitting with 100 other men and discussing theology for 4 years, but not in the days before deodorant. These guys did precisely that.

What they produced in the end was not a revision of the 15 Articles. Instead, these men authored the mother of all doctrinal confessions: a huge statement that summarized the Christian faith, The Westminster Confession of Faith, plus a Larger Catechism (it is pretty large) and a Shorter Catechism (it is also pretty large). The Shorter Catechism was written for kids; that's why I can understand parts of it. In its very first question/answer, the Shorter Catechism asks, *"What is the chief end (purpose) of man?"* and answers, *"To glorify God and enjoy him forever"*.

Several years ago, the American theologian, John Piper, claimed in his book DESIRING GOD that the Shorter Catechism would have reflected biblical teaching equally well, if not better, had it answered the first question, "To glorify God BY enjoying him forever."[11] The point is that God feels glorified by us when we find enjoyment in him. It is the same as when my wife feels honoured by me, when spending time with her gives me enjoyment. She would not say that I am being self-absorbed when loving her brings me delight. Quite the opposite! The same is true of God. He is honoured and esteemed when loving and enjoying him becomes the gratification of our souls.

Piper found this theological thought expressed in Jonathan Edwards (18th century), as well as in C.S. Lewis (20th century). Lewis criticized the philosophy of Kant and his concept of 'disinterested morality.' Kant claimed that the morality of a good work loses its value when the action is motivated out of self-interest. He said that actions of love must be done without any thought of personal gain or pleasure or they are no longer love. This stoic philosophy has seriously influenced us, especially in Germany, with a strict and serious pietism that frowns on personal gratification, pleasure, hilarity, and enjoyment of the world around us. Lewis' point was that it is impossible for man to do anything without some thought of and desire for personal gratification in the deed. In a letter to his friend, Sheldon Vanauken, Lewis wrote, *"It is a Christian duty, as you know, for everyone to be as happy as he can."*[12]

The French philosopher, Pascal, who stated that in every person there is a god-shaped vacuum that only God can fill, also wrote similarly, *"All men seek happiness without exception. They all aim at this goal however different the means they use to attain it... They*

---

[11] John Piper, DESIRING GOD: MEDITATIONS OF A CHRISTIAN HEDONIST, Portland: Multnomah Press, 1986, p. 14.

[12] Sheldon Vanauken, A SEVERE MERCY, New York: Harper & Row, 1979, p. 189.

will never make the smallest move but with this as its goal. This is the motive of all the actions of all men, even those who contemplate suicide."

Jonathan Edwards, who died when Kant was 34, expressed it like this: *"Resolved, To endeavour to obtain for myself as much happiness in the other world as I possibly can, with all the power, might, vigour, and vehemence, yea violence, I am capable of, or can bring myself to exert, in any way that can be thought of."*[13]

So the question we face in our quest for a Christian spirituality is this: why would Edwards, Pascal, Lewis and Piper see the matter of 'doing something that brings personal pleasure' differently than Kant? I think it is because they saw that in the Bible 'deriving personal pleasure' from an action and 'honouring God' in that action are not mutually exclusive. In fact, they complement each other.

God is a God of pleasure

God is a God of pleasure and delight. He is a happy God! I want to highlight what John Piper has already written in THE PLEASURES OF GOD.[14] First, God delights in himself. It is a fact that you delight in what you treasure most, and what you delight in most is that around which your life revolves. God is the greatest treasure there is, and beside him there is no other God. Consequently, God delights in himself. He delights in being God. He takes pleasure in the brilliance of his own glory. How good it is to know a God who is perfectly content with himself! It is the assurance that there really is nothing more delightful than what he is.

Secondly, he delights in his creation. The creation account in Genesis 1 goes through the days of creation, ending every day with a reference to God's sense of pleasure in his own action. Whether the sea, with all the fish squiggling and darting here and there, or the brilliant sun by day and the gazillion stars lighting up the night, or the tremendous variety of animals (I am sure that some of them give heaven a good laugh), or the vast array of flowers, bursting forth in manifold colours, at the end of every creation day, God saw what he had artistically put together and probably

---

[13] Hickman, p. xxi.
[14] John Piper, The Pleasures of God: Meditations on God's Delight in Being God, Portland, Oregon: Multnomah, 1991.

enthusiastically exploded "It is good!" But after creating man and woman, with all the physical complexity, the mystery of the soul and the synchronization of body and soul, God celebrated, "It is *very* good!"

Thirdly, God takes great pleasure in the second Person of the Trinity, Jesus. Matthew 3:17 tells us that when the Son of God was baptized and came up out of the water, the Holy Spirit was seen coming upon him in the form of a gentle dove and anointing him to his messianic ministry. Then the voice of God the Father boomed throughout the universe, *"This is my beloved Son, in whom I am well-pleased."* God's passionate love for his Son gave the Father a deep sense of personal pleasure.

As grief-stricken as heaven must have been when Jesus was crucified, and as much as the Father looked away from Jesus in horror over our sins loaded onto his most holy Son, the Bible teaches that God found pleasure in the cross of Jesus. Isaiah 53:10 says, *"But the Lord was pleased to crush Him, putting Him to grief."* *(NAS)* This is not some blood-thirsty, sadistic God with whom we have to do. The Bible text goes on to explain that as Jesus was being crushed, God was able to see the tremendous result of Jesus' death. Father and Son were in covenant with each other; they had agreed that the Son would purchase (redeem) a people for the Father by paying the infinite price none of us can pay. God delighted in Jesus' death because he knew—even as Jesus himself cried out, "It has been finished"—that the death of this One would, for millions, lead to the happy reconciliation with the Father and eternal life.

Similarly, God delights in the death of those who belong to him. Psalm 116:15 says, *"Precious in the sight of the LORD is the death of his saints."* Again, this does not mean that God is unable to identify with our grief or the pain and agony that many must go through in the process of dying, but God looks at everything through a boundless wide-angle lens. He knows and controls how one thing leads to another and to another and to another and to another until at some point--maybe even 300 years later—the cause has effected something beautiful and precious.

But that is not the only reason why God finds the death of those who are safely his to be precious. The Father's covenant with his Son was not merely that the Son should purchase us through his death, but that as the Father's possession, we would belong to him and be with him forever. The sting that God removed from death through the death of his Son is that death no longer threatens God's children with the cessation of all that is bad or good, but has become the entrance for us into all that is perfect. Through his death and resurrection, Jesus has saved us with a goal in mind. Death essentially gets us to the finish line, to the end of a victorious race and the beginning of an eternal victory party. God knows that. Therefore, when one of his own dies, God says, "Welcome home. Everything I, the Trinity, did to make you our possession, everything for which you were saved, is now here for you to enjoy." This moment brings God inexhaustible pleasure.

God is a happy God, who takes pleasure in all that is about him. And in the end, it is all about him.

Christians are called to participate in God's pleasures

Here is an amazing truth in Christian spirituality: God wants to share his inexhaustible pleasure with us. In Psalm 16:11, King David celebrates, *"You have made known to me the path of life; you will fill me with joy in your presence, with eternal pleasures at your right hand."* God is stocked full of pleasures right to the brim of his being. Psalm 36:8 describes the Almighty as the one *who "give[s] them drink from your river of delights."* Psalm 46:4 says, *"There is a river whose streams make glad the city of God."*

God is so delighted when our souls are gratified by him that he commands us to delight in him: Psalm 37:4 commands *"Delight yourself in the Lord."* This is why Jesus God-incarnate said in John 15:11, *"I have told you this so that my joy may be in you and that your joy may be complete."* The goal of his coming to earth was that you would begin to taste the gusto. John 10:10 states *"I have come that they may have life, and have it to the full."* The writer to the Hebrews says (Hebrews 11:6) that we cannot come to God, unless we believe that he is, and that *"he is a rewarder of those who seek him."* (NAS)

Christian spirituality, it turns out, is God's invitation to step into the pleasures of God, and to find pleasure in the things that fill God's heart with delight. To that end, the Bible commands us to do things in the revelry of enjoyment.

Note the following commands:

- Micah 6:8: LOVE kindness
- Psalm 1:2: DELIGHT in the law of the Lord
- Psalm 40:8: I DESIRE to do your will, o my God, your law is in my heart
- 2 Corinthians 9:7: God loves a CHEERFUL giver
- 1 Timothy 6:6: There is great GAIN in godliness with contentment
- Nehemiah 8:11: The JOY of the Lord is your strength.

God hates heartless, joyless service. He abhors deeds that are done—no matter how good and generous they appear—out of a mere sense of duty. I know this destroys a million homilies, but God is terribly displeased in sermons that simply tell people to obey God because that is what good Christians do. If my wife is sad when I want to take her to Heidelberg out of a mere sense of duty, then God is even more furious over offerings brought to him out of routine and from hearts that are cold.

The key is to have God so cemented into your life as a cornerstone that your heart gets shaped around his heart. When that is the case, you begin to love what God loves, hate what God hates, and feel what God feels. God LOVES to be kind. When you love being kind to the neighbour who is unkind toward you, you know you have stepped into the pleasures of God. God gives CHEERFULLY to people; it is simply a delight to him to share all that he has. When you happily give things away to people, you know you have entered into the pleasures of God.

Participating in God's pleasures leads to passionate living

Many people have misunderstood Christian spirituality as a joyless living according to rules and regulations. The misunderstanding arises either because someone prominent exemplified a rigorous, pleasure-denying life and called it 'Christian', or because categorizing Christianity as „nothing but rules and regulations" is merely a way to justify their own autonomy and selfish pursuit of pleasures.

As a matter of fact, Christian spirituality has a rule and a regulation. Here it is:

Whatever is, is created by God, is given by God or is a reflection of God and is to be fully enjoyed by you.

We will deal in more detail with the practical outworking of this in the chapter on decision-making and obedience, chapter 10. For now, let us understand that Christian spirituality is a gracious summons to participate in God's pleasures, not a pressing into some pietistic prudishness nor a repudiation of life's good things. Let us underscore this biblical truth: Ecclesiastes teaches us that the pleasures of life without God at their centre are nothing but vanity. Why? Because without the God of pleasure at their core, they can only give happiness for the moment but bring disappointment in the end. But what about with God at their centre? *"I know that there is nothing better for men than to be happy and do good while they live. That everyone may eat and drink, and find satisfaction in all his toil—this is a gift of God"* (Ecclesiastes 3:12, 13). Strachan and Sweeney, in summarizing the teaching of Jonathan Edwards' teaching on the pursuit of happiness, write: "Swept up in happiness, we exude not a self-righteous, judgmental spirit but a deep joy rooted in conviction and love for God and man. This kind of life is available to all of us, but many of us practice a deficient Christianity ruled less *by grace and more by rules, less by happiness and more by performance.*"[15]

At this juncture, we should make two analytical points about the Christian world and life view. To some of my readers these will appear revolutionary.

First of all, the age-old distinction between sacred and secular is false. (see more on this in chapter 12). This claim may severely challenge the way you have thought about things, or threaten to destroy neat categories into which you have safely placed this or

---

[15] Owen Strachan and Doug Sweeney, JONATHAN EDWARDS ON THE GOOD LIFE, . Chicago: Moody Publishers, 2010, p. 69.

that idea. The distinction between sacred and secular is the result of a particular world view, but it is not a biblical view.

In the beginning was God and all that God had made. That means that originally, all was sacred. There are statements in Scripture which point to the sacredness of everything in its pristine condition—we will look at several of them later. Suffice it to say for now, Titus 1:15 says, *To the pure, all things are pure, but to those who are corrupted and do not believe, nothing is pure."* The author, Paul, is operating from a basic principle in a God-created but sin-infiltrated world: All that is created by God, is given by God, is a reflection of God and is in and of itself pure. It is sacred! Man was created with a taste for the sacred. His entire appetite was for the satiation in all God had made. His longing for happiness was daily and richly satisfied in his delighting in God's world.

But since the fall of man, his inclination has always been to place himself at the centre of things. His taste for the lower and godless life has him trying at every turn to take God out of the centre of life. You might say he de-sacralized everything originally sacred. The result is that he takes God out of everything that originally was pure. This is the process of secularization. When God is taken out of art by the artist, his paintings end up being nihilistic, pornographic or dehumanizing. Take God out of sex, and man thinks he/she can sleep with whomever he/she wishes whenever he/she wishes, and in autonomy determine his/her own sexual identity. Take God out of food, and appetite becomes the master, eating too much or too little, eating unhealthily, or eating merely for comfort. Take God out of alcohol, and it is used to soothe pain or relieve boredom. Take God out of drugs, and they're used not to get well, but to numb sadness or to feel high...Take God out of sports...take God out of politics...take God out of the environment...and you have the process of secularization!

None of these things—art, sex, food, alcohol, drugs, sports, politics, the environment—are in and of themselves bad. Just the opposite! They are originally good, because they are originally from God. That means they are sacred, holy, and a delight to God. It is when we take God as creator and master out of these things, that as self-centred and self-consumed humans, we turn them to selfish interests.

Christian spirituality teaches us that our role in this world is to re-sacralize what was de-sacralized or secularized. Christian spirituality calls us to bring all things under the lordship of our holy God. When we do that, we begin to use all things in a way that reflects God, and that fulfils the original intent of those things. This way we join God in taking pleasure in the things in which he takes pleasure.

The second revolutionary implication of joining God in the pleasures of God is the lifestyle that results from it: you will begin to enjoy God in everything, right down to the smallest detail. Let's be as blatant about this as the Bible is!

The Old Testament book Song of Solomon is about romance and intimacy, about the sexual delight in your spouse's body. The pleasures of God include your enjoyment of your wife or husband's body. If you are physically able to enjoy sex, but are too prudish or hung-up to have an exciting sexual relationship with your spouse, you are not living in God's will. You need to lighten up. You need to get with the party God wants to throw for you!

The same goes for food. I already mentioned 1 Corinthians 10:31 and the command to glorify God through eating and drinking. In the Old Testament, Ecclesiastes 2:24-25 prescribes for us the same: what you eat, how you eat it, how much you eat and drink...all has to do with honouring the Giver of the food and the drink. In Proverbs there are commands to enjoy wine and to be merry, as well as prohibitions against getting drunk. Wine is a gift from God. Why you drink and how much you drink, determines whether you are joining God in the pleasures of the vine.

Take music: God is not found in one kind of music and which then is labelled 'sacred music', is played behind cathedral walls with a classical or baroque sound to it. Nor can we say that rock 'n roll with lyrics about Jesus is 'Christian rock' while other lyrics are necessarily non-Christian rock. Where songs celebrate life's pleasures devoid of God's centrality in them, they are non-Christian. When songs espouse the values of God's character, even if they do not mention Jesus, they can be called 'Christian' or 'sacred'. God's creativity is discovered and enjoyed in the details of music, be it the rhythm, harmony, poetry, softness or the power of the tones. All music that points to the creativity of God behind the creativity of the composer and resulting composition can and should be labelled 'sacred music', whether it be jazz, classical, rock and roll, hip-hop or whatever. All can be used to praise God. All can be enjoyed.

A number of years ago I suggested to my friend Stephan that we go see a football (soccer) game in one of Germany's great stadiums. He was hesitant at first. Being a fairly well-known Christian in Germany, he wondered what other Christians might think if they discovered that he had mingled with beer-guzzling, cursing football fanatics. Using my special powers of motivation I said, "Hey, you are a football fan and a Christian. Let's go glorify God at a football match!" He chuckled and said, "Beck, you are stretching it a bit. Cheering like two crazies amidst drunken fans about a ball and a bunch of feet that kick it has nothing to do with glorifying God."

"It has everything to do with glorifying God," I said, smiling. "When the right wing drives down the right side of the pitch with the ball perfectly controlled at his foot, swerves to the left, dribbles the ball to the right, then drives the ball in the air, perfectly placed into the centre, where his teammate soars above the other players and in a split second knocks the ball with the centre-left part of his head into the upper right corner of the goal, you not only have 65,000 fans cheering the goal, you have a right winger and a centre forward whose artistry with the ball glorified God. Now when we join the 64,998 other fans in cheering, we are not only cheering two great players and a great play, we are cheering our great God who gave them their creative skills."

"But those two players don't even think about God in that moment. So how is it glorifying God?"

I answered, "Hey, some players do think of their Creator when they score a goal. That is why they immediately point upward to say to the crowd, 'cheer vertically, cheer the Artist who gave me my artistry and allowed me to score that fabulous goal!' But the fact is, even if a football player is not thinking about God when he makes a great play, in reality the play points to the One who made it possible. Even if nobody were to give God the credit for that play, the credit goes to God. God is taking pleasure in the fact that he made that play possible. So, let's go to the stadium and join him. Let's glorify God by cheering like two crazies who are giving him the credit for a great sport and the great skill that is being displayed on the pitch!"

Since that discussion, Stephan and I have visited numerous stadiums in Germany. He often takes his son along to help us glorify God. Every time I am at a game, I think of the lady at the conference the other year, who admonished me for my use of the word 'pleasure', a word that ought not to be used for God. And yet, 'pleasure' is a word that can be used to describe the feeling you have when the right winger dribbles the ball down the sideline with amazing skill, and the player in the middle skilfully heads the ball into the goal. In that moment you celebrate what a glorious God we have, who takes great pleasure in our joining him in the enjoyment of everything that he has given us. And when you are done cheering and screaming your voice dry, you reach for your cold beer on a hot summer day, thanking God that he made such a great brew possible, and glorify God all over again.

■ What's in it for me?

1) **Pleasure:** At this point, many will argue, "I do not need God for this; I have found plenty of pleasure, happiness and good luck without God, thank you." True, God's *general love* and common grace allows even secular-minded, godless-living people many moments of bliss. The point is that with God at the centre of everything you enjoy, you will enjoy everything to the absolute fullest. It's grabbing the gusto to the max. It is going back to the original, uncontaminated fountain and drinking deeply. With God at the centre as the giver of every perfect gift (James 1:17), you will enjoy art, sex, food, nature, family, career and sports. But more: you will enjoy all these things in their sacred purity, which means you will enjoy them to the fullest and no less. The great runner and Olympic champion from Scotland, Eric Liddell, whose life was made famous through the film "Chariots of Fire," once said to his sister: "Jenny, God has made me to run fast, and when I run, I feel his pleasures!"

You can apply that feeling of pleasure to anything that is a gift from God or reflects him.

2) **Passion**: Stepping into the pleasures of God is the secret to developing passion. When you begin to delight yourself in the things in which God delights, whether his creation, his Son Jesus Christ, his crucifixion and resurrection, the greater purposes of God even in the sad situations of life, the display of God-given emotions, bodily pleasures, physical exercise, good and healthy food and drink, rest, relationships and the community of God's people, you develop passion.

3) **Joy:** Jesus came to give you joy in fullness. When you enter into the things that make God's heart glad, you will feel his gladness.

4) **Humour**: Being released to the enjoyments of God, a lowered brow can be raised and a sombre spirit lifted. You begin to not only rejoice with those who rejoice, but to laugh over things that even God finds funny. And there are a lot of funny things in the world! Learning to laugh is part of Christian spirituality. "A cheerful heart is good medicine, but a crushed spirit dries up the bones" (Proverbs 17:23).

4th motivation:
I want to be thrilled by the most enjoyable thing there is

---

1. God is a passionate God. He enjoys with great pleasure everything that comes from him and that reflects his holiness and reveals his beauty. Being a Christian means that you step into his delights, live in his delights and take pleasure in the things in which he takes pleasure. In what specific ways does this guiding principle of spirituality change your life?

2. In review, look over the following verses in the Bible. In what all does God take pleasure?

- Matthew 3:16-17; John 17:24, Colossians 1:19
- Genesis 1:4, 10, 12, 18, 21, 25, 31; Psalm 19:1-2, 104:31
- Deuteronomy 10:14-15; 1 Samuel 12:22; Luke 10:21; Ephesians 1:4-6, 11-12
- Isaiah 53:10
- Zephaniah 3:17; Psalm 147:10-11
- Psalm 135:6, 115:1-3; Isaiah 46:9-10.

3. Memorize Psalm 37:4-5.

4. Memorize Question/Answer #1 of the Westminster Shorter Catechism:
- Question: "What is the chief end of man?"
- Answer: "To glorify God and enjoy Him forever!"

5. How is your joy? In Luke 4:14-21, Jesus explained that he is the expected Messiah, who came to bring joy and liberation. That is why followers of Jesus are exhorted to be people full of joy. In Philippians, Paul commands the church in Philippi three times (2:18, 3:1, 4:4) to "rejoice". In Galatians 5:22, joy is listed as an aspect of the fruit of the Holy Spirit in our lives. Where you notice aspects of your life where joy is missing (work, marriage, studies, worship, etc.), ask God to reveal to you the reason for that. Ask God to show you how to enter into his joy in that (those) aspect(s) of life.

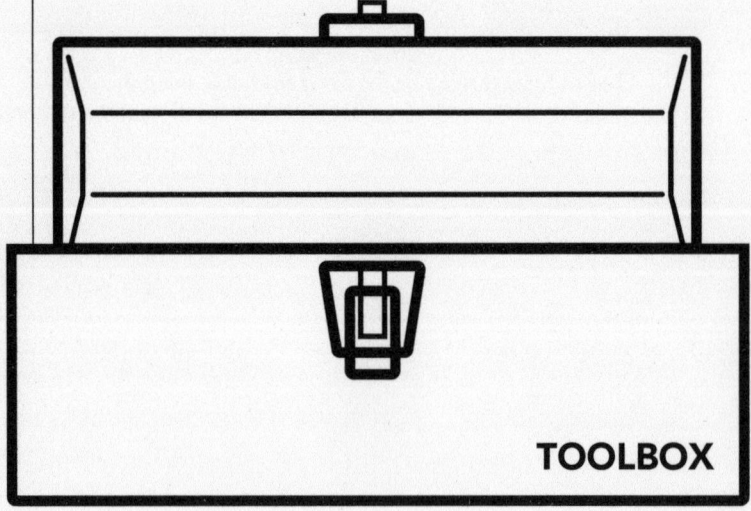

TOOLBOX

Maria's Journey #4
Discovering the costliness of unconditional love

I sat with my wife, Susan, in Karina's kitchen in Toronto. The year before, we had moved across the big pond to Germany. It was great to have been called by God to return to the country of my childhood. But at that moment, it was good to be back in the great metropolis of Toronto for a visit. We were pleasantly chatting with Karina and Maria, who was holding Monica in her arms.

Home from work, Rob suddenly came through the door with his big smile. He gave Maria a hug. "Hey daughter, have you taken good care of my granddaughter?"

"Sure dad!" Maria grinned

Then Rob gave Karina a kiss and walked over to Susan and me with a hug for us. A feeling of amazement swept over me. This family had experienced a lot of pain and sadness in the past years, but was now visibly enjoying harmony. Maria's younger brother joined us as we sat down for supper, which meant the conversation immediately turned to ice hockey and how poorly the Toronto Maple Leafs were doing. Then Maria asked me if I had read a new book on Christian spirituality that was attracting a lot of attention at that time. I had.

"What did you think about it?" I asked her. For Maria, as for me, the book had been enjoyable to read because it was funny in many places.

"I liked that the author tries to communicate with people of my generation who have grown up with no knowledge of God, the Bible, or the Christian faith. It speaks to people who are on one side of a large river and don't know that the other side of the river is their real home. A year ago I would have said that there is only one side to the river, and if there is another side, we can't know anything about it. I would have said that we all must build our own house to suit ourselves. And then I hit the resurrection of Jesus head on. The more I thought through the implications of that historic happening, the clearer it became to me that the only spiritual place where the soul will ever be at home is there where Jesus is. And he is on the other side of the river. The only way to get across is for God to cross over to us, which he did in Jesus. The author makes that pretty clear."

"Sounds like the book was an inspiring read for both of you," Karina said.

I answered, "There were some things that represented Christian spirituality well, like his statement that the heart and soul of Christian spirituality is being one with Jesus. He stressed the core of the gospel message when he said that spiritual life comes from Jesus working inside me, not me working up something for him. But I was bothered by the way he says a person gets to Jesus, that if we just follow the radar inside us, we will end up by God. We do have radar for God by virtue of God having created us, but in our drive for self-autonomy, we naturally suppress this radar. Our only hope is for God to confront us in such a convincing way that we want God."

"I was bothered by the statement that Christian spirituality can't be explained," my wife jumped in, "because it is something you feel. Christian spirituality is something you feel, yes—maybe that is his emphasis—but Christian spirituality is not true simply because you can feel it. It can be explained. That God is ultimately mysterious, incomprehensible and unsearchable does not mean he is irrational, illogical and unexplainable. Precisely because he has revealed himself in the incarnation…"

"In the what?" Maria's younger brother suddenly looked up from his food, though most of it had already disappeared from his plate through inhalation.

"Incarnation", Maria answered. "It means God became flesh, referring to Jesus."

Susan continued: "Right, the incarnation. It is so foundational to Christian spirituality. Due to the incarnation, there are many things about God we can know for certain. When the author writes that Christian spirituality cannot be explained, he plays right into the postmodern lie…"

"Into the what?" the young hockey player raised his head again.

We all laughed. "Postmodern," Maria answered.

"Well that's a dumb word," he remarked. "How can anything be postmodern?"

"Hey, you're not as dumb as I thought you hockey players were," Maria said. We laughed some more. She explained, "It's a crazy word that points to the craziness of life without any sort of objective reality outside of the subjective experience. Get it?" The expression on his face told us he didn't get it. Susan added: "The postmodern premise is that we have to work from within our subjective experience to get to God. But the incarnation explodes that. God explained himself in the historic person of Jesus and in historic events like his birth, crucifixion and resurrection. Christian spirituality can be explained precisely because God has given us a rational, historically verifiable basis for believing in Jesus."

Maria said, "The author made it sound so easy to get to the bridge that takes you across to the other side. He talks about having spiritual insights into God while hanging out with a bunch of hippies who are getting drunk and having an orgy in the woods. I think my generation needs an intelligent confrontation with the facts. Hanging out with funky people who have sweet experiences and a 'feel-good' way of filling the soul's void will not cut it. We all create barriers to God, barriers like deep-seated pride and self-righteousness, rebellion and unwillingness to believe in God, intellectual arguments, or growing up in a culture where faith is never mentioned. You don't just remove all this darkness by having sweet spiritual experiences. Meeting God is an experience, even a wonderful and fulfilling experience. But there are big boulders in the path that we have to be willing to scale if we are going to make it to the bridge. Getting past those boulders means admitting you were wrong, that you have been self-righteous. Part of the experience is wrestling with tough questions before you can decide that Jesus' outrageous claims must be the objective truth that informs your subjective feelings. You have to struggle with historic facts to be able to see things Jesus' way, that he is not one of many alternatives but the only way, the only bridge to God."

The passionate speech continued. "While I am thinking about Jesus' exhortation to all of us to love God with heart and mind, I've learned that love is not simply a nice, warm feeling. I mean, look at my parents. They stuck me into a drug rehabilitation centre against my will, and I accused them of hating me. The fact is they loved me and understood what I, in my rebellious state, could not comprehend. It was love that drove them to do what I hated them for. Later I realized love is based on truth, not truth on love. Sometimes, real love loves in a manner that the loved one does not consider loving. It can cost you everything to love somebody truthfully. Without my parents I would not be here, but it has cost my parents unbelievably much to love me.

"My generation needs to know that the costliest love of all is the love of Jesus, that Jesus' sacrifice of himself on the cross is the most loving thing ever done by anybody. The eternal God dies for dying people, the holy God dies for sin-filled, rebellious people, the most self-sacrificial God offers himself up for self-consumed people. What a love! But people think—as I did—that this Christian faith is just a few fundamentalists wanting to force on others what nobody wants. It is actually a call to lay down our self-righteous rebellion and open our hearts to the greatest love there ever was. This author presents Christian spirituality as a good feeling about Jesus that anybody can achieve, and still go with the flow politically and morally, and be trendy. But love based on the truth of God is not trendy. To follow Jesus can cost you everything, because it cost God everything. It will cost you things you hold dear and want to keep on doing, *things that are out of line with the truth and holiness of God. It will cost you your self-righteous attitude about other people. It may cost you the approval of friends and family, or even cost you your life. But it will gain you the way to the bridge and the crossing over into home. If God loved us so much that he butchered his own Son on the cross because our rebelliousness against him is more awful than we will ever realize, then following after Jesus is going to be much more than having a faith based on good feelings."*

Maria had been down that path and it had left her impoverished. She wanted a holistic faith, one that was both intellectually true and emotionally alive, one that informed and transformed all aspects of life. She had concluded that next to Jesus there was only one alternative: to follow the lie within.

It would be awhile before we would see Maria again, and she would experience more heartache in the meantime.

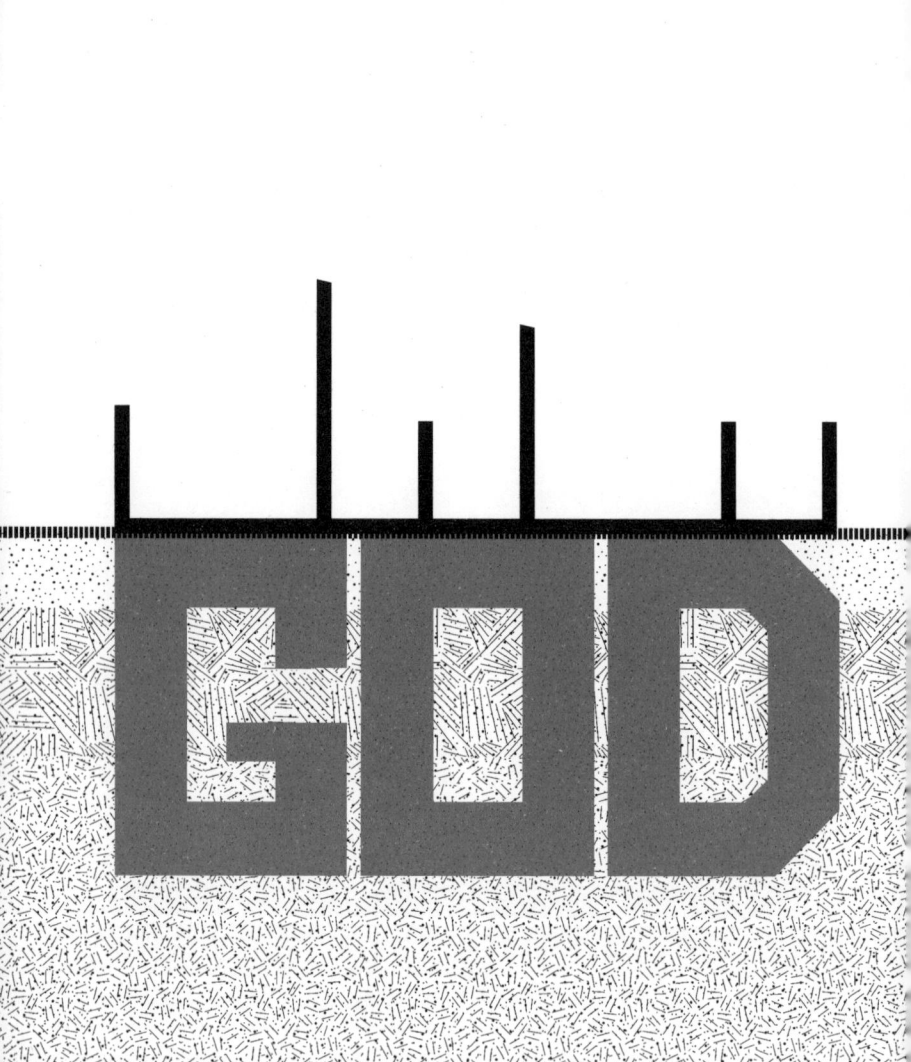

SECTION 3

The floor and the 4 walls of our house

Here we come to the practice of Christian spirituality, as it is built on a proper foundation and fitted around the cornerstones. In Sections 1 and 2 we have developed Christian spirituality around the presupposition that we can only know and walk with God as God has revealed himself.

It is not impossible for a human being to develop his own spirituality. It is impossible for any human being to develop a *true* spirituality from within himself. If God is God, eternally self-existent and self-defined, then a true spirituality can only be developed if we build it in response to God. Luther called God the Durchbrecher, the One who breaks through to us that we might be able to break through to him.

C.S. Lewis said somewhere what I will paraphrase: *If you want God because you want him to work for you, he will not work for you; if you want God because he is true, he will work for you.*

God is what he is! Alister McGrath stated the implications of God's self-revelation like this:

> *"God is gently pointing out the limitations of reason. We ought to attend to God as he actually is, rather than constructing ideas of what we would like him to be like...The self-revelation of God is a demand for self-humility on the part of the theologian. We must learn to respond to God. God has taken the initiative away from us, pulling the rug from under our neat preconceptions of what a god ought to be like. In part, faith is a willingness to apprehend and respond to God as he has chosen to make himself known. It is a form of humility (a characteristic for the young Luther), in that it amounts to a willingness to submit to*

God, rather than to assert the validity of our own stereotypes of divinity (wherever these may have come from). True spirituality is not a human invention, but a response to God."[1]

For that reason, we have emphasised in Sections 1 and 2 that Christian spirituality is based on the spirituality of God. We come now in Section 3 to the working-part of a Christian spirituality. How does it function? As we continue to build our house of spirituality on the rock of Jesus' teaching, we now move to the visible, above-ground part of the house, the part that is experienced daily by you, seen by others, and influences the scenery around you. Even here we will realize that, while we do the building and shape the practice, the practical part of Christian spirituality will only work for you if it is gospel-driven and based on an understanding of God and his revelation of himself.

Enjoy building the first floor of your spiritual house!

---

[1] Alister McGrath, Spirituality in an Age of Change: Rediscovering the Spirit of the Reformers, Grand Rapids: Zondervan, 1994, p. 78

07
The Floor
Running Your Life according to the Word of God

Learning spirituality by the book

Rocco is a blind man. But that is not what intrigued me about him. He and his brother had picked up a land mine in Italy when Rocco was 5. It had exploded in their hands, killing his older brother and blinding Rocco for life. The story is tragic and so is the result. But that is not what at first intrigued me about this man.

As I watched Rocco 41 years after that terrible incident, he was jogging around an indoor track filled with other runners. It was cool how he did that: he would take the inside track, hold his cane out in front of him with his right hand, to preserve a proper distance between himself and other runners, while barely touching the railing with his outstretched left hand. I watched this week after week as I also jogged.

My admiration for Rocco grew so much that one day I approached him after we both had finished jogging and said, „Hi, I know I am a complete stranger, but I see you here all the time and really admire your courage. The way you jog with the rest of us is quite ingenious. You also illustrate for me a very important lesson in life. Thank you very much." Rocco smiled and kindly responded with the question I was hoping for: „And what lesson would that be?" I said, „The way you use the railing to guide you along the track, well, it reminds me of the fact that we all are spiritually blind by nature." I waited for him to jump on me and try to strangle me for using the s-word. But Rocco just stood there smiling, so I decided it was safe to continue, "In order to be able to run through life successfully, we all need to be guided by something that is firm and dependable, and perfectly in keeping with the reality of the track we are on." „Wow," my listener responded, and then asked, „and what kind of a guide might that be?" I hesitated a little, wondering if I really wanted to die by strangulation. „Uh...well...the Bible," I answered. „I read it every day and God speaks to me." I thought to myself how strange my statement must sound to this little balding Italian. Instead another big smile crossed his face, as he said, „So do I, and he speaks to me, too."

How does God speak to us through the Bible?

This question is absolutely basic, because its answer determines how you handle the Bible and what place you give it in your life. Basically, there are 4 different views of what the Bible is:

- The Bible is a human book that TESTIFIES to God's work in the authors' lives. It is therefore, no more divine than the Koran, the Book of Mormon or any other sacred literature or holy books written by people. In this view, divine inspiration of the text does not exist, since it did not come from God. Inspiration lies in the human writer who records his illumination of God. It can inspire the reader to discover ways in which God—however you define "God"—can be experienced. This is the *modernist view* of S7cripture, which developed in the mid-18th century and is the prevailing view in many theological faculties of universities today.[1]

- The Bible BECOMES the Word of God when the Holy Spirit makes a passage inspiring to the person who is reading it. This is the *dynamic view of Scripture*. Theologians in the first half of the 20th century developed this view as a corrective to the *modernist view*.[2] Known as 'neo-orthodoxy,' it presupposes the human, and therefore fallible, origin of Scripture ("to err is human"), but insists that God the Holy Spirit makes the words of the Bible come alive to its readers, illuminating the reader with an understanding and application of the text. Barth wrote, "The Bible is God's Word to

---

[1] Prominent proponents are Friedrich Schleiermacher, Adolf von Harnack, Rudolf Bultmann, Paul Tillich, Karl Rahner, and Edward Schillebeeckx.

[2] Early proponents were Emil Brunner, H. Richard Niebuhr, and Karl Barth.

the extent that God causes it to be his Word, to the extent that he speaks through it."[3] In this view, the Spirit's inspiration of what is written and the illumination of the reader are considered to be one and the same thing.

- The Bible IS the Word of God because the Holy Spirit inspired its content. This is the *organic view* of Scripture, the oldest of the four views.[4] It corresponds to what Luther originally meant with Sola Scriptura: the authority for faith and life resides alone in the writings of the Bible. But how can a book be the authority for life? According to the *organic view*, the Holy Spirit inspired the very words themselves that were written down. Rarely dictating the words, the Spirit instead directed each one of the writers to express in the writer's own words, in his individual style, with his own background and with his desired emphasis exactly the content God wanted us to receive from him. This means God authored the Bible, but used humans, so that divine revelation could be read by humans in their language. Over a period of 1500 years the original 66 books were revealed by God in Hebrew, Aramaic and Greek. Since then the Bible has been translated for numerous people groups to read in their own language. In the *organic view,* inspiration and illumination are two distinct concepts: divine inspiration is the Holy Spirit breathing God's intended meaning into every word written down by human authors—making the meaning of the words authoritative and without error—while illumination is that same Spirit helping the reader to understand, interpret and apply the text according to God's original intent.

- The Bible GUIDES THE COMMUNITY to God's word for today. Some call this the *postmodernist Christian view*, others the *post-evangelical view.*[5] In this view there is a desire to preserve

---

[3] Barth, Karl, CHURCH DOGMATICS, Edinburgh: T&T Clark, 1975, I.1.109

[4] Well-known proponents include Augustine, John Calvin, Martin Luther, the Puritans, and, more recently, F.F. Bruce, John Wenham, John Stott, J.I. Packer, Mark Driscoll, and Tim Keller. According to some scholars Dietrich Bonhoeffer also held this view. (See Willberg, Faix and Gableske, EINER VON UNS? VTR, 2006, pp. 56-57; cf. research by Georg Huntemann, Rainer Mayer)

[5] It is held by Thomas Oden, Stanley Grenz, John Franke, Brian MacLaren, Donald Miller, Karen Ward, Doug Pagitt, Rob Bell, Spencer Burke, and Dave Tomlinson. (A very helpful

the inspiration of Scripture, but the words used by proponents of the organic view to describe the text of Scripture—authority, inerrancy, objective, absolute, and literal—are frowned upon. So is the concept of 'propositional truth'. To be sure, these so-called 'emergent' thinkers do not devalue propositional statements—one cannot do so without devaluing the meaning of his own words—but they decry turning propositional statements of the Bible into static truth or doctrinal absolutes that replace the person of Jesus as the embodiment of truth. In the words of one proponent, "Christianity is a relationship with a person, not affirming a set of propositions… We worship the Word made flesh, not the words on a page."[6] A friend of mine recently summarized the *postmodernist view* of biblical authority in an email to me like this: *"The Reformation doctrine of Sola Scriptura is a heresy. Biblical authority rests on a 3-legged stool: the original text + one's personal experience with the text + the church community's collective agreement to the meaning of the text for the culture in which it operates."* Doug Pagitt meant the same thing when he wrote, *"The Bible is not reduced to a book from which we extract truth, but the Bible is a full, living, and active member of our community that is listened to on all topics of which it speaks."* [7] The *postmodernist* approach to the Bible allows for and even celebrates doubt, uncertainty and mystery. God cannot be put in a box. Neither can truth. It is fluid. It all depends on the shaping of the 3-legged stool at any given time. Since God has not only spoken but still speaks, revelation is not closed but ongoing. Biblical inspiration becomes continuous illumination within the Christian community. Theology is not truth about God as revealed in Scripture, but the task of expressing communal beliefs and values in an ongoing conversation.

---

summary and critique is Kevin DeYoung and Ted Kluck, WHY WE'RE NOT EMERGENT (By Two Guys Who Should Be), Chicago: Moody Publishers, 2008).

[6] Sally Morgenthaler, as quoted in DeYoung and Kluck, WHY WE'RE NOT EMERGENT, p. 73

[7] Doug Pagitt, REIMAGINING SPIRITUAL FORMATION. Grand Rapids: Zondervan, 2004, p. 32.

Now the question confronts us: which one of these four views on biblical authority is the true one?

Approach #1: Decide each claim in the Bible individually. Look at every historical-geographical-scientific detail mentioned in the Bible, and each time decide if it is true or not.

This is how many have arrived at the modernist view. The problem with this approach is that it is simply impossible. You can never know everything there is to know about history, geography, archaeology, biology, astronomy, linguistics, or anything else And from that consummate knowledge of the known and yet-to-be known, it is impossible to make an objective assessment about every detail in the Bible. To think you can—and many think they can—is in my estimation a highly evolved form of scholarly arrogance.

Approach #2: The normal and logical way to solve the question is to consult an appropriate authority.

That calls for a 2-step approach:

Step #1: What claims does the Bible itself make for its authority? In 2 Timothy 3:16, Paul writes that "all Scripture is inspired by God". The word "inspired" means "breathed out." This in turn means, the Spirit of God breathed out truth into "all Scripture". With "Scripture" (the word means "writing"), Paul meant at least all that was written down and accepted as Scripture in his day, namely the Old Testament.

Years after the disciple Peter had walked with Jesus, he made this claim in the Bible about his record of experiences with Jesus: *"We did not follow cleverly devised tales when we made known to you the power and coming of our Lord Jesus Christ, but we were eyewitnesses of his majesty...And so we have the prophetic word made more sure, to which you do well to pay attention as to a lamp shining in a dark place... But know this first of all, that no prophecy of Scripture is a matter of one's own interpretation, for no prophecy was ever made by an act of human will but men moved by the Holy Spirit spoke from God"* (2 Peter 1:16-21).

What a brazen claim! Yet the apostle Peter makes the same claim about Paul's writings: *"...As also our beloved brother, Paul, according to the wisdom given him, wrote to you, as also in all his letters, speaking in them of these things, in which are some things hard to understand, which the untaught and unstable distort, as they do also the rest of the Scriptures..."* (2 Peter 3:15, 16 *NAS*).

Other authors of Bible books make similar and explicit claims to their writing being a word from the Lord.

Step #2: Does Jesus confirm the Bible's understanding of itself? Though Jesus professed to be one with God and God in the flesh, he placed himself under the authority of the Bible. When tempted by Satan three times (Matthew 4), Jesus resisted temptation and obeyed God each time according to the passages he quoted from the Old Testament. The Scriptures were to Jesus the authority by which he let himself be guided. The only way that he, to whom God gave authority over heaven and earth, would submit to the authority of Scripture, is if Scripture had an authority on the same level as the authority of God himself.

In the Sermon on the Mount, Jesus said that every last word, even down to the smallest letter of the Hebrew alphabet, would be fulfilled, because it came from God (Matthew 5:17-19). In statement after statement throughout the rest of the Gospels, Jesus quoted from the Old Testament, and always with the sense that the Old Testament verse confirmed the truthfulness of Jesus' words (e.g., "just as the prophet Isaiah wrote..."). To Jesus, the Old Testament was on the same level of truthfulness as his own words of truth. Even Old Testament stories that the modernist disregards as mythological stuff, like the swallowing of Jonah by a large fish, are referred to by Jesus as historical events (Matthew 12:40).

My handling of this subject here falls short of the many scholarly and helpful insights and answers others have brought to the table. A very helpful book is by the English scholar, John Wenham, CHRIST AND THE BIBLE. Let me humbly suggest that while the other three views have important factors every reader of the Bible should take into consideration, I think the evidence points us to the *organic view of inspiration.* The Bible *in its original* is what it claims to be and what Jesus accepted it to be, namely the Word of God, that in every culture and for every period of history it is *"sufficient for teaching, warning, correction, and training in righteous-*

ness; that the man of God may be thoroughly equipped for every good work" (2 Timothy 3:16-17).

We want to be honest. Embracing the *organic view* opens us to severe criticism and accusations. Let's look at a few arguments, as well as possible ways to answer them:

1) The *organic view* is not reasonable for our secular, rational, scientific world! It is just as reasonable for God to reveal himself through a fully divine/fully human book, as it is for him to reveal himself in a fully divine/fully human person. If God can wrap perfect humanity and perfect divinity into one body and call him „Jesus"—and he did—God can wrap divine revelation and human authoring into one book and call it "all Scripture breathed out from God". In both cases you have something perfect and divine being revealed in humanly understandable form. Secondly, the *organic view of Scripture* makes perfect sense. If God loves us so much that he wants us to know who he is, if he wants mankind to know his plan for turning Paradise Lost into Paradise Regained, if he wants every human being to know how to become part of God's salvation plan and how to experience the satisfaction of glorifying God, then God would certainly want us to have his revelation not only in words we can understand (i.e., human authorship) but in words we can fully trust (i.e., divine authorship). Bottom line: if there is a God who wishes to personally reveal himself to mankind, the *organic view* is completely reasonable.

2) The emphasis in the *organic view* on the Bible's infallibility—specifically, that the Bible must be without error—is ridiculous. The Bible was written by humans, and 'to err is human.' I would suggest that that statement simply is not true! Not everything humans do has to include error. Especially if God is overseeing a human activity that is supposed to have his name on it and guide his creation into a relationship to himself, he will want to supervise the human au-

thors to not give erroneous information. It is reasonable to believe that God would want that and can accomplish it.

3) There is no good reason in our day and age to hold to the *organic view*. The real issue is how to properly explain some of the supernatural and profound occurrences in the Bible. For example, Genesis 12:1–3 is introduced with the words *"the Lord said to Abraham."* *(NAS)* The words that follow are introduced in Galatians 3:8 with the preface, *"The Scripture ... announced ... to Abraham."* "The Lord" and "The Scripture" functioned interchangeably. The same thing occurs between Exodus 9:13 *("This is what the Lord ... says [to Pharaoh]")* and Romans 9:17 *("The Scripture says to Pharaoh")*. Another sign of the supernatural at work in the Bible is the many Old Testament prophecies that have already been fulfilled, either in the New Testament or in our own day. The inner unity of the 66 books by 40 different authors, with one theme running through all the writings without a single contradiction points to a reasonable conclusion: this is a divine book, in which God speaks to us in a human language.

4) There are apparent discrepancies in the Bible! Let me suggest, that the apparent discrepancies are just that: apparent! First, we must be fair toward the Scriptures. The trustworthiness of the Bible has to be judged on the basis of the authors' intentions. It also must be viewed in the context of the truth standards of its own time and culture. We should not impose 21st century standards of literary precision on biblical statements anymore than we would on any other ancient literature. Secondly, archaeology has done us a great service in recent years to clarify difficult texts or mysterious claims in the Bible. Walter Kaiser, Professor of Old Testament and Chairman of the Archaeological Study Bible published in 2005, wrote: *"No previous generation has witnessed so high a degree of collaboration of Biblical events, persons and his-*

torical settings as we have during the past century of ongoing, successful archaeological exploration. The quantity, quality and relevancy of the artifacts and epigraphical materials impinging upon the story of the Bible from the ancient Near East have been so staggering that few have been able to incorporate them into one place, let alone link them side by side with relevant Scriptures." Then he goes on to explain, how the publishing of the Archaeological Study Bible is *"...a unique opportunity to see firsthand how archaeological discovery helps us to make sense of some of the heretofore difficult texts of Scripture... Cultural allusions and settings have in the past plainly eluded us – simply because the context belonged to another, completely 'foreign,' place and time...The Biblical narrative comprises the greatest story ever told, but that story is so much more than an impersonal, third-person, ancient account. Indeed, it is both about and for each of us."*[8]

In summary, if we come to a Bible text in which there appears to be a discrepancy or problem, we may presuppose this: Since the Bible originated with God as the written revelation of himself, it must be like its divine author: without error, totally reliable and completely sufficient to guide us through every question, issue, and ethical dilemma in life.

5) Truth is not to be found in a written proposition (Biblical sentences) but in the experience of a person (Jesus Christ). I believe the *modernist, neo-orthodox* and *postmodernist* distinction between proposition and person is a false one. God's way of revealing himself, in person and in proposition, are not two separate categories, but two forms of revelation married into one holy couple. The proposition reveals the person, the person reveals the proposition. In John 15:7, Jesus declares the union this way: "...you remain in me and my words remain in you." Person and proposition (*words*) go arm-in-arm. However, the concern that lies behind the *postmodern* apprehension toward 'propositional

---

[8] Walter Kaiser, INTRODUCTION TO THE ARCHAEOLOGICAL STUDY BIBLE, Grand Rapids: Zondervan, p. XI.

truth' deserves a careful hearing. Truth be told, many of us who have embraced the *organic view* of Scripture have sought to defend the integrity of propositions to the point of making the Bible text an end in itself. Preaching, teaching and analyzing the propositions is right, but if that is all we do, and if that is all we leave with the hearers of the Word, we have done precisely what the Bible does not allow us to do: we have forced a divorce between proposition and person.

Biblical propositions are there to explain to us Jesus, God's Saviour to mankind, crucified, resurrected, and reigning. If we cast our eyes so high that we see the person and ignore the proposition, we create for ourselves an indefinable Jesus.

If we cast our eyes so low that we only see the proposition and not the person, we end up with bone-dry statements that cannot quench the thirst of every soul nor satisfy the human heart with God's banquet. Every student of the Bible does well to follow the advice of a proponent of the *organic view* of Scripture, who was a great preacher in London, Charles Haddon Spurgeon: *"Don't you know, young man, that from every town and every village and every hamlet in England, wherever it may be, there is a road to London?...So from every text in Scripture there is a road towards the great metropolis, Christ. And my dear brother, your business is, when you get to a text, to say, now what is the road to Christ?...I have never found a text that had not got a road to Christ in it, and if ever I do find one...I will go over hedge and ditch but I would get at my Master, for the sermon cannot do any good unless there is a savour of Christ in it."*[9]

How do we read the Bible?

Remember the Westminster Shorter Catechism? In it the authors ask the question, "How we should read the Bible so that it is effective in our lives?" The answer these men wrote down is a word

---

[9] Quoted from Charles Haddon Spurgeon, "Christ Precious to Believers", New Park Street Pulpit, vol. 5, London: Passmore & Alabaster, 1860, p. 140.

of advice as good and practical in the 21st century as it was in the 17th. Here it is, one Catechism line at a time:

1) *Read the Bible with diligence*: Put some energy into it if you want to get something out of it. Have a reading plan and stick to it as much as you can. Read the Bible regularly. Just like a marriage relationship works well when husband and wife communicate with each other every day, God wants to talk to us daily. Set a regular appointment time with Him, when you open your Bible and read. Read a paragraph or a chapter in one sitting, maybe a section in an Old Testament book, and then one in a New Testament book. There are Bible reading plans that will guide you through the Bible in one year. But if you have very little or no experience in reading the Bible, start small, with bite-size helpings daily. Over a long period of time, work your way up to the discipline of reading through the Bible every year. It will change your life.

2) *Read the Bible with preparation and prayer*: When you open the Bible, remind yourself that you are entering into a conversation with Jesus. Take a moment to pray, asking Jesus to speak to you that which you need to hear. Ask the Holy Spirit to guide the Word to your heart and illuminate your mind to understand what God is saying. Sometimes, for example, I pray Psalm 139:23,24 before I start to read the Bible: *"Search me, O God, and know my heart, try me, and see if there is any hurtful way in me, and lead me in the way everlasting."*

Another way to prepare yourself for reading the Bible is to recognize what kind of literature you are about to read. The Bible is really not one book, but a library of 66 books. Not all the books are written in the same genre. To say we interpret the Bible literally is simply too simple to be accurate. We need to read the Bible naturally, meaning that we read each passage within the rules of the genre in which it was written. Some passages, like the Psalms, are written as Hebrew poetry. There are rules for how to read and understand Hebrew poetry. There are books in the Bible that are written as historical accounts, such as Chronicles, Kings, Samuel, the four Gospels, and Acts. We may read these like a newspaper, taking the written to mean exactly what it says. There are some portions of Scripture which are apocalyptic. This is a special genre, which we most certainly do not read like a newspaper account. The apocalyptic genre was used when the author wanted to describe a cataclysmic in-breaking of God into the affairs of man. The last book of the New Testament, Revelation, is like that, but parts of Isaiah, Daniel and Ezekiel in the Old Testament are too. Usually the plot is pictured in the large strokes of a paint brush, the detailed specks of paint having no meaning except to add colour and background to the main message. To interpret the small specks as major events or personages that will rise up on the canvas of end time history may sell a lot of books, create scary movies, and bring drama-hungry people to a fever-pitch, but it does violence to the biblical text.

   3) *Receive what you read with faith and love:* We need to be able to trust God when we read His Word, because sometimes God relates truths to us that are hard to swallow. He might challenge your world view. In fact, you can be sure that he *will* challenge your world view, because we are products of our society as well as of all that has happened before our time. But God is not the product of anything and he lives in eternity with a timeless perspective. This means that our views of right and wrong, gender and sexuality, love and hate, forgiveness and anger, priorities and preferences, leadership and submission, are all warped by our upbringing, surroundings and culture. Through the Bible, God comes to us out of the eternal into the temporary, out of the transcendent into our finite spaces, in order to give us the straight line on something that without His Word will remain crooked. That is why C.S. Lewis used to say that God does not turn your world upside-down as much as he turns your upside-down world right-side-up.

When we notice that His Word says something different than we or the society around us has been thinking, we can do one of two things: we can either seek to twist the Word to our liking, so that we do not need to change or look like an oddball to the rest of the world, or we can recognize that something in us must have gotten twisted and needs straightening. Receiving the Word of God in faith means responding to God humbly and acknowledging, "God, I must not have seen the full picture, because my way of thinking has been different than what you are saying in this passage. Help me to see the bigger, better, more beautiful picture that must be in your mind, but is not yet in mine." When we react in this way to truth in the Bible, we are not only receiving it in faith, we are expressing our love to God.

4) *Lay the Bible up in your heart:* Psalm 119:11 says, *"Your Word have I hidden in my heart, that I may not sin against you."*[(NKJ)] Internalize Scripture. Let it seep down into your heart. When the Holy Spirit cuts or comforts you with a verse, stop! Meditate on that verse. In fact, thank God for having spoken to you in that moment. Maybe you want to write the verse on a card. You may even want to take that card with you into the rest of the day, reading it over from time to time and asking God to impress its truth into the depths of your soul, and to form your character through it. Take the Colossians-challenge to heart: *"Let the Word of Christ dwell in you richly!"* (Colossians 3:16) That is why in this book's toolboxes, I suggest passages you can practice meditation on and verses you can learn by heart.

5) *Practice it in your life:* God has given us the Bible not so that we merely know it in our head and are shaped by it in our character, but so that we follow it in our daily actions and reactions. Like a wise builder of a house, you do not simply take the blueprint from the architect, get thrilled about it and memorize it. You actually build your house according to it. The Bible is God's Word, given with the purpose that it may shape our way of thinking, our attitudes, our actions and the way we respond to people and situations. *"But prove yourselves doers of the word, and not merely hearers who delude themselves,"* says James 1:22 [(NAS)].

■ **What's in it for me?**

1. Jesus speaks to you

The Bible is the written Word of God. When we read it—no matter which verses between Genesis 1:1 and Revelation 22:21—Jesus speaks to us. The good news is, the Bible is not a textbook for ivory tower thinkers but a love letter from God to us. For that reason, Bonhoeffer tells his sceptical brother-in-law in the balance of the aforementioned letter, that reading the Bible critically will not reveal to us the heart of God in it... *"just as we do not grasp the words of someone we love by taking them to bits, but by simply receiving them, so that for days they go on lingering in our minds, simply because they are the words of a person we love; and just as these words reveal more and more of the person who said them as we go on, like Mary, "pondering them in our heart," so it will be with the words of the Bible, as though in them this God were speaking to us who loves us and does not will to leave us alone with our questions, only so shall we learn to rejoice in the Bible."*[10]

Bonhoeffer speaks here of an approach to Bible reading that echoes the advice of the 18th century English theologian and pastor, Horatius Bonar: *"The study of truth in its dogmatical more than in its devotional form has robbed it (the Bible) of its freshness and power."*[11]

We need to be clear about this point: Doctrine is essential for the Christian life. Never should we disclaim its importance with foolish statements like, "I don't need doctrine, just give me the Bible" or, "Who needs theology, just give me Jesus!" While well-intended, these are nonetheless ignorant statements. Doctrine is like the bone structure of a body. Without it, there is no backbone behind the movement, no stride in the step, no direction in the motion. Doctrine is the content, the truth, of the Bible. Every Christian needs to know biblical doctrine or he is like a butterfly without wings.

The goal of reading the Bible is not that we might know doctrinal systems. The goal is to know Jesus, to hear Jesus, to follow after

---

[10] Metaxas, pp. 136-137.
[11] Horatius Bonar, WORDS TO WINNERS OF SOULS, Phillipsburg, NJ: P&R Publishing,1995, p. 31-32.

Jesus in obedience, and to become more and more like Jesus. Just like Jesus told his disciples that the entire Old Testament was about him (Luke 24:27, 44), our reading of the Bible is to lead us into a deeper devotion to and greater love for Christ.

Bonhoeffer concludes the letter to his brother-in-law accordingly: *"And I would like to tell you now quite personally: since I have learnt to read the Bible in this way—and this has not been for so very long—it becomes every day more wonderful to me. I read it in the morning and the evening, often during the day as well, and every day I consider a text which I have chosen for the whole week, and try to think deeply into it, so as really to hear what it is saying. I know that without this I could not live properly any longer."*[12]

Martha was a good woman. And when Jesus came to her house, she did what many good women like to do: show good hospitality and put on a great meal. I honestly do not know what was in Martha's heart while she was scurrying about the kitchen and getting more and more frustrated with Mary. Maybe Martha was like some people I have experienced, who want to prove their goodness to themselves in how much the guests enjoy their cooking. Maybe Martha was upset because she wanted to put on the finest meal possible, and a little help from Mary in the kitchen would have brought the quality of the food and hospitality to perfection.

I don't know.

Maybe what was bothering Martha was that she would have welcomed some appreciation. One friend of mine, whenever I would ask him what his greatest longing in life was, would say that he would just like to be appreciated for what he was doing at work. I think many people would echo that remark. Maybe Martha in the kitchen would have appreciated some recognition from the living room. An affirming comment from Jesus, "Whatever it is you are cooking in there, Martha, it sure smells good," or an encouraging word from Mary: "I am so glad you are doing the cooking today, sis, because if I were doing it, Jesus would end up getting burnt offerings."

I don't know.

---

[12] Ibid.

Whatever it was that was bothering Martha, her feeling of frustration reached a boiling point and she burst into the living room where Mary was sitting quietly at Jesus' feet, taking in each of Jesus' words. "Uh, excuse me, how about some help in the kitchen," she demanded. But Jesus had a different view of what was important in that moment. He responded to Martha something like this, "Your sense of what is important right now is oriented around what makes you look good, and you want to look like a good hostess. Stop! Get off the 'let-me-serve-Jesus-the-way-it-makes-me-look-good-merry-go-round', sit down beside Mary, get quiet like Mary, and open your ears like Mary. Mary has chosen what is really good in this moment, namely, listening to me, because I have something very special to tell both of you." I know he didn't say it like that (they did not have merry-go-rounds back then), but I think this captures the meaning of his words.

I do know that I would not have been happy with Jesus' exhortation to me, had I been Martha, who was trying so hard to make everything just right for the prized guest. But...

Christian spirituality teaches us the importance of having those moments, in which we drop everything we are doing 'in the kitchen' and sit down at Jesus' feet, in order to listen to what he has to say. The 1560 Scots Confession echoes this biblical principle in a lovely manner, when it says in chapter 19, *"In listening to the instruction of Scripture, the Church hears the voice of her own Spouse and Pastor."*[13] That is the first thing that happens when we read the Bible: we come out of the busy kitchen, sit at Jesus' feet and listen to him speak to us: the Living Word of God through the written Word of God.

2. The Holy Spirit illuminates our minds, applies the words, and changes our hearts

Hebrews 4:12 says, *"The word of God is living and active. Sharper than any double-edged sword, it penetrates even to dividing soul and spirit, joints and marrow; it judges the thoughts and attitudes of the heart."* The fact is, you cannot divide soul and spirit. The latter is part and parcel of the former, and both are invisible and indivisible. Hebrews 4:12 is making a point by exaggeration: God's Word

---

[13] http://www.creeds.net/reformed/Scots/scots.htm.

can pierce the deepest part of our inner being, including those parts we want to hide, protect or pretend we don't have. Nothing is safe from God's sword.

And the living Word wields this weapon. Fearsome is the picture painted in Revelation 1:16, where the resurrected and ascended Jesus is described as one whose face shines like the sun, with a double-edged sword extending from his mouth. When Jesus speaks to us through the Bible, the words sometimes soothe and comfort, but many times they hurt. If we read the Bible the way we should—with hearts open to hear what the Spirit of God wishes to say to us—it can convict us of sin. It can point to cancer cells of faithlessness in the world of our private thinking and fantasies. It can cut into the wounds of long-held bitterness in our memories. It can pierce through the lack of self-control in the use of our tongue. The 17th century Anglican preacher in London, Richard Sibbes, once told his congregation at Grey's Inn, *"The Bible is the chariot upon which the Holy Spirit rides to the heart."*[14] When the Sacred Knight of God, the Holy Spirit, arrives at our heart and thrusts his sword, we might feel the pain of conviction, of humbling, of having been found out. It can also be the beginning of transformation, of becoming spiritually healthy and whole.

3. God gives you direction in life

While the Bible calls God *"light, and in him is no darkness"* (1 John 1:5 *NAS*), and says that Jesus is *"the light that shines into the darkness"* (John 1:5), the Bible, too, is called *"a light unto my path"* (Psalm 119:105). The Bible is the written light which the living light holds out in front of you to show you the way forward.

In May 2009, the German media reported of a young man who had gone missing. He was in Spain at the time, on holiday with several friends. The first evening out, he and his friends had gone to a night club and danced for a few hours. At 3 a.m. the young German decided to go back to the hotel and get some sleep. He told his friends "good-bye," and left the night club. He never made it to the hotel.

---

[14] Alexander Grosart, ed., WORKS OF RICHARD SIBBES, Carlisle, PA: Banner of Truth, 1983, Vol. 3, p. 455.

Four days later, a worker at the hotel made a sad discovery in some bushes behind the hotel: the young man's battered and lifeless body. What had happened was on his way back to the hotel, he had turned left one street sooner than he should have. Instead of ending up on the street in front of the hotel, the man had turned down a street that led in the direction of the back of the hotel building. That street dead-ended in a meadow. There were no lights. It was so dark in the grassy area that it was impossible for the young man to see his own feet. What he also could not see, as he kept going forward in the black darkness, was that the meadow came to an abrupt end with a 25 meter drop. The poor man never saw that his next step—his last step—led to death.

There are many roads we walk on in life. Every decision we make in life leads us another step forward. We decide—consciously or unconsciously—and hope for a good outcome, for success and happiness at the end of our path. Nobody knows ahead of time if his path will lead to the peace or the joy he hoped for. But God knows, and He knows where we will find peace and joy. His Word is a lamp unto our feet and a light unto our path (Psalm 119:105). When we order our steps according to the principles of Scripture, we may not take the easy way or a short cut, but we take the safe road to the entrance of that for which our souls long.

4. The Bible gives you a desire for more of the Bible

A normal Christian is a Bible-loving Christian, someone who cannot get enough of it. Psalm 119 trumpets this fact over and over again: *"Oh, how I love your law! I meditate on it all day long"* (v. 97)…*"How sweet are your words to my taste, sweeter than honey to my mouth"* (v. 103)…*"Your statutes are my heritage forever; they are the joy of my heart"* (v. 111)…*"I love your commands more than gold (insert: paycheque plus a huge Christmas bonus), more than pure gold"* (v. 127).

That is Steve's story. He had started coming to our discovery group in Toronto, quite frankly more interested in the good food than in God. But on a full and content stomach the first evening there, he became intrigued by the content of the group discussion. Subsequently, he made it his weekly routine to join the experience.

One evening after many months of attending, Steve was sitting in a group in which the topic was the nature of the Bible. Several people, especially a young Buddhist man, were attacking the reliability of the Bible. This was perfectly acceptable, because the agreement in discovery groups is that anybody may say or believe whatever they want, so long as they respect the viewpoints of all others. But on this evening, Steve found himself getting frustrated with those who opposed the view that the Bible is of divine origin and, therefore, perfectly reliable. He found himself vigorously defending the integrity of the Scriptures. He felt his insides twisted in knots, as he vehemently disagreed with the young Buddhist.

When the group gathering was over, and after everyone had left, Steve was alone and started to think about his reaction. He was a bit surprised with himself. What was going on that he had reacted so heatedly toward a view he himself had held a few weeks earlier? Then it started to dawn on him: he had fallen in love with Jesus and with the Bible. As I was locking up the building, I found big, bulky Steve sitting on the steps, crying like a baby. I sat down beside him and asked what the trouble was. He could barely get the words out. Between sobs of joy, he stammered something about Jesus having come into his life that evening. After he composed himself a bit, he told me about the 'battle for the Bible' that had raged that evening, and how it had awakened Steve to a change of heart that had quietly occurred in him over the months. The following Sunday Steve was baptized in our church community. That was 13 years ago.

After I had moved to Germany, I was back in Toronto in 2009 for a visit. There was Steve. Thinner, from a serious illness, his heart was still the same: he has never stopped loving the Bible. Like a child on Christmas morning, receiving the toy he wished for so badly, and jumping up and down with delight, Steve expresses a Christmas-like thrill for the Bible. He reads it every day. He takes it with him wherever he goes. In fact, he explained to me, he has one Bible at home, from which he reads daily before he goes to work, another Bible in his van, a third copy at his desk at work, and a fourth copy – a pocketsize version – on his dresser by his wallet, so that he never forgets to carry it with him wherever he goes. He can never be found anywhere without the Bible.

People throw accusations at Steve. Some religious people have scolded him, "You should love Jesus, not a book, man; you have practically turned the Bible into an idol," while some more reserved 'Christians' have admonished him, "It is Bible-fanatics like you that make the rest of us get a bad name in the media." Steve seems undaunted by such haranguing, and quietly responds with statements like, "I do love Jesus, and I love this Book because God gave it to me so I can know Jesus." Or he says, "I can't help it. If those journalists could experience the Bible the way I have, if they could see how it fills me with joy, how it has made me a better employee, how I treat people much better, how I have internal strength in the hard times and when I get really sick, and all because of this Bible, they probably would say that being a Bible-fanatic makes more sense than being a Harry Potter freak!"

One of those people who have thrown accusations at Steve is Dave. Steve laughs now, when he tells the story about his friend, Dave. At first, Dave was angry at Steve for having become a 'Bible-man'. Steve remained unfazed. He told Dave, "Hey, I don't love the Bible because I am into religion; I love the Bible because I am in love with Jesus. You want to hear Jesus talking to you today, man, you have to read the Bible." That did not sit well with Dave.

Dave and Steve frequently drive together to their favourite fishing hole. Unfortunately for Dave, they always go there in Steve's van. Once in awhile, when Dave would climb into the van, Steve would reach for his "van-version", open it up and say, "Listen to this, man; this is so great!" and then he would read some verses out loud. Since they were friends, their discussions along the river bank would turn into conversations about challenges in life. Steve would often reach for the little Bible in his back pocket, turn to a passage of Scripture and say, "This verse really gave me some direction in that matter, man," and would then read the verse.

At first, Dave was terribly frustrated about his friend's obsession. But over time, Dave gained a respect for the helpful insights he heard from the Bible. Once Steve noticed Dave's newfound respect for the Bible, he gave Dave one of his four Bibles (and bought another one to replace it). Dave started to follow Steve's example. He started to read daily. Soon the two would be travelling in the van to their fishing hole together, and it would be Dave who would open his Bible and say, "Listen to this, man. I just read this the other day, and it is so great!" Sometimes he would ask Steve questions about passages Dave found hard to obey or understand, and the two would have long discussions. Finally, through reading the Bible, Dave came to embrace Jesus and was baptized in 2009.

Steve is an example to me of a normal Christian: someone who has gained such a thrill for God's Word that he loves it more than all the riches or reputation a person could ever wish for. He reminds me of those verses in Psalm 119, like, *"Oh, how I love your law! I meditate on it all day long," (v. 97)* or *"Your statutes are my heritage forever; they are the joy of my heart,"* (v. 111) or *"Your testimonies are my delight; they are my counsellors"* (v. 24).

Not only has his delight in and hunger for the Bible given Steve's soul an abundant life, but his love for God's Word has even given others, like Dave, a new start on life.

When you open the Bible, you are joining Mary at Jesus' feet. You and I can join them. We will hear his words and find rest for our souls and direction for our lives.

Even a blind man like Rocco can see that!

1. Look up several Bible passages and review what they say about the origin of the Bible and how it is to be interpreted: 1 Chronicles 28:12, 19; 1 Thessalonians 2:13; 2 Peter 1:19-21.

2. In 1 Peter 1:22-25 the disciple Peter speaks of the „living and abiding word of God" that was implanted like a seed into the hearts of the readers and caused them to be „born again." He then contrasts God's word with grass. Grass withers but "the word of the Lord remains forever" (a quote from the Old Testament). Then Peter says, "This is the word which was preached to you." On the basis of Peter's correlation of the word of God with the preached word, what conclusions might you draw about preaching, its legitimacy, necessity, and truthfulness?

3. In this chapter I briefly spoke about the importance of doctrine. The word means „teaching." The same goes for „theology." a word that essentially means „a word about God." Doctrine or theology is basic for gaining a proper understanding of Christian spirituality. The letters of Paul, 1 Timothy, 2 Timothy and Titus, are called Pastoral Letters, because of the practical and pastoral way they were written. Yet in them, Paul speaks repeatedly of the intricate relationship between what we know and teach and what we live and become, i.e., between doctrine and practice. Read through 1 Timothy 4 and write down any insights you glean on the effects that doctrine should have on your personal life and spirituality.

4. Memorize Psalm 119:9, 11, 105; 2 Timothy 3:16, 17.

5. Make a plan: What will be your strategy for reading the Bible regularly?

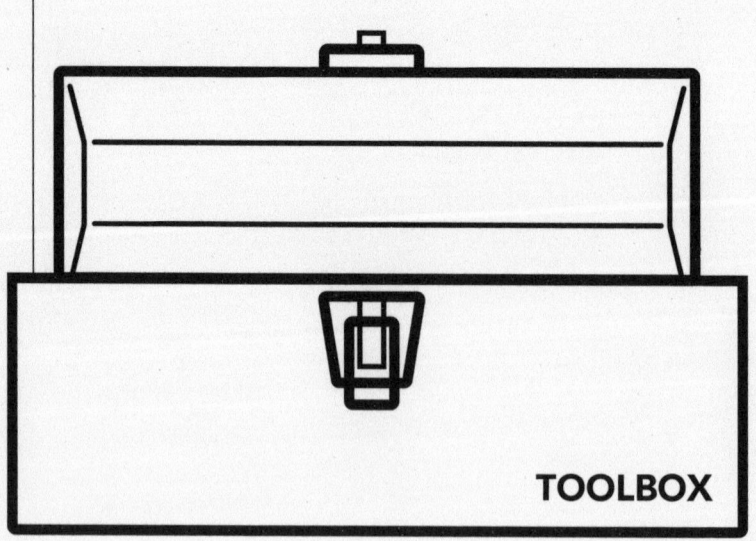

TOOLBOX

08
1st Wall

Connecting in 'No-Man's Land' with the Heart of God

Learning a spirituality of communion with God

Her name is Maria Elisa and his is Manuel, and Manuel was still in touch with Maria Elisa.

She had moved from Peru to Canada with her son several years earlier. She wanted a new life, away from the place in which she had experienced so much pain. Actually, there had been pain before Manuel, but now he had also turned into a pain, you might say. It was a little complicated. She longed to leave Peru and start all over, but had met her high school sweetheart Manuel after a disastrous marriage had left her traumatized. The old romance fanned into a new flame. He proposed marriage to her, but, because he had a career in the military, he was not allowed to leave the country. Under those conditions, Maria Elisa said, „No". Heartbroken she came to Toronto with her son but without Manuel.

E-Mails went back and forth between her and Manuel for a number of years. Then Manuel decided to retire from the military. He loved the military; it had been a good career. But he desperately wanted to spend the rest of his life with the woman he was deeply in love with.

They met on the Rainbow Bridge at Niagara Falls, between the USA and Canada. Neither had the visa to cross into the neighbouring country; Maria could not cross into the USA, Manuel could not enter Canada. So they met in "no-man's-land," a small area on the bridge between the borders that belongs to neither country, for the maximum-allowed four hours a day.

175

On the first day, Manuel got down on one knee and asked Maria Elisa to marry him. Neither one knew how it would work out; they just knew they wanted to have the deepest possible relationship to each other for the rest of their lives. This time she yelled, "Si", jumping into the arms of Manuel who had not yet gotten up off of one knee. He fell backwards on the hard cement, Maria on top of him, and they both laughed. Fortunately, no official investigation was started to uncover why two people were rolling around on the hard macadam of the Rainbow Bridge in 'no-man's-land'.

After four hours, they went back to their respective hotels to dream of the next day when they could see each other again. They did this for 5 days. They would hurry out of their hotels, cross into no-man's-land, run into each others' arms. They would talk and share their longings, aspirations, sorrows and regrets. Shortly thereafter, Maria Elisa received permission to sponsor Manuel in Canada, where they married.

After Maria Elisa proudly introduced her husband to Susan and me during a visit to Toronto, I began to think of how much the spiritual discipline of prayer is like Maria Elisa and Manuel's hours of communication in "no-man's-land."

There are grand and long definitions for prayer. But I am a simple man who likes things simple, so I will simply say: Prayer is the love language used in the spiritual conversation between the spirit of man and the Spirit of God.

That means it can happen without a movement of the lips, because it is a conversation that takes place in the human spirit and in the spiritual realm. It also means, whether audible or inaudible, it happens like a normal conversation between two parties seeking to communicate with each other.

But more than that, prayer is the communication between two persons in love with each other. It is intimate talk between the bridegroom and the bride, between God and His wife (the Old Testament analogy), between Jesus and His church (the New Testament analogy).

It is you and the God who laid aside His glory and came for you, who proposed to you on the Rainbow Bridge, meeting with you for honest, heart-to-heart communication. That is prayer!

Prayer is essential for the spiritual life

Like fluids to the body, prayer is essential to the soul. The Bible teaches us about prayer, by introducing us to men and women who prayed much and effectively.

We can learn from Abraham, who exemplifies for us bold and intense 'bargaining prayer' to God. It was not manipulative—you cannot manipulate God—it was prayer for the awfully wicked city of Sodom, through which he stepped into the gap between the city and God, pleading with God to spare Sodom on account of a few righteous people who lived in that city, namely the family of his nephew, Lot (Genesis 18).

Moses is also a mediator through prayer. He stepped into the gap between God and God's own people, the Israelites (Exodus 32). God was about to give Israel over to its constant, insistent disobedience, and abandon the nation. Moses, out of love for the wayward yet chosen people, tells God bluntly that he is unwilling to move forward without God's presence and blessing. It is this extremely bold prayer of the 'meekest man on earth' (as he is called in Numbers 12:3) that turned God's favour back on God's people, and His presence remained with them.

We can learn from Daniel, another man of prayer. He managed his time well, disciplining himself to prayer three set times a day. Even the threat of his godless persecutors to end his life if he did not end his prayers to God, did not deter him from keeping up his practice. He, too, understood God's calling to step into the gap through prayer, and to pray for a wayward and errant church. Noteworthy is Daniel's prayer for God's forgiveness of Israel in Daniel 9, where over and over again, he identified with the sinning people in his prayer. He did not refer to "they", but spoke of "we". He had a collective outlook on the nation when he prayed.

Then there was Elijah. This sometimes eccentric individual exemplified for us 'persevering prayer' (1 Kings 18). It had not rained for 3 years. Elijah prayed repeatedly for showers to fall. He kept asking and asking and asking and asking God for rain. He kept sending his servant to the mountain top to check for rain clouds. Each time he was told that there were none—and for 3 years that is what he was told—he would go back to prayer and ask and ask and ask for rain...until finally God broke open the heavens and sent the long-needed rain.

There are many things that happen only after God's people pray persistently and perseveringly. That may be a mystery to us. Why would God not answer right away? Why does he make us build up calluses on our knees and get weary by constantly asking for the same thing? I do not know. For some reason God blesses persevering prayer. Somehow, it works on God's heart.

We learn about other kinds of prayer from David. He had a long and successful reign as king in Israel, but he also had a very hard life. This man of God had constant, sometimes extremely painful, opposition. He faced strong temptations, not always holding strong, either. He had large mood swings, sometimes flying to the heavens with his emotions, other times plummeting into deep despair. His is a normal life. That is why his prayers, contained in the Psalms, are so instructive to us. They include prayers of adoration to God (for example, Psalm 65), prayers of petition (Psalm 67), prayers asking for forgiveness when he sinned (Psalms 38, 51), prayers for God's righteousness and peace to triumph over evil and chaos (the so-called "imprecatory psalms", e.g. Psalm 68), and prayers in which he poured out his heart to God (The English Puritans called these kinds of prayers "holy complaints"; for example, Psalms 42 and 43).

All these Old Testament believers show us that faith without prayer is like a relationship without communication. It is simply impossible—at least if you want a relationship with depth!

It seems to me, however, that the one who showed us the vitality and necessity of prayer more than any of the aforementioned, was Jesus, the Son of God—God in the flesh—mediator between God and man. Yet he was a man of much prayer. In looking through the 4 gospel accounts of his life, we find:

- Jesus prayed for wisdom and guidance before significant decisions.
- Jesus prayed for strength to accomplish God's will, including obeying God's will when it cost Jesus everything, like going to the cross.
- Jesus prayed in worship to the Father.

- Jesus prayed with thankfulness for God's goodness.
- Jesus prayed out of sadness over his people's unwillingness to receive the Messiah.

For me personally, this became many years ago the driving motivation to seriously develop the discipline and enjoyment of prayer: If my great Master and sovereign Lord over all the universe found it necessary to pray daily, sometimes nightly, sometimes all night through, how much more do I—a fragile, feeble and fickle follower of Jesus—need to be in much prayer!

The apostle Paul, throughout his 13 letters in the New Testament, throws additional light on this mysterious aspect of Christian spirituality. He views prayer as essential to our personal growth, essential for being victorious in daily spiritual battles, essential to the salvation of others and the evangelization of the world (Ephesians 6:18,19).

At this point, some may ask, „If God has determined the end from the beginning—and He has (see Isaiah 46:10, 11)—why pray?" I love this question, because I love the answer. I learned years ago from the writings of some of our forefathers in the faith a lesson that revolutionized my prayer life: God has not only determined the end from the beginning, he has also determined the means to the end. The means he has determined, by which he would accomplish the determined end, is prayer – my prayers, your prayers, our friends' prayers, our children's prayers spoken in child-talk before climbing into bed, the prayers in our church services, the prayers spoken spontaneously in any given circumstance, the prayers all around the world. Each and every prayer has been foreordained by God to be the trumpet blast toward heaven that rouses him to action.

I know it does not answer all the mystery the sovereignty of God leaves us with. Not by far! But it does tell me that God seeks our prayers as the very instruments through which he wants to bring about what he has predestined. This means prayer is not only essential to your and my spiritual growth and vitality, it is also essential to God's doing of his will. He has honoured us by making our prayers the means through which he will accomplish things big and small.

I will tell you something about my own development in this matter. I picked up a book of sermons once by the 17ᵗʰ century English pastor, John Flavel. I had read a few pages, when the preacher moved into an analogy. He said that prayer is like a ship that is filled with much costly cargo and sails around the world, dispensing its goods into every harbour. Then he said we may not be able to personally go to all the cities of the world, not be able to physically run to every person we are concerned about, or be at every place where help is needed. But through prayer we can go everywhere and touch any person. Prayer is the way we can call God down into every place, every situation, and to every person. Whenever we pray, it is as if we are steering the ship of God's costly cargo to some place or some person where God's Spirit unloads the goods.

It was this realization of the power of prayer that became for me what a fuselage is to a rocket.

But how should I pray?

1. Let your prayer life take two forms

First, have *organized prayer* every day. That means, set a time in the day when you are alone with God, and tell him how much you adore him, confess your sins to him and receive his cleansing, thank him for his goodness toward you, and talk to him about the things that burden your heart, decisions you have to make, and people for whom you care. I am one of those people who finds early morning with a cup of coffee in my 'prayer chair' (my rainbow bridge?) the best time to meet with God in concentrated prayer. It is not the easiest time, because I am not a 'morning person'. But it is, for me, the best time. That quiet time with God before the noise, the pace and the demands of life start in on me—that is how I can move into my day with calmness, peace, and perspective.

Other people find other times of day more conducive to a quiet conversation with God, maybe lunch time alone, or late afternoons after work, or at night before going to sleep. What's important is that you 'make a date' to regularly talk with God, and then you work at letting nothing interfere with or squeeze out your appointment with him. Nothing, not even your phone! It is the most important conversation of the day.

Second, fill your day with *spontaneous prayer.* Perhaps this is what 1 Thessalonians 5:17 means when it says, *"Pray without ceasing!"* [(NAS)] Always be ready to pray. Pray on the go. Learn to respond to every situation with prayer.

A woman, whom I never saw before and have never seen since, taught me this way of life. I was walking out of a bookstore years ago. A young woman with 3 little children was leaving the store ahead of me. Just as we reached the sidewalk, an ambulance rushed by us with the deafening sound of its siren. The woman quickly called to her children, "Kids, let's take hands and pray. Somebody is in big trouble and needs us to pray for them." I stopped and watched the scene unfold in front of me. As if the children had practiced this before, all took one another's hands, stood still on the sidewalk, closed their eyes, as their mother began to pray, "Dear Lord, please come to the person in that ambulance, protect and comfort that one, and please heal him. Most of all, let the person experience your power, comfort and presence in these unsettling moments. Please protect the ambulance driver and give the doctors wisdom in treating this patient. We ask this in the name of Jesus our Healer, Amen." With that, the four continued walking. God had just taught me through an unknown mother how to be alert in prayer, how to spontaneously call God into situations and unload the cargo from his ship on my surroundings.

Pray spontaneously throughout the day! Pray for the person on the bus or subway who looks to be sad or in pain. Pray for the people coming toward you on the sidewalk. Pray for the individuals involved in the accident you are passing on the highway. Pray for the people who are experiencing the tragedy you are reading about in the newspaper or hearing about on the news. Pray in your car (with your eyes open, please), pray at work (while doing your work, of course), pray with the person on the phone, pray at the football game for the drunk people cheering beside you (and Stephan?). Pray without ceasing!

2. Just say it like you feel it

No matter if you have had a personal relationship to God for two days or twenty years, prayer is and remains the language of the human spirit. Whether you are a baby in Christ, a wild, sometimes unruly adolescent in Christ, or a seasoned, wise warrior for Jesus, God does not look for scholarly or high and lofty language. Just simple, authentic expressions of the heart will do.

Sometimes someone in a group will turn to me and say, "Why don't you lead us in prayer—you're the professional!" If you do that to me, I will respond, "There are no professionals, only priests. And in Jesus we are all priests. So in your own language, wouldn't you like to have the honour and lead us in prayer?"

When you pray to God, say it like you feel it. If you feel like screaming, scream. If you feel the need to dance, dance. If you want to fall flat on the floor, don't fall too hard. This is what I love about inaudible prayer: I can do all those things in my spirit, without anybody accusing me of "losing control" or being disturbed by the noise. There are prayer settings, however, in which loud and emotional prayer is expected and practiced. Us quieter, more reserved Christians need to respect such flights of the soul. God created our emotions; they are the way we communicate what lies beneath. To numb or disallow our emotions from giving expression of pain or praise is to call 'bad' what God has created 'good'.

3. Pray boldly

God is glorified when we come to him expecting great things from him. Wouldn't you feel honoured if three people showed up in your office and said, "Look, we have this situation, and we don't know how to solve it, and we have looked the world over, and we think you are the only one who can get this thing done"? God is honoured when we show up in his office and tell him, "We know you can do this!" Jonathan Edwards said, "That which God abundantly makes the subject of his promises, God's people should abundantly make the subject of their prayers."[1] Robert Murray McCheyne, in writing on this topic, said, "Every 'I will' on God's lips should become a 'Wilt Thou' on our lips, for promises should

---

[1] Eric Alexander, „Plea for Revival," Message at the Philadelphia Conference on Reformed Theology, Philadelphia, PA, 1982, p. 6.

provoke prayers."[2] In other words, we may boldly bring back to God what He has promised us, with the expectation that he will deliver on His promise.

4. Pray kingdom-centred prayers

Jesus taught us to pray to God the Father, *"Your kingdom come!"* Let God's reign over this world and every part of it be the centre out of which all your requests come in concentric circles:

- 1st concentric circle—Pray for yourself. Lay everything about yourself before God. Don't ask Him to make your life easy for you; rather, ask Him to reveal and bring honour to Himself in every situation you find yourself (i.e. *"your kingdom come"*).

- 2nd concentric circle—Pray for your family. I learned years ago not to pray, "Lord, keep my children from pain and suffering," when I realized that suffering is a normal part of how we encounter God. Instead, I started praying, "Lord, when my children go through pain and suffering, please hold your hand over them, that in their suffering they remain faithful to you and through their suffering bear fruit for you."

- 3rd concentric circle—Pray for your church, its leaders, its challenges.

- 4th concentric circle—Pray for your friends, for people who need God.

- 5th concentric circle—Pray for your town, its mayor, its issues, your neighbours.

- 6th concentric circle—Pray for the cities, for their renewal.

- 7th concentric circle—Pray for your country.

- 8th concentric circle—Pray for the world, for specific countries in the world.

As you pray in ever-widening circles, keep Jesus' kingship over the hearts of people as that which determines the content of your prayer. You could actually pray for yourself for hours that way, without being selfish, because you are actually praying that God's

---

[2] Ibid., p. 5.

kingdom come to you. There is nothing selfish about that, and everything honouring to God.

Four complicated situations in which prayer can take you into a deeper walk with God

1. Listen to God's response to and involvement in your prayer

Sometimes God speaks to us during our time in prayer. That is one reason why an organized time of prayer is important: we remain still long enough for God to whisper in our hearts. This is a very personal and subjective aspect of prayer. We must learn to deal with it cautiously and wisely. It can come in the form of a new idea in your mind, or a sudden burden you feel. Sometimes it is a desire that was kindled inside of you during a previous time of prayer, which now suddenly becomes a flame that burns with deeper conviction and passion.

It's not always easy! In fact, the question quickly asked at this point is: How can you know if it is God and not your own thoughts speaking to you? Here are a few tips that have come down to us from wise, experienced and prayerful Christians over the ages:

- Test the thought: Do the morality and integrity of the thought fit within the boundaries of Scripture? Is it a thought that glorifies God and exalts Jesus?

- Test it with time: Does the idea or burden go away after awhile, or does it return and, in fact, grow?

- Remain flexible in implementing the idea: I have found that I can get the idea from God right, but get the details wrong (such as timing or place).

- Never tell others that they must carry out your idea simply because God gave it to you. This robs people of the opportunity of being used of God to confirm or negate your idea. Confirmation from others is an important part of knowing if the idea is of God or not. Therefore, do not say to a group, "The Lord has told me that we should…" You may not mean it as manipulation, but it essentially functions that way. If God wants the others to join in 'your' idea, then he will lay it on their hearts as well. You might say to the group something like, "In my times of prayer, I have repeatedly felt a conviction regarding…Maybe this is what God would have others in our group do. What do you think? Has he given anyone else this conviction? Would you be willing to start asking God if he would like our whole group to do this?"

In fact, if God has given you a message that applies to someone in your church community, take the matter to the elders first, and let them test it through their own prayer and wisdom, before a matter God has laid on your heart becomes a matter that is laid on others.

2. When you are in situations in which you feel helpless, pray

Susan and I got married the summer of 1976. We worked part-time, went to university full-time and lived in an apartment building that had been condemned by the city. Rent was only $119 a month. I am sure the owner needed at least $40 of that to feed the rats in the basement.

Once, on the last day of the month, Susan and I sat at the supper table and she informed me that we only had $59 for the rent which was due the next day. We decided to take the matter to God through prayer. It was a brief conversation we had with the Father. Something like, "we are trying our best to earn as much as we can without forsaking our studies…we only have $59…we do not believe it is good to be late paying our rent…could you please provide us with another $60 by tomorrow morning? Amen!"

An hour later there was a knock at our door. When I opened it, there stood friends of ours, another couple with the same names as ours. Stephen said, "Hey Stephen, Susan and I were praying for you an hour ago, and as we were praying, we suddenly felt a real burden for you and Susan, like you might have a financial need or something. So we gathered up what we had and put it in here for you." He handed me an envelope, then turned and left, as I called after them to thank them. I closed the door, went to (my) Susan, and opened the envelope. There was $60 inside.

A few months later, we had the same challenge. Again, we were $60 short for our rent payment. Again we asked God to provide

for us like Jesus taught us to pray, *"Give us this day our daily bread."*
Again we waited for a knock at the door. But nothing like that
happened this time. We went to bed discouraged, and asked God
again to take care of us. The next morning on my way to class I
stopped by my mail box. I turned the combination to the lock,
swung the little door open and pulled out several envelopes. One
simply had the word "Becks" on it. I opened it and unfolded a
piece of paper on which a guy who did not like me had written,
"God wants me to give this to you, as you might need it." In the
envelope were (This is no lie, seriously, I am not making this up)
5 tens, 1 five and 5 ones.

Later in life we had bigger needs and more challenging situations. But what we learned in our first year of marriage became
our pattern. We learned not to decide matters on the basis of what
was in the bank today but on the basis of what we believed God's
will for us was.

People often respond at this point: but we are to make responsible decisions and not be presumptuous toward God. This response is correct. Christian spirituality includes making decisions
on the basis of facts. Fact is, we are to work hard, earn money
and be responsible with what we earn. The fact is also that we can
suddenly find ourselves in a place of need. My point is that it is
good once in awhile to be in a situation in which the personal need
is greater than your ability to cover it. You learn to pray, to trust,
to let the God of providence be your Provider, instead of placing
your trust in your skill, the strong company, healthy economy, job
security and people to never let you down. Christian spirituality
is not a lifestyle for control-freaks. It is an adventure of walking
humbly and trustingly with a God who is generous, dependable
and full of surprises.

3. Ask all your hard questions in prayer, even if you get no answers

I have already made reference to Athol Dickson's wonderful book, THE GOSPEL ACCORDING TO MOSES: WHAT MY JEWISH
FRIENDS TAUGHT ME ABOUT JESUS. In the opening chapter he
speaks of how he learned to ask God the hard questions. God delights in hearing our hard questions, because "asking is not doubt-

ing. It is trusting."[3] Sincere questions are a way of showing God respect. They basically communicate, "You are incomprehensible, so infinitely different from me, your ways are so high above my ways, and your thoughts so much deeper than I can ever grasp with my mind, that I simply do not understand you." That honours God.

Hard questions can sound like these:

"Why did you take my little boy? Why did you not take me instead? He had so much potential. I simply do not understand your harsh way with me, God!"

"Are you really the King seated on the throne? Why will you not protect your church in Iraq? Why do you allow these people who are willing to follow you to be murdered? In the Psalms you say that the righteous will not stumble or fall. Why are they falling like flies in Iraq?"

"Why have you only saved me into a relationship with you? My three teenagers make fun of me. My husband does not want me involved in my church for more than Sunday morning worship. But I want to give you so much more. In the Bible I see that you are a covenant God who brings salvation to the family? Why not *my* family?"

"It seems so senseless, God! She was the most encouraging person in our church community. Nobody could uplift people like she did. Nobody brought as many non-Christians to our church as she did, nor lead as many people to Jesus as she has. Of all the people to be cut down early in life, why did you ravage her body with cancer and take her from us so quickly? It makes no sense!"

"We did everything right, Lord! Not that we were without sin, not that we did not make mistakes. But God, we loved every one of our kids the same, and we loved them deeply. Each one was loved gently, with healthy hugs and kisses. We were clear about Christian integrity. We talked openly as a family about everything. Each one of the kids saw how deeply Harry and I love each other. How could our sweet little girl grow up, hate us and become a prostitute?"

These are some of the hard questions I have heard people ask God.

---

[3] Dickson, p. 19.

Usually the answer from God—at the time the question is asked—is silence. Loud, screaming silence. And the silence hurts!

Dickson writes, *"One reason I might feel God has not answered is because I rudely demand an answer, and another is my own inability to understand. (But) here is a third explanation for divine silence: I am probably unable to safely handle some of the answers out there."*[4]

When God's answer to your question is silence, it is important that you keep asking the question over and over. Sometimes silence *is* God's answer. Sometimes he is honoured by your repeatedly bringing the confusing and humbling matter before him. Sometimes he means for you to ask for a long time until peace has entered your heart, and you feel that you do not need to understand; you can trust him.

Imagine, a little 5 year old boy asks his daddy, who works for NASA, how a rocket can fly. He simply says to the child, "Someday you will understand." And it is true! Someday he will understand, but right now the boy cannot understand the intricacies of the highly complex answer the father gives when he lectures aeronautics in university. The father is honoured by his child's question, anyway. He gives him bits of the answer, but in child language, mind you. Since he does not have the full answer, the child keeps asking. It is a way for the two to communicate. It spells father-son communication, while at the same time honouring the difference between father and son. And someday, when the little boy has grown up maybe he will understand, too.

4. Be prepared for seasons during which you cannot pray

Every follower of Jesus has times when he cannot pray. These are hard times in which it feels like the prayer is stuck in your throat or is bouncing off the ceiling. Or days in which your mind and heart go blank as soon as you decide to pray. When this happens, it is easy to feel guilty. You might feel that you have a spiritual problem in your life, maybe unconfessed sin, maybe you are under attack from the devil, maybe God has removed himself from you out of disappointment or anger.

---

[4] Ibid., p. 25.

Before you fault yourself or give too much credit to the devil or doubt that God holds true to His promise to never leave you nor forsake you, recognize that seasons of prayerlessness happen in the Christian life. God even said they would. In Romans 8:26, 27 he expressly said, *"In the same way, the Spirit helps us in our weakness. We do not know what we ought to pray for, but the Spirit himself intercedes for us with groans that words cannot express. And he who searches our hearts knows the mind of the Spirit, because the Spirit intercedes for the saints in accordance with God's will."*

God even gives these lonely times of prayerlessness in our Christian experience, so that we learn to yearn for him, to thirst after communication with him. This desire for God, for his nearness, for communication with him, honours God.

The English pastor, Richard Sibbes, who died in 1635, wrote in his famous The Bruised Reed and Smoking Flax, *"A Christian complains he cannot pray: 'O I am troubled with so many distracting thoughts, and never more than now.' But has he put into your heart a desire to pray? He will hear the desires of his own Spirit in you. 'We know not what to pray for as we ought' (nor do anything else as we ought), 'but the Spirit helps our infirmities, with inexpressible sighs and groans,' Romans 8:26, which are not hid from God...God can pick sense out of a confused prayer. These desires cry louder in his ears than your sins... Let us not be cruel to ourselves when Christ is thus gracious."*[5]

I had a phase when I could not pray for weeks. Under constant attack from fellow church leaders, I fell into deep depression. Daily, I sat in my white prayer-chair and tried to pray. No words or thoughts rose from my soul.

When something like that happens to you, do as I did: sit quietly, think about the things that trouble you and place your confidence in the Holy Spirit. He is doing something precious in those moments of prayerlessness: He is translating your confused thoughts and struggles of the soul into powerful expressions to God the Father. His descriptions of your sorrow and imploring for the Father's intervention, is better, more accurately and more passionately stated than you could muster in your strongest moments of prayerfulness. Besides, the Father has never turned away

---

[5] Ibid., p. 65

his own Holy Spirit, and he will certainly answer in time to his Spirit's pleading for you.

Of course, being lazy in prayer is a spiritual problem. Refusing to develop the discipline of regular prayer is a sign of a rebellious and self-righteous heart. But when a prayerful Christian moves into a time of 'blocked prayer,' it is either God's work in his life (for which he relies on the Holy Spirit) or a symptom of depression (for which he should see his doctor), or both. It is not a spiritual problem.

■ What's in it for me?

Francis Schaeffer challenged us in his classic TRUE SPIRITUALITY, *"If we woke up tomorrow morning and found that all that the Bible teaches concerning prayer and the Holy Spirit were removed…what difference would it make in practice from the way we are functioning today? The simple tragedy is that in much of the church of the Lord Jesus Christ—the evangelical church—there would be no difference whatsoever. We function as though the supernatural were not there."*[6]

None of us is an exception to the rule. Nobody has reached a point in their spiritual growth that he has attained all the strength needed for heated battles with the Enemy, and has achieved a degree of self-sufficiency with which he can feel safe about tomorrow. If Abraham, Moses, David, Elijah, Daniel and Paul could not live without prayer being an essential part of their day; if Jesus, Son of God and our Lord and Saviour, felt the need to take everything to the Father, then you and I cannot deceive ourselves into thinking we can make it without prayer, both organized and spontaneous.

Prayer is essential to life. It is the spark that ignites other vital aspects of Christian spirituality

- **Much prayer makes for great VISION**: What God wants to accomplish through you for the benefit of others and to God's glory.

- **Much prayer increases your WISDOM**: Wisdom is the ability to practically use the knowledge of truth you have. Through prayer God shows you how.

---

[6] Schaeffer, p. 363.

- **Much prayer increases your FAITH in God**: C.H. Spurgeon once said, that much prayer is a sign of great faith, while little prayer is a sign of little faith.[7]

- **Much prayer with your spouse will increase INTIMACY with your spouse**: Spiritual union through prayer makes for a deep uniting of souls.

Remember, Christian spirituality is about a romance with God. Just as Manuel went after Maria Elisa, God came for you, proposed to you, and wants to have you as his bride.

Now go meet him in 'no-man's-land'!

---

1. Memorize the Lord's Prayer (Matthew 6:9-13). It is the prayer Jesus taught his disciples. He did not necessarily give it as a prayer Christians are to repeatedly recite, but more as a model from which to shape the contents of our prayers. Still, it is good to memorize it, as some churches like to use it as a prayer that draws all Christians together.

- **Our Father in heaven:** While God is personally God of every individual, he is the Father of the collective community of disciples world-wide: "our Father".

- **Hallowed be your name:** "Hallowed" is an old word meaning "revered".

- **Your kingdom come:** "Kingdom" is not a reference to a place but to the "kingdominion" or "rule" of God over people. This phrase has a missional meaning, as we will see in chapter 12. This is a request for God to rule over every aspect of your personal life as well as expanding his rule over all the world.

- **Your will be done on earth as it is in heaven:** A declaration of ultimate discipleship. As these were the words of Jesus to the Father shortly before his crucifixion, they are the declaration of allegiance and obedience to Jesus even unto death.

- **Give us this day our daily bread:** The community of Jesus' disciples knows that for everything big and small in life, they are completely dependent on the Giver of every perfect gift (James 1:17). This request shows that it honours God when we ask him for things we need.

- **And forgive us our sins as we forgive those who sinned against us:** A vital element of worship is for the community of Jesus to ask God for forgiveness. Only those are forgiven of their sins whose hearts are so broken by their own sinfulness and God's incredible grace, that they are ready to forgive their wrong-doers.

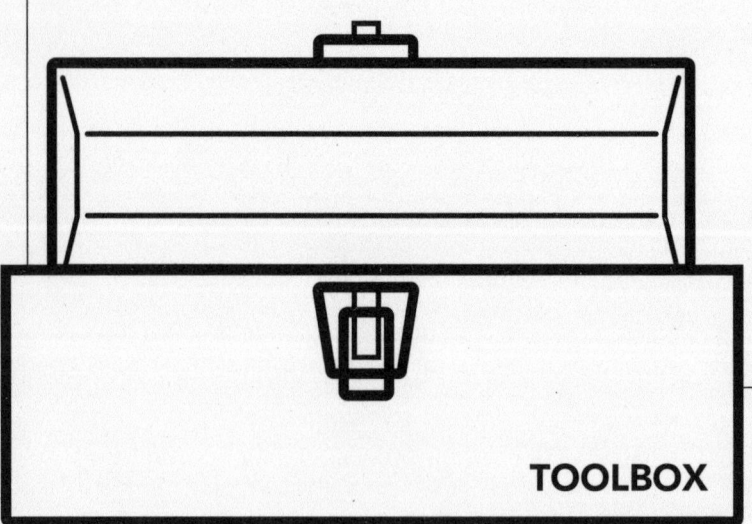

TOOLBOX

- **And lead us not into temptation but deliver us from evil:**
  "Temptation" here is not a reference to temptation to sin, but temptation
  to give up our faith. "Evil" can be a reference to the system of evil that
  prevails throughout the world, but could also be translated "evil one",
  meaning Satan, who through his army of demons and the many sly
  strategies he uses, attempts to destroy our faith in and faithfulness to
  God. This line is a prayer for perseverance in faith.

- **For yours is the kingdom, and the power, and the glory forever:** The
  Lord's Prayer ends where all our building of our spiritual house takes
  us: the glory of God (chapter 13). Everything about us is about God;
  everything about world history is about God's rule.

- **Amen!** This little word means "so be it!" It is a way of saying, "everything
  I have prayed in this prayer could have been prayed by Jesus, therefore,
  O God, I may expect great and gracious things from you."

**2. What are different kinds of prayer that you read and learned about in this
chapter?**

**3. Isaiah 62:6-7 is a call to take God at His word and to pray until we get
results:** *"You who remind the Lord, take no rest for yourselves; and give Him no
rest until He establishes and makes Jerusalem a praise in the earth."*
What are promises you know that God has made, the fulfilment of which you
long for? What are good and righteous things you would like God to do, for
which you would like to regularly and boldly begin to ask Him? Start a list, and
start to pray!

4. Memorize Philippians 4:6-7.

09
2nd Wall

Growing through Others into Maturity in God

Developing a spirituality of community

For Christmas 1999, friends gave Susan and me a gift certificate to one of the finer restaurants in Toronto. As we sat by candlelight with snowflakes falling outside, I felt anything but romantic or sentimental, because I was in depression. Those were dark days, where I could not pray, sleep or find the energy to do anything. I felt the raw harshness of life. And with that, I felt—for the first time in my adult years—a sober sense of what were the most important and essential things in life.

"Honey, I've been thinking," I started.

"That's dangerous," my wife quipped, as she looked at her food and wondered what half-brained idea I might spill onto the middle of our finely decorated table.

"No, seriously!" I countered. "I have been thinking that life is really like the Preacher said in Ecclesiastes: you know, this-that, this-that and 'this too is vanity' and blah-blah-blah and 'this too is vanity'. I've come to the conclusion that there are really only four things that are important to me; everything else is just a puff of air. Four things that I still want to have or enjoy or still be doing when I am 80 years old."

"And what are they?" my wife asked, half-afraid of finding out that she might not be one of the four things.

"First, when I am 80 years old, I want to still be romantically in love with you, sit as an old geezer in the subway (we are urban people), hold your hand even if you don't know anymore who is holding your hand, and know that it was good being married all these years to the girl who turned my head and set my heart spinning when I laid eyes on you the first day in college in 1973."

"I like that. Is the second one as good?"

"When I am 80 years old, I want to be preaching God's Word, even if it is in a shaky voice, even if the only listeners are church mice, even if nobody is converted to Jesus through my preaching. I want to still have the honour of unfolding those deep truths of God's Word and unload on the listeners (mice?) the richness of God's grace and truth."

"When I am 80 years old, I want to have a little house by a lake, to which I can regularly go and enjoy the quiet, away from all the noise of the city, the madness and rush of life, the stress of deadlines. Beside the lake I want to feel peace, tranquility and quietness. I want to be able to quietly talk to God, with the waves making their rhythmic splashing sounds to remind me that God is still in control. And I want to sit there and write books about God and life.

"That one I like! And where do you think we will get the money for a house by the lake?" my always practical, down-to-earth wife asked. When I did not answer, she smiled, patted my hand, and asked, "What is the fourth and final thing that is important to you, honey?"

"When I am 80 years old, I want to have had 3 or 4 really good friends. Friends who stuck with me over many years, with whom I can talk honestly and openly about anything, even the bad stuff in my life, without being judged. Friends with whom I can share vacations, friends who give me energy, have fun and laugh with me and who will weep with me when you die."

"How soon do you hope that last part will happen?" my wife asked.

"Sometime after I have had the opportunity to hold your hand on the subway when I am 80," I smiled.

That was over 11 years ago. A year after that dinner by candlelight I had—with the help of a doctor—climbed out of my deep depression. What has remained unchanged throughout all the years, however, is that I still am pursuing those 4 things essential to my short existence. In reflecting on them, you might notice, that all 4 points, in one way or another, have to do with relationships. The second and third essentials are about my relationship to God, whether resting in him, hearing him or explaining him, and points one and four have to do with my relationship to others.

Truth be told, everything, in the end, has to do with relationships. Relationships are everything. Yet precisely at this point, we are facing a tremendous crisis in our multi-everything age. Technology—which has so many marvellous benefits to it—has deeply curtailed our ability to be relational. Facebook is great, but face-to-face relationships are essential. Add to that, in Western society our fragmented homes, the undermining of the family, clueless parenting, high divorce rates and lovers drifting disillusioned in and out of relationships, have produced a generation that is at worst, relationally dysfunctional and at best at a loss how to have deep and lasting relationships. A German psychiatrist has concluded that while in 1970, 10% of the population was "societally challenged" (gesellschaftsunfähig), in 2010 it is 70%. He speaks of an implosion of the relational fabric of society taking place right now.

Yet precisely this point of relationship-building is an essential part of the Christian spirituality.

Relationships are essential for maturing in Christian spirituality, because others are essential for achieving your own individual wholeness.

The BASIS for lasting relationships

Earlier in this book, as we analyzed the love of God for us, I mentioned the word 'covenant.' This concept—it can also be translated 'testament'—is so basic to understanding Christian spirituality, that the entire Bible is divided into 'the Old Testament (covenant)' and 'the New Testament (covenant).' The word appears over 300 times in the pages of Scripture, and runs like a thread through the entire contents of the Bible. Why? The warp and woof of the Bible's content is how God has taken a universe in fragmentation, and relationships in alienation, and by 'covenant' is putting all things back together again.

Someone might sceptically say, "We don't do covenants today! We are modern or late-modern or postmodern. Covenants are premodern!"

That is not entirely true. Today we still sign contracts; we still say, "I promise"; we still expect the other person to honour an agreement. That is what a 'covenant' is. One catechism defines it as "an agreement between two or more persons." It is an agreement, but the force of that agreement is more like a 'commitment.'

With that we come to the basis of the problem we are facing today. We still do covenants or agreements, but we do them without commitment. Commitment has died. When I worked in retail in 1981, a young co-worker expressed to me his surprise that I had survived the first 5 years of marriage. "Commitment," I explained. His response was unforgettable to me, and marked our new way of defining the word: "Hey, I believe in commitment, too. I believe in being committed until I am no longer committed."

One of Germany's heroes on the national soccer team told the German public during the successful 2010 World Cup, that he promised to remain with his Stuttgart club for the next year, as he was still under contract. A few days later, one of the richest and most popular teams in Europe made the young German an offer of a few million to play on their star-studded team. Basking in the glory of newfound stardom, he apologized to disillusioned Stuttgart fans, "I know I made a promise, but I know you will understand, because it is an offer I cannot refuse."

Apply that to marriage, to work and to everything else involving relationships, and we have a disaster on our hands: a fast-growing mass of deeply wounded and relationally disoriented individuals, and—well, as the psychologist said—a society that is socially imploding.

The basis for healing, for restoring relationships, for staying connected when other things tear at the friendship, for making it through the dark nights of incompatibility, for being patient with someone who is being difficult, is in learning to live 'covenantally.' Commitment!

The solution is not in ourselves; it is in God. He is a covenanting God. He covenanted within himself to go after us when we had alienated ourselves from him. He stepped into the relational gap through Jesus. He approached us as rightful king over our hearts by his Holy Spirit. He soothes our woundedness. He heals us. He is the One from whom we learn how to treat one another 'covenantally'. From his example, as well as through his love in us, we are empowered to bring commitment that endures, heals and restores into our relationships.

You were created for relationships with others

God is a relationship. This is what I find so exciting in the biblical teaching and mystery: that God is one substance, yet three Persons in that one substance. The three Persons are in relationship to each other. They talk to and about each other, the Father speaking about his beloved Son during his baptism (Matthew 3), the Son addressing his Father in the high-priestly prayer of John 17, the Spirit groaning to the Father the burdens that are on our hearts (Romans 8:26). The three Persons work together: *"Let US make man in our image"* (Genesis 1:26). The Father creates the world (Genesis 1:1) by his Son (Colossians 1:16), and the Spirit moved upon the face of the world and gave it shape (Genesis 1:2). The Father sent the Son into the world (John 3:16), and the Son asked the Father to send the Holy Comforter to us (John 14:16). What the Father is already working at is what the Son joins him in working, and he is led by the Spirit to accomplish that work (e.g., Matthew 4:1). What revelation is in the Father is in the Son, and the Spirit makes it known to us (John 16:15).

You see then, the Trinity is a harmonious community of three Persons in deepest relationship to one another.

Here is why this theology is so essential to understanding our own make-up: When God created us, He made us in his image (Genesis 1:26). That means He created us to reflect God, to reflect God's character (holiness, love, justice, compassion, kindness, anger, etc.), and God's way of functioning. And the way God functions is socially. He is a relationship in himself, and he extended himself to make a relationship with each one of us. From this you know that being created in God's image means you are a social being. You were made for relationships.

That social aspect of your true self expresses itself on two levels:

1. Relationship on the vertical level:

That you are meant for a relationship with your Maker, Protector and Friend was emphasised in the first part of this book. Jesus, in his high priestly prayer, spoke of how deeply intimate this relationship is: *"Father, just as you are in me and I am in you, may they also be in us"* (John 17:21). This union with God is spoken of also as God's residing in us personally. Jesus stated that He will send us another Comforter, the Holy Spirit, and that this One would not only be with us—as Jesus was beside his disciples when he said this—but in us. Paul emphasises the intimacy of our relationship with God, when he speaks 3 times within 4 verses of the *"Spirit who lives in you"* (Romans 8:12, cf. 8:9,11). Yet in that same paragraph the apostle says, *"Christ is in you"* (v. 10). What deep intimacy! The Son, who is in the Father, and the Spirit who is in the Son and the Father, reside in you.

Christian spirituality, as earlier chapters have shown, is about growing in this intimacy with the triune God in us. How does that happen, so that our relationship with God leads to the gratification and fulfilment of our selves?

Years ago I officiated at the wedding of a young couple in our Toronto church, both of whom were heavily involved in serving the love of Jesus to people living on the street. For the wedding sermon, I chose a rather unusual Bible text, the last verse of Genesis 2: *"The man and his wife were both naked, and they felt no shame"* (Genesis 2:25). I could not know that Erinn and Dion had invited a whole host of children from one of Toronto's neediest neighbourhoods to attend their wedding. These kids all sat in the last row together, children of every colour. Picture the reaction of these already high-strung kids when I read the Bible text. Loud laughter bellowed from the last row of seats ("The priest said 'naked', man!"). Every time I quoted the verse—and it was fairly often, in order to make my point about nakedness and the lack of shame—a wave of laughter erupted from the rear of the sanctuary.

The point of my sermon was that when a person can stand over against his opposite and bare it all—that means, show everything there is in his or her life; all the warts, the scars, the sins, the failures, the deep, dark secrets—and not feel ashamed, the door is open for intimacy. When you know that the other sees you as you really are, yet you are sure you will not be judged but one hundred percent accepted, approved, even appreciated the way you are, there is intimacy.

200

When Adam and Eve sinned against God, and God came into their Paradise Lost, they were both naked and ashamed. They reached for fig leaves and ran behind a bush. They did not want God to see them as they were. When God asked them what they had done, they both tried to cover over their fault by putting the blame on the other, on the devil, or even on God himself. God's response was to inform them of the horrible and ugly consequences of their sin, and then to speak about grace and forgiveness and the coming of the Messiah. Then God did something beautiful to comfort Adam and Eve. He gave them a sign that our covenant-God would hold His promise. He slew an animal, took the bloody skin, and clothed over the shame of two guilt-ridden people, so that they would feel safe in the presence of the Lord.

The fulfilment of that sign came in the person of Jesus at the cross. There God slew the Animal of Heaven, the Lamb of God. In the moment you turn to Jesus in faith, God dresses you in the perfect righteousness of Jesus. Protected by that righteousness you now can stand before God *naked, but not ashamed.* You can be honest with Him about all the ugly things you have become, thought, said or done. Because the Lamb of God was slain in your place, you stand in his righteousness while being completely undressed of any of your own. This way you have absolute confidence that the Father will not judge you or think less of you for who you are or what you have done.

That fulfils the longing of every soul. That creates intimacy with God. Enjoy!

2. Relationships on the horizontal level

What you learned about relationship and intimacy with God, you now carry over to the horizontal level. The need for closeness with another human is underlined in the account of Adam's creation. God told this lone individual to go hang out with the animals he had created, which is what Adam did. Yet all the animals in Paradise could not still Adam's hunger for meaningful connection. He did not need more pets, he needed a woman (Genesis 2:18). She was the counterpart of his creation: *"Male and female he created them"* (Genesis 1:26).

201

Here are some thoughts on meaningfully connecting in relationships:

- Only in relationship to others, can you come to know yourself well. Seeing the scars of the fall of Adam in the lives of others helps you realize that those scars must be present somewhere in your life as well.

- Only in relationship to others can you mature to the individual God wants you to be. *"As iron sharpens iron, so one man sharpens another"* counsels Proverbs 27:17. Rubbing shoulders with others shapes Christian traits in you, such as considerateness, sensitivity, kindness, goodness and loyalty, also stamina, resilience, brokenness, and sympathy. Only a fool despises the advice of others.

- Only in relationship to others do you learn to respect personal boundaries. This principle is inherent in the 8th commandment, *"You shall not steal."* You can steal from others in many different forms: by taking a possession that rightfully belongs to someone else, by robbing them of their dignity through physical mistreatment or cheating on them, by taking away their privacy, by not respecting the borders of countries or your neighbours or by sexually engaging with someone who is or will be the spouse of another.

- Only in relationship to others do you learn to submit to authority. This principle is included in the 5th commandment, *"Honour your father and your mother."* In this time and in our culture authority is suspect. But even though we can all point to horrible abuses of authority, the fact is that no person can live without authority. The opposite of authority is not freedom but chaos, not self-expression but personal confusion. Let's be real about this! Everybody needs something or someone that will guide him, explain things to him, protect him, stand up for him or represent him to others. We need good parents, good teachers, good politicians and good police. Instead of trying to get rid of authority because we have authority-hating hearts, we need to learn and teach good authority.

Relationships are essential for maturing in Christian spirituality, because others are essential for achieving your own individual wholeness.

You were created for friendships

Friendships are great when they function well, but they rip us apart when they don't. We cannot function as true humans without functional friendships. Friendships are meant to communicate to us, in very concrete and visible ways, the invisible love God has for us. Friendships are an avenue through which we can experience God's friendship with us. In fact, the vertical friendship with God is the source for everything we need to enjoy meaningful friendships horizontally: acceptance, security, significance and connectedness. Real friends communicate to us imperfectly the perfect characteristics of our best friend, Jesus. The German poet, Marie von Ebner-Eschenbach, wrote: *"Real friends are people who know us exactly and still stick to us faithfully."* That's precisely what Jesus does as our friend.

Knowing our need for friends, the Bible celebrates good friendships. That the almighty and pure and holy God would call the father of our faith, Abraham, a "friend" (James 2:23)—and our faith-father did some pretty nasty things in his lifetime—shows less what a friend Abraham was and more what a tremendous friend God is. Abraham grew up a complete heathen, yet for reasons we will never know, God picked this common man with a lot of flaws out of a crowd of a million, and committed himself to being his intimate friend.

Nineteen hundred years later, Jesus picked a rough group of people to be His followers, and in a tender moment turned to them and said, *"I have called you friends"* (John 15:15). He was, for them, the fulfilment of Genesis 15.

Jesus shows us various degrees of friendships: there was his friendship to his disciples and then there was an even deeper friendship with three of the disciples. Jesus must have a felt a need in especially meaningful times (like Matthew 17, on the Mount of Transfiguration) and the most excruciating moments (like Matthew 26:36-46) to only have Peter, James and John at his side. He also had a special friendship with Mary (not Magdalene), Martha and Lazarus as well as several women who joined Jesus and the twelve disciples to personally take care of the travelling band.

Besides Jesus' varied kinds of friendships, there are other companionships described in the Bible that open our eyes to the importance of befriending someone covenantally. One friendship, whose depths I am still trying to plummet, is that between David and Jonathan. These two men had a remarkable love for each other. Some have tried to sexualize this love. The Bible gives no indication of that, and we ought to be careful not to assume that such deep companionship as theirs can only be possible if sex was involved. The sex act is not the ultimate expression of intimate friendship. The ultimate expression of friendship is the willingness to offer yourself up for the other person. This is the covenantal approach to friendship which God has modelled in Jesus for us on the cross. *"Greater love has no one than this, that he lay down his life for his friends"* (John 15:13).

This is precisely what Jonathan was willing to do for David: his love for David translated into a willingness to give up his life for the future king. It is almost strange by today's standards how this friendship is described in the Bible: *"Jonathan became one in spirit with David, and he loved him as himself…and Jonathan made a covenant with David because he loved him as himself"* (1 Samuel 18:1, 3).

The two men covenanted with each other not only to be there for each other, but to stand firm together in the righteousness of God. This stand on integrity set Jonathan at odds with his own father, Saul, the current king, who was opposed to David. It cost Jonathan his life.

When Jonathan died in battle, David was virtually inconsolable. With his gift for poetry, he cried to the heavens, *"I am distressed for you, my brother Jonathan; you have been very pleasant to me. Your love to me was more wonderful than the love of women"* (2 Samuel 1:26 *NAS*).

Hold the horses! Stop the wagons! Did this married man just say, *"your love to me was more wonderful than the love of women"*? Was his wife such a disaster?

This is where some people make the assumption that these two men must have been homosexual. But as I already said, I think that is short-sighted and superficial, not taking into account the depth and meaning of 'covenant.' David and Jonathan had an extremely deep friendship. Covenantal friendship can be a bonding at such a deep level David's son Solomon would later write how *"a friend loves at all times"* (Prov. 17:17), and how *"a real friend sticks closer than a brother"* (Prov. 18:24 [NLT]).

To be practical about this, let's think through some principles of 'making friends':

1. Giving to the other, not needing from the other, makes for healthy friendship.

Healthy friendships exist when two people fill their need for security and significance from God and not from each other. You have to be gospel-driven and let God, through Christ, be the source of your significance and the refuge for your security.

If a friendship—in or outside of marriage—is conducted on the basis of need, there is a progression the friendship goes through, where one person is demanding that their needs be filled, while the other seeks to fill those needs, because he gains his sense of worth from filling those needs. Both demander and giver are operating from a need-base. The demander operates with manipulation ("if you love me…"), but the giver also gives out of manipulation ("I give so that you will like me…"). Me-centredness creates need-based friendships, and need-based friendships generally do not survive. Persons end up feeling exploited, abused, rejected, or unappreciated. The cord is torn in two, because the tension between the demander and the giver has grown to the point where the friendship cannot handle it anymore.

Now imagine a triangle with God the Giver at the top. Two people (bottom right and left points) daily go to the Giver. They are driven by the gospel. Recognizing their bankruptcy and inability to give from any self-created resources ("in and of myself I am more sinful than I ever dared to believe"), they place themselves under the waterfall of God's love in Christ and refuel ("in Christ I am more loved than I ever dared to hope"). Each person is now in a position to give to the other from the fullness received, able to approach the other with an attitude of ministry and service, instead of need. When you have the right chemistry, you have the beginning of a friendship. When you have the mindset of ministry, you have the ongoing motivation for a healthy and ever deepening friendship.

2. Follow certain steps to slowly form friendships...slowly.

1) Go to places where you can meet people. Plan social times, where you are in a "fishing pool" of potential relationships: your church community, your school, your work place or a place where people go to pursue the same interests (e.g. a club pub or a café).

2) Take the need for friends to God in prayer. Remember, God wants you to have friends, through whom he wants to communicate his special love for you. Remember that God, the giver of your best friend, Jesus, is also the giver of the friends you need: *"He who did not spare his own Son, but gave him up for us all--how will he not also, along with him, graciously give us all things?"* (Romans 8:32).

3) Schedule time to get together with people with whom you feel chemistry or a spark of interest.

4) Take your time getting to know people. Suggest that you get together. Do not demand time or affection from another person—that is manipulation that points to a hole in your soul for which you have not yet looked to God (see #2 above).

5) Put yourself into various situations where you can experience the other person in various modes, and let him/her experience you in times of fun and relaxation, times of sorrow and times of serious contemplation or learning.

6) Start to open yourself to a person, revealing something sensitive in your life. Make yourself vulnerable. If the person judges you, you know that this person is not constructive for your life. If this person begins uninvited to correct or instruct you, you know that this person may serve your spiritual growth as a counsellor or spiritual director in the future, but not as a friend. If this person listens, sympa-

thizes, identifies with and accepts you as you are, you may have gained a special friend.

7) Enter into a covenant (spoken or unspoken) with your special friends. That means:

- You accept each other the way you are.
- You hold each other accountable to grow spiritually.
- You plan time with each other just hanging out, doing special and fun things together, delighting together in the pleasures of God.
- You will be there for each other in the hard times.

You were created for a big, bad, but beautiful community

I love the church! I really, really, really love the church. Not the building with a steeple, not a certain tradition, not a particular denomination. What I love is church as the gathering of people into a community. The Bible envisions the church as one big collective whole that plunges itself into the glories of God, soaks them up, shares them with each other and goes out from each other to bless the world. It is rich and rewarding to be part of such a community.

There is so much I still have not figured out. I know that we in the West are extremely individualistic, while people in the eastern and southern hemispheres are strongly group-oriented. I understand that group-oriented people have some things to gain from our individualism, and that we individualists are somehow not fully grasping God's ways with mankind because we lack the group-mentality. I'm sure I will be working at this for years.

In the meantime, let's latch on to this reality: If you are "in Christ" you are connected to him as an individual, but being "in Christ" as an individual makes you concurrently part of something much bigger than any individual. You are part of a world-wide community, a universal group, a collective mass of millions. You are not swallowed up into an insignificant nothing by that mass. You are still an individual without whom the other members of the mass are incomplete. But by the same token, your individuality cannot exist apart from your connection to the collective rest. It is a mystery, and it is called 'the church.' *"In Christ, we who are many form one body, and each member belongs to all the others"* (Romans 12:5). In the community of God, individuality and being a part of all the others come together in an unparalleled dynamic.

Tim Keller writes that when we are converted to Christ, the first change that happens in us is a grammatical one: our focus shifts from "I" to "we", from "me" to "us".[1] *We* become part of a new community. It is Jesus' community, in which everyone has the righteousness of Jesus credited to his account and the life of Jesus flowing through his being. Our numbers are innumerable. Reach to the left and right and you are connecting with all your brothers and sisters of this present time. Reach behind you and you are connected to the millions who have gone before us. Reach to the front and you realize you are linked up with all who will come into the community after us. We all have something in common: the blood that flows from our head, Jesus, courses through us all, cleansing us from sin and curing us from all our spiritual sicknesses. As we all have the plague in us, we are all in "a hospital for sinners"—as the 17th century preacher, Richard Sibbes, used to describe the church to his congregation in London. Being sick, we are an ornery, obnoxious, self-serving, spiteful and unrighteous group of people. That means, we are not only an amazing community, we are a frustrating one, as well. This is why the other thing we all have in common is the Holy Spirit of Jesus. He resides in every one of us as the physician of our souls, working into us the character of his own holiness. We need this treatment for the rest of our lives, until we are discharged from this hospital community and sent home completely healed.

I love the church! I need to stop here and say something to you, the reader:

- If you have been hurt by the church, I can understand your pain. I have also been deeply hurt by the church. And I am sure that I have also deeply hurt others in the church.

---

[1] Keller, Timothy & Thompson, Allen, CHURCH PLANTER MANUAL, New York: Redeemer Church Planting Center, 2002.

- If you have been hurt by the church, I doubt very much that you have been hurt as much as Jesus has been. And it's his church. And you are that church. And together, we have hurt Jesus a lot and we have hurt him deeply!

- About that statement, that you are the church: Everything bad that you can say about the church lies in some form in your own heart. If my experience tells me anything, what others have done to you, you have probably done in some form to others. You just don't notice it so quickly, because it didn't hurt you. It hurt them.

What I am driving at is this: There must be something for us to learn from our Lord's example, when he refused to walk away from this mangled mess called 'the church' and, instead, died for it. There are reasons for leaving a church, and I will list some under Toolbox. But gospel-driven spirituality calls us to get behind the action and ask what the motive is. If the motive is me-centredness, the action will lead to disappointment, frustration, and hurt within the church community and then you walk away from her. If the motive is God-centredness, the action will bring with it a willingness to die for the church community, even while feeling disappointment, frustration, and hurt within her.

1. You need to be part of a church community

The reason is simple: you *are* part of the church. Union with Christ the head means you belong to Christ the body. You are a very tiny part of the body, but you are an important part. 1 Corinthians 12:18 teaches us that the Holy Spirit gives you spiritual gifts and then places you into the body of Christ where your gift will benefit others. Become part of a church community, but not from the consumerist perspective, "What will this church do for me?" but from the ministry perspective, "What can I do for this church?"

Choose a church that unapologetically esteems, worships, and proclaims Jesus as God, as God in the flesh, as the only way to God, and as the only one who died for our sins and rose again.

Choose a church that is gospel-driven instead of legalistic towards its members and self-righteous toward the world.

Choose a church that is God-centred in worship, that has you coming away from every worship service amazed at the greatness of our God. Choose a church that reveres and teaches the Bible!

2. You need to be part of a church that is flawed and imperfect

This is good news, because there is no other kind of church. Imagine what would happen, if after all your searching for a perfect church, you suddenly found one. The people are perfect, the preaching is perfect, the worship is perfect, the community groups that meet throughout the week are all perfect. The ministries to your children and to your teenage kids are perfect. Everything about this church is perfect, so much so, that you never ever have to feel frustrated, irritated, disappointed or hurt.

There are two problems with this perfect church:

First of all, how are you going to be challenged to grow in holiness if your church community is perfect? If everybody is perfect, how will you learn to deal with difficult people? If nobody wrongs you, how will you learn the cost of forgiveness? If everyone is perfectly pleasant, how will you learn to be patient? If the decisions of the elders are always perfectly right, how will you learn to submit to people who decide different from what you would prefer?

Secondly, the description above of the perfect church is a description of heaven. It is perfectly wrong, even arrogant for anyone to expect that there might be a church community that should be handed the prize before it has crossed the finish line. Until we get there, we may view the flawed and imperfect church as God's gift to us. It is a sacred workshop in which we are chiselled and shaped by the hammer blows of challenging people and difficult situations. And the one holding the hammer is the Holy Spirit! Even Paul, when given the choice between going to the perfect(ed) church in heaven and dwelling amidst the imperfections of the Philippian church, said, *"It is more necessary for you that I remain in the body...I know that I will remain, and I will continue with all of you for your progress and joy in the faith"* (Philippians 1:24, 25).

If 'ministry to' not 'getting from' is your approach to the church community, then you will want to take the attitude of Dietrich Bonhoeffer. After he announced to his sceptical family in 1920—

at the age of 14—that he had decided to study theology, his older brother Klaus reacted, calling the church nothing but a "poor, feeble, boring, petty, bourgeois institution." Dietrich quickly responded, "In that case I shall have to reform it!"[2]

3. You need a church that expects you to live out Jesus' guidelines for healthy relationships

Be part of a church that keeps things in balance: On the one hand, it is open and honest and pro-active about problem situations and problem people in its midst, and does not sweep conflicts and controversy under the carpet. It recognizes that conflict is a normal part of relationships (i.e., a church that is experiencing conflict is not a bad church), and that conflict resolution is a normal part of community life (i.e., a church that is not experiencing conflict resolution is a bad church).

On the other hand, it expects every member to be open and honest about his own sins and his need for accountability and correction, and to be pro-active about his responsibility toward all other members:

- to forgive freely when wronged, even if not asked for forgiveness;
- to forbear patiently with another person's faults, if it is something that irritates you personally but is not bringing harm upon the whole community;
- to gently confront a fellow-Christian, if his false teaching or persistent sin is causing the church a bad reputation, or is bringing harm to several or all in the church community (see Matthew 18:15-17; Galatians 6:1; James 5:19, 20);
- and to pray regularly to God to give you his love for those who are hard to love (and impossible to like).

4. You need to become a member of a church community

The matter of 'membership' in the church is a bit controversial in some circles, complicated in others. In the German state church, for example, you are a member by virtue of living in the church's town and paying the church tax. You do not need to believe in

---

[2] Metaxas, , p. 38

God or participate in the church's community, but you can get hatched-matched-and-dispatched (as the English express it), that is, baptized as an infant into the church, and married and buried by the church. This form of 'membership,' to say the least, poses certain challenges.

There are churches that prefer the other extreme. In response to the so-called 'institutionalization' of the church, they feel that keeping things loose is attractive to a generation that has difficulty with tight structures and top-down authoritarianism. Besides—so the argument goes—'membership' brings with it too much of an in/out or we/they categorization, which only brings feelings of estrangement to outsiders or visitors.

I personally think you need to be part of a church community that takes 'membership' seriously. The reason for this takes us back to where this chapter began: the foundation for a healthy relationship is a 'covenant,' a commitment to love others even if it costs us our lives. A church community is in a position to function best when those who make up the community have sworn their allegiance to Jesus, and their undying love, loyalty and service to one another.

A church covenant is important in order to clarify lines of communication, establish community-wide sense of responsibility toward one another, and grant leaders the authority to pastor the members. It is good for you and others, and it embraces the principles of relationships discussed in this chapter, if you officially, publically and formally make a commitment to the local church you decide to be part of.

Relationships are essential for maturing in Christian spirituality, because others are essential for achieving your own individual wholeness.

1. Read "the love chapter," 1 Corinthians 13. Then pick 3 characteristics of love expressed in this chapter that are still missing in your life. Begin to ask God to give you these characteristics of his love.

2. Read Romans 12:4-21 three times. After each time, write down principles you see for conduct or attitude in relation to others in the "body of Christ", the church. Then pray through each one of those principles to God, asking Him to help you make them part of your ongoing relational way of living in community with others in the church.

3. Conflict in relationships is a normal part of living in a sinful world. We should always seek to resolve the conflict, and God has given us guidelines and principles in Scripture to help us accomplish that. Many times a conflict can be resolved. But there are times when the only solution is to go separate ways. This, too, can be God's will in a situation. **Read Acts 15:36-41** about several godly men who could not come to a harmonious conclusion and went their separate ways as a result. What good do you think came out of this conflict situation?

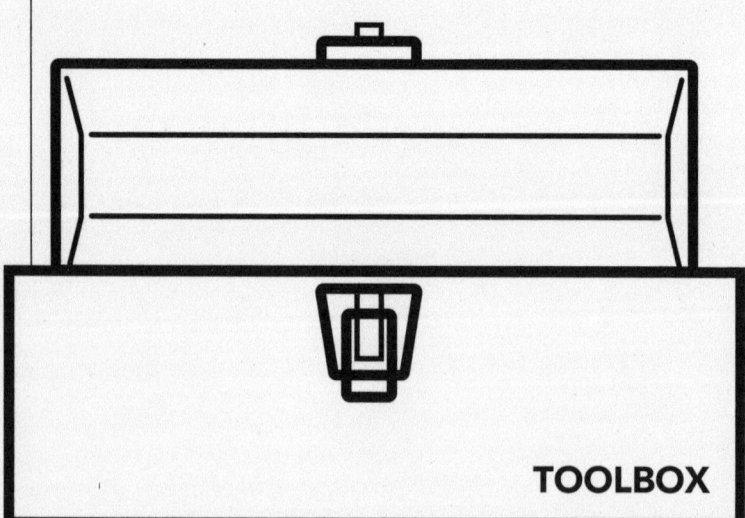

TOOLBOX

4. Our connection to God's covenant community is to be built on a covenant commitment. We stick together through thick and thin, through the great times and through the difficult times. Our unity in the church is a testimony to a watching world of who God is and what He has done (John 17:23). I think there are a few legitimate reasons to leave a local church for another:

- if the church has become so moralistic, legalistic, authoritarian or emotionally abusive toward its members, that it is chronically destroying one member after another, leave the church

- if the church does not take the teaching of the Bible seriously nor Jesus as God in the flesh, you will – along with all others in the church – begin to starve spiritually. Before you starve to death, leave the church (Romans 16:17, 18)

- if the church has no room for your gift of evangelism and your passion to reach non-Christians in the city, if it has no desire to engage with non-Christians nor to feel a sense of honour when non-Christians show up because they are curious or searching, then before many people go to the grave without having heard the best news there is, leave your church and join one that will catapult you into the lives of the spiritually dead

5. For further reading: Dietrich Bonhoeffer, Life Together. London: SCM Press, 1954; Ken Sande, The Peacemaker: A Biblical Guide to Resolving Personal Conflict. Grand Rapids: Baker Books, 1997.

10
3rd Wall

Deciding to Live in the Will of God

Learning the spirituality of obedience

When I was 7 years old and very attached to my father, he went away for 3 days to speak at a conference. I could not accompany him, because I had more important things to do, like going to school or pestering my older sister until she screamed for my mother to come and save her (this was always a highlight in my day!).

After two days of life without my dad, I had had enough. "When is Daddy coming home," I whined at my mother. She answered, "Tomorrow, son." "Well, tomorrow is too late," I protested. Then I went to the bread box, took out a loaf of bread, and declared, "I am not coming home until my daddy comes home!" I tucked the loaf of bread under my arm and walked out the front door. I don't know what my mother did, since I do not have eyes in the back of my head like some mothers do, but the fact is, she did not keep me from going out the door. If I were my mother, I would have at least wanted the loaf of bread back in the bread box.

I walked across the street (my mother was probably watching), and started up the pathway into the forest across from our house in Alsbach, Germany. About 50 metres up the path was a large boulder, and that is where I sat down. Today there is a golden sign on that rock on which is inscribed, "Here rested Stevie Beck in 1962." No, I am just kidding; there never was such an engraving. But the rock is still there—nobody has removed it since that historic day in 1962. On that rock I sat down, me and my loaf of bread. Together we would keep an eye out for when my father would return home the next day. I was determined to spend the evening and the night up on that rock and protest my father's absence. When he came home, I would come home. Not one moment sooner!

Two hours later, as the first signs of incoming darkness and a chill in the air were making themselves felt, my sister walked out of our house, down the steps, over the street and up into the woods to visit me. I knew she was coming to comfort me and assure me that I was right. "Hey stupid," she said, "why don't you stop being so childish and start to grow up! Get your butt off that rock and come home."

Quietly I slipped off the rock and followed her home. My mother was very glad to see the loaf of bread safely back in the bread box.

This book is about building the "house of your spiritual life" on the solid rock that is Jesus and his teaching. But let us now change the picture a bit. While we would never want to forsake *that* rock, because it would mean certain destruction when the storms of life hit, we need to see ourselves as growing up in spiritual maturity by getting off of our old rock on which we used to sit in personal autonomy and protest against God, and go home to where we grow up in God's family.

That raises the question: how do you know if you are growing up? How do you know if you are spiritually where you belong? How do you decide what your next step of growth should look like? These are questions every follower of Jesus faces in this present time during which the Master of the house has gone away.

What is spiritual maturity? In Hebrews 5:11-14, the author really digs at his readers. He is disappointed by them. He would love to tell them deeper things regarding Jesus, Son of God, but the recipients of this letter have not yet matured out of their spiritual infancy. They received Christ in the faith of a child, but they have never grown into spiritual adulthood. The sign of maturity, says the author, is to have your mind so well trained, that you can distinguish between good and bad and make decisions that please God. Let's define maturity in a gospel-driven manner:

Christian maturity is the freedom to use your biblically informed mind to make decisions that glorify God, out of motives that honour Christ, and that are carried out in the fruit of the Spirit.

**The MORAL WILL is your basic
parameter for decision-making**

In the chapter on God's holiness as a cornerstone to our lives, we already stated that sin is any thought, attitude, word or action that falls short of, or transgresses against, God's measure of holiness. The moral will of God has to do with your decision in any given situation to obey God and conform to his holiness, instead of following your own selfish path and thereby being out of conformity to his holiness.

In a lot of situations, it's easy to know God's will for your life, because for many things God has already clearly stated what his will is. He made it so easy for us that He had it written down. Deuteronomy 29:29 states, *"The secret things belong to the Lord our God, but the things revealed belong to us and to our children forever, that we may follow all the things of this law."* This verse speaks of two parts to God's will: there are *"secret things"*, and these do not "belong to us." There are the *"things revealed"* and they *"belong to us and to our children forever."* More than our possession, they become our lifestyle: *"that we may follow all the things of this law."*

Where might we find these revealed things we are to obey? Deut. 29:29 points to *"this law."* A few verses later, in Deuteronomy 30:14, God explains, *"The word is very near you; it is in your mouth and in your heart so you may obey it."* The Law of God, as a guideline by which we lead our lives, is the Word of God. It contains all the guidelines every person on earth needs to live a life pleasing to God. This moral law of God is unchanging. It remains the same from one generation to the next. It transcends cultures, times and trends.

In the New Testament, Paul re-states this point in the passage we analyzed, even memorized earlier, 2 Timothy 3:16, 17. In referring to *"all Scripture,"* he says that it is *"profitable for teaching, for reproof, for correction, for training in righteousness; that the man of God may be adequate, equipped for every good work"* (NAS) Every good work would mean all the good works God could possibly wish you to do. The 'moral will' of God covers the entire territory of your life.

Where I used to live in Toronto, there is a major street downtown called University Avenue. It is four lanes wide going each way. Driving north on University Avenue from the financial district with its huge bank towers, one drives by a number of hospitals, then crosses over College Street, and has the Ontario Parliament building looming large in front of him. Approaching it by car, you could think that the whole volume of traffic might drive right through its front door, were it not for the fact that a hundred feet before the entrance, University Avenue makes a very sharp curve to the right and continues in a circle around the large government building and the park in front of it. During rush hour cars drive side by side in all four lanes around the parliament building. Fast. It is nerve-wracking. You have to keep your eyes on the lines that mark the right and the left of your lane. You have to keep your car between those lines. If you start looking to the right or the left at the other drivers, or if you take your eyes off of your lane and look at the majestic architecture of the parliament building or the lawn in front of it with all its beautiful flowers, you will quickly cross into another lane and sideswipe another automobile, bringing injury to yourself or the other driver.

God has revealed to us in writing what his holy nature and character are like. All the commandments in Scripture are nothing other than the extension of God's holiness to us and descriptions of holiness God desires in us. These commandments are his moral will; they are the white lines to the right and the left of the car of our lives. If we obey them, we will arrive safely at life's destination. I am afraid that viewing God's moral will or the Bible's commandments as mere freedom-inhibiting 'rules and regulations' is just as naïve and disastrous as the driver who rounds the parliament building in Toronto with the perspective "These lines only limit my freedom; I can decide for myself how I want to drive my car, thank you!"

The SOVEREIGN WILL is life's big adventure

Deuteronomy 29:29 also referred to *"the secret things of God"*. God's secrets take us back to the first cornerstone of our spiritual house, the sovereignty of God. As I showed there from Isaiah 46:10, God has determined the end from the beginning, and from the start what will come to pass, right down to the smallest detail, such as which bird of prey will pick apart which field mouse, and what man will move from one country to another. The wrong implication to draw from the sovereignty of God is that man is not free to choose. To say you will create man in your own likeness, but then not create him free to choose, would not only be an unethical creation, it would not be a creation in God's likeness. Therefore, when people put God's sovereignty and predestination on one side, and man's responsibility and freedom of choice on the other side, they are creating false categories, the separation of which is not found in Scripture. The right implication of God's sovereignty is to realize that since God controls every detail of every movement of every being, we are not only free to choose; we are also safe in choosing. People who know themselves to be kept safe in the sovereign oversight of a good and loving God are not inhibited by His sovereignty, but are freed up to make decisions. Why? They know that as long as the human is human, he is created by God to choose and decide. And they know that as long as God is God, he is sovereign to protect and keep them in their decisions.

The previously mentioned Scottish theologian, John Murray, once wrote that one cannot know God's will until after it has happened. He was not referring to God's moral will, as that has already "happened". Murray was referring to God's sovereign will about the everyday events of our lives. Not one of us knows what will happen next, no one knows what tomorrow will bring, no one of us knows where we will be living next year, or *if* we will be living next year. But God knows! He knows everything, and in knowing these actualities of our lives, he has planned them. But he is not telling us what he has planned. It is all part of his *"secret things,"* all part of this journey we are on, trusting God with our lives moment by moment, trusting Him for strength and grace when we discover what the next moment brings.

This turns life into a big adventure with God. It also allows us to make decisions about our unknown future. Whether it is choosing where to attend university, where to live, whom to marry or what job to take, here are some practical principles for making decisions about *"the secret things of God"*:

- First step: Be sure you are living within the moral will of God. This is always basic to your ability to follow the guidance of the Holy Spirit. If you are persistently not living within the moral will of God, you are quenching the Holy Spirit. It will rob you of needed spiritual sensitivity; it will cloud your judgment in situations that require the Spirit's wisdom.

- Second step: Be in touch with the desires of your heart. Often God leads us to do something by giving us the desire for it. It may be an occupation, a particular person, a place or a thing. At this point, one might well ask, "But how do I know if the desire in my heart is from my own flesh or from God?" The answer is that God often leads us by placing His desire on our hearts, so that we will begin to desire in accordance with His desires. (a) Test the desire by asking yourself if it is within the moral will of God as revealed in the Scriptures; (b) test the desire by analyzing if there is evidence that you have the gifts or skill to carry out the desire; (c) test the desire by regularly asking God in prayer if he would have you move forward on your desire. If it is from him, chances are, the desire will only grow into a deep conviction; and (d) test the desire by asking wise Christians for their counsel.

- Third step: Decide. Make a plan for how you will proceed, always asking the Holy Spirit for guidance (James 4:13-15).

- Fourth step: Start moving toward the goal you desire to reach. Go according to plan, always in prayer, always ready to change your plan if the Holy Spirit changes the course or blocks your way (Acts 16:6, 7).

- Fifth step: If you reach the goal (the place, the person, the school, the occupation), thank God that his sovereign will has come to pass.

But in a fallen world you will face various disappointing scenarios:

- Scenario #1: What about situations where you have a strong desire, the desire is completely within Scriptural norm, others think it is a smart move, but every door to the opportunity closes? Those can be discouraging, disappointing and painful times in life. Here, too, we may trust in our sovereign

God that the closed door—painful as it may be—is God's sovereign will at work for us. It means that God has something even better and more constructive or fruitful in store for us.

- Scenario #2: What if you are in process toward a goal you want to reach, but shortly before arriving at the finish line everything falls apart (like a broken engagement just before the wedding, or making it to the final two candidates for a job and the other person is chosen)? Here, too, you acknowledge your deep pain to God, ask him for wisdom to recognize the lessons you should learn and thank God for what unknown disappointment he has protected you from.

- Scenario #3: What about the situation where the goal is met, God's sovereign will is thereby revealed, but it very quickly becomes obvious that you have walked into a difficult situation (like finding out that the person you married has some scary ghosts in the closet of his soul, or discovering that the job or ministry you had longed for and received has some impossible people you have to work with)? Here, too, you may trust that God's sovereign will for you was not a mistake. Difficult situations and disappointing relationships can be the very thing God wants you to live and work through, so that he can shape your character. Maturity is not the ability to be joyful when things are going well. Maturity is the ability to be joyful and content even when things are going painfully bad for you. It is the will to be and react in a godly way, independent of your circumstances.

As long as God is sovereign, you are safe. You are safe to make decisions and you are safe to live with the decisions you have made. You are safe to learn from your decisions, and to grow from bad decisions. You are safe to take good risks, and when something does not work the first, second or tenth time, you are safe to try again. Like I said, it's an adventure!

Life in the grey zone requires spiritual fitness

Many people I know think in black-and-white. They believe that as long as God is absolute truth, everything must either be absolutely right or absolutely wrong. The "black-and-white" people and churches find a black-and-white world very convenient. God stays in a black-and-white box, life becomes predictable, people can be categorized as either 'belonging to us' or 'not belonging to us', and everything feels like it is under control.

Thankfully, reality is not like that, neither is Christian spirituality, neither is God. There is a grey zone.

The Bible teaches us that one of God's absolute truths is that everything he has created is absolutely good. But how a sinful person decides to put it to use either keeps it good or makes it bad. These are "matters of indifference," or *"adiaphora,"* as the old theologians called them in Greek—a whole area of life, where every Christian has the freedom to decide for himself. The grey zone. Things in this area become right or wrong as soon as sinful man touches them with his life, but—and I admit that for the "black-and-white people" who like simple answers to everything, this is hard to swallow—they are not right or wrong for everybody. They may be right for one person and wrong for someone else, good in the one situation and bad in another.

In fact, Hebrews 5:14 speaks precisely to this category of spiritual decision-making: *"But solid food is for the mature, who by constant use have trained themselves to distinguish between good and evil."*

As if we are part of an athletic team, we need to go to training camp. We need to get in shape and learn how to run certain plays. Then when the actual game is to be played, we know in matters of indifference precisely how to "distinguish between good and evil."

Let's practice some plays:

Practice-Play #1: Always follow the Bible's command! Where God has pointed to something in his Word as sin, it is sin regardless of how you or others feel about it or the value your culture places on it. We need to trust God that behind the command is God's understanding of what is good, what destroys and what benefits. Certainly the creator of all good things knows how they work. We may trust him, who is good, not to command because he loves to kill our joy and fun in life, but because he loves it when we feel the delight of living life to the fullest.

Practice-Play #2: Develop your conscience to a high degree of reliability. The conscience is part of the human self that God created. While our consciences can be shaped by our surroundings, parents and culture, the conscience is an innate part of every human being since conception. It is like a built-in voice God placed into our psyche to guide us to him.

We train our conscience by continuously feeding it biblical information. As this happens, our conscience may "change its mind" on things. What it once regarded as objectionable, it may begin to see as permissible and enjoyable. Or what it once applauded with no second thought, it may, through biblical information, come to see as adverse to the holiness of God. *"Blessed is the man who does not condemn himself by what he approves. But the man who has doubts is condemned if he eats (meat sacrificed to idols), because his eating is not from faith; and everything that does not come from faith is sin."* (Romans 14:22, 23).

Practice-Play #3: Learn to think positively not reactionary. Everything God has made is intrinsically pure and good. In Christian spirituality we begin, not with Genesis 3 and the cosmic fall into sin, but with Genesis 1 and 2, the original goodness of all created things: nature, the body and every one of its shapely parts, bodily movement (whether it be sports or dancing), sex, music, wine, food...everything is originally pure. According to Titus 1:15, *"To the pure, all things are pure."* 1 Timothy 4:4 adds that *"everything God created is good, and nothing is to be rejected if it is received with thanksgiving."* Romans 14:14 says *"nothing is unclean in itself"*. (NAS)

This is the reason...

- ...why in the Bible, a whole book is devoted to the beauty of the body and the enjoyment of sex in marriage (Song of Solomon): it is pure!

- ...why there is the call in the Old Testament to sound the instruments and to dance: it is pure!

- ...why there are biblical passages (e.g., in Proverbs) encouraging us to enjoy the fruit of the vine: it is pure!

- ...why Paul commands us to eat anything sold in the meat market (including meat that has been offered to idols) without raising questions of conscience, for, *"the earth is the Lord's, and everything in it."* (1 Corinthians 10:25, 26; Psalm 24:1).

...why Paul refuses to let highly religious people reduce Christian spirituality to a religion of 'do this' and 'don't do that': *"They forbid people to marry and order them to abstain from certain foods, which God created to be received with thanksgiving by those who believe and who know the truth. For everything God created is good, and nothing is to be rejected if it is received with thanksgiving, because it is consecrated by the word of God and prayer"* (1 Timothy 4:3-5).

Practice-Play #4: Look behind the action and see what is in your heart. Here we return to the cement mix of your spiritual foundation; to the idea of being gospel-driven. What is your motive for wanting to do or say something?

Are you acting out of self-righteousness? That means, do you want to do something in order prove yourself, to attain a certain image, or to please or fit in with others?

Or are you acting out of the gospel? In that case, you will do something, having placed your identity in the righteousness of Christ and the accepted standing it gives you with God. You will remind yourself in any given situation, that you do not need to prove yourself. You want to do what is right because it reflects the righteousness of Christ that has covered you. You want to do something (like go to the football stadium with Stephan), because it is a way for you to enjoy a righteous God and all the gifts he has given us to enjoy.

Practice-Play #5: Be on the lookout for how your actions affect others. Paul told the Corinthians who insisted on the use of their freedom in indifferent matters, but ended up unnecessarily hurting others, *"Everything is permissible to me, but not everything is beneficial"* (1 Corinthians 6:12). That means spiritual maturity calls the Christian to think before he acts. He is to discern every action with the question of whether or not it is necessary and useful. Someone will object, "Hey, I have the right to freely do as I please wherever the Bible does not forbid it, don't I?" The Bible answers, *"Not everything is constructive. Nobody should seek his own good, but the good of others"* (1 Corinthians 10:23, 24).

The more we practice these things, the more we mature spiritually. *Christian maturity is the freedom to use your biblically informed
mind to make decisions that glorify God, out of motives that honour
Christ, and are carried out in the fruit of the Spirit* (Hebrews 5:11-14).
Let's take a 'matter of indifference,' and put our training with the
practice-plays to work! Let's take an issue that in many parts of the
world remains controversial, regardless what religion you belong
to: the consumption of alcohol.

You are in a group of people and everyone is enjoying a pint of
beer. The host of the party has placed a full glass of full-bodied
stout in front of you as well. You have never drunk beer before.

As a follower of Jesus your...

- ...first step is to ask yourself if the drinking of beer is ex-
  plicitly forbidden in Scripture. You know that drunkenness is
  mentioned as contrary to God's character of self-control. You
  know that there are passages in Proverbs that encourage the
  enjoyment of wine as part of merrily enjoying our King and
  Creator God. You have not signed any agreements or received
  any orders to not imbibe, which Scripture would command
  you to honour. You might, therefore, conclude that drinking a
  few sips of beer is not outside of God's moral will.

- ...second step is to check your conscience. If your conscience
  has always sought to bar you from drinking beer, ask yourself
  if this is due to biblical information or due to your upbringing, peer pressure or moralism that characterizes your community and its teaching. You might, in all fairness, decide that
  your conscience has been shaped by God's Word on this matter, and politely decline the glass of beer. But you also might
  decide in this moment that a more extensive search of the
  Bible has led you to conclude that your conscience has been
  wrongly informed and needs to be informed by the broader
  boundaries of Scripture.

- ...third move is to ask yourself if beer is innately good. You
  think through the ingredients of beer. You might conclude
  that God is the Creator and Giver of the ingredients which
  someone has brewed. Beer in and of itself must be pure, and

Scripture says (Titus 1:15), *"To the pure all things are pure"*. But that is precisely the question: the beer is pure, but are you?

- ...fourth step, therefore, is to look behind the action of drinking the beer to what is in your heart. What is your motive for drinking this beer? Is it because you want to 'fit in' and be like everyone else in the group? Then you would be bowing to the idol in your heart that promises you the feeling of security if you remain in harmony with the group. Is it because you would attain the approval of those in the group or would feel grown up or macho? Then you would be bowing to the idol in your heart that promises you the sense of significance when others signal to you acceptance or desirability. Is it because you would like to get drunk? Then you would be bowing to the idol of rebellion that promises you happiness by following an ethic other than that which reflects God's holiness. Or do you want to drink the beer because you would like to know how it tastes; and if it tastes good, you would like to add beer to your list of drinks that nourish, satisfy and bring you into an enjoyment of its creator?

- ...fifth step is to celebrate your freedom in Christ. Being free means you are free to drink what is pure and good. But you are also free NOT to drink the beer, if wisdom would lead you to conclude that it is not beneficial.

So before your fingers wrap themselves around the glass' handle and lift the desired ale to your lips ask yourself if this beer is really beneficial to you personally? While it is pure and good in and of itself, it might be harmful to you. It might add calories at a time when your health requires you to seriously limit your calorie intake.

Consider the fact that Christians around you may be weak in the area where you wish to enjoy your liberty. Pulling them into your liberty may cause them to sin against their own conscience. You may enjoy beer as much as Luther did, but if you know that a person in the group is an alcoholic and will take your liberty as permission to down a cool one, and a second one, and then get drunk, that is *"causing your brother to fall"* (Romans 14:21). The Bible calls us to be sensitive toward others, not insisting on our own rights of freedom, but looking out for the spiritual well-being of others.

But let's consider a completely different scenario: Imagine, the host of the party has served everyone beer, but none of the people around the table think kindly of Christians swallowing the "liquid from hell." To the other guests, anyone who drinks beer is abysmally low on the holiness chart. You know that, and you also know that you like beer, and are convinced beer is innately pure.

My counsel is, we need to help other Christians stop acting in 'matters of indifference' out of self-righteousness. This is a sticky point, I admit. But Jesus abhors any behaviour that is done or not done in order to prove "what a good Christian I am." Where a brother hangs his sense of righteousness on how he has decided in a 'matter of indifference,' he is dabbling in a false gospel. Here we must not show tolerance. To paraphrase Luther: If a Christian in the group says, 'I will not drink beer, because I cannot stop with just one glass, nor can I resist drinking if other Christians around me are drinking, be sensitive and courteous toward your 'weaker brother' and do not encourage him to drink the beer by your drinking your glass of beer. If he says, 'I will not drink beer, because good Christians do not drink such sinful stuff,' then out of love for that Christian drink 3 glasses of beer in front of him, unless 3 glasses gets you drunk. Then drink only 2!

■ What's in it for me?

Decision-making within the will of God makes you FREE!

- When you order your life according to *the moral will of God*, following and obeying his commands and prohibitions in the Bible, you can be absolutely certain—regardless of what others think of you—that you are doing what is right, what is healthy to yourself and helpful to others. That's a wonderful freedom with which to handle life's challenges! Where God has clearly spoken, follow his will.

- When you trust the *sovereign will of God* to guide and protect you, you become free to make decisions and plans in the present and for the future on the basis of what you think is good for yourself, good for others and good for the reputation of the God who runs your life. You can make decisions in the confidence that God wants to bless you, he will guide you, and he will re-route your path if your good plan was not his good and perfect plan (the sovereign will). That's being free!

- When you confront a matter that is in the grey zone, use the considerations we outlined to decide. You are free: free to be yourself, free to do what is good and enjoyable, free to respect the opinions and convictions of others, free to look out for the good of others, free to sacrifice your 'right' so that others might not sin. There is a lot of power in that freedom.

So you see:

Christian maturity is the freedom to use your biblically informed mind to make decisions that glorify God, out of motives that honour Christ, and that are carried out in the fruit of the Spirit.

For anybody who thought that living within God's will was as simplistic as compartmentalizing everything and everyone into categories of don'ts and do's, you have done no more than create a religion of legalism instead of following a gospel-driven Christianity. It may look like you are building your spiritual house on a solid boulder, but I can already hear my sister's approaching voice:

"Get your butt off that rock, go home where you belong, and start to grow up!"

1. Read Romans 6:15-23 and meditate on each line. Note the emphasis – you WERE slave to sin, you ARE slave to righteousness. What are results of being a slave to sin?
What does living out of the righteousness of Christ do for you?

2. Meditate on Proverbs 28:13, 14. What hidden sins are in your life? What would renouncing those sins look like?

3. In our definition of spiritual maturity, we said that our moment-by-moment decisions are to be carried out in the fruit of the Spirit. The 'fruit of the Spirit' are traits that make up the character of Christ. They are the result of the Holy Spirit's work of reproducing Christ's character in us. **Read Galatians 5:19-26**, noting the contrast between the acts of the sinful nature and the fruit of the Spirit.

4. Memorize the 'fruit of the Spirit' in Galatians 5:22-23. One way to do that is to bring this list of Christ's characteristics to God in prayer daily, asking him to let these be what characterize your personality and decisions.

5. Here is another way to discern the motive in your decisions: James 3:13-18 lists the characteristics of two kinds of wisdom and ambition. Read the passage and learn 'wisdom from above' by asking God in prayer to instil these characteristics into your decision making processes.

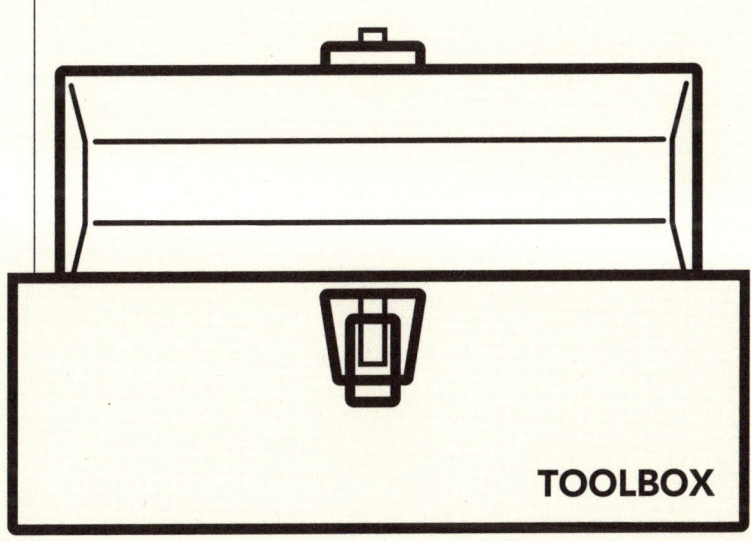

TOOLBOX

11
4th Wall
Carrying Your Cross through the Harshness of God

Learning a spirituality of suffering

There is a reason why Joni Eareckson broke her neck at age 17 and became a quadriplegic for life.

There# is a reason why Joe Pinzka, a wonderful husband to Karen and tender father to their one-year-old daughter, was diagnosed with sarcoma. There is a reason why we had to watch Joe deteriorate within 6 months from a robust 27-year-old to a skeleton that looked like something out of a labour camp, until he died one Sunday morning.

There is a reason why the baby son of colleagues received a deficient amount of oxygen in the birth process, leaving him permanently unable to use his arms and legs.

There is a reason why in 2009, two German girls went to Yemen to serve less privileged Muslim families in a hospital. Together with a doctor, his wife and four children, the two ladies were kidnapped and ruthlessly shot to death by a group of Muslim terrorists. The German media jumped all over this case, labelling the two young ladies "Christian fanatics" and the Bible school at which they had studied "irresponsible" for letting them go to Yemen. There is a reason for their martyrdom in Yemen, as well as for their being slandered by the German media for their good deeds to Muslims.

There is a reason...

"Why does a good God allow good people to suffer?" This is the question philosophers and theologians have wrestled with as long as there has been suffering, philosophers and theologians. It is not the purpose of this chapter to answer that question. Atheists, and all others who are looking for a reason to justify their rejection of God, often use this question as a reason for not believing in him. But there is—in the opinion of man—more difficulty in explaining the existence of evil without the existence of God than there is explaining the existence of evil with the existence of God.

Suffice it to say, Christian spirituality reaches out with both hands and holds a particular consideration of reality in each one:

On the one hand is the reality of the fall: man, whom God ethically created free to choose his destiny, chose a self-centred spirituality in place of a God-centred life, and through this decision brought death into God's living and life-giving creation. Death mastered everything, soiled everything, corrupted everything, twisted everything and debased everything, from nature to human bodies to human souls to emotions to intellect to relationships to thoughts to words and deeds. Nature began to destroy nature and to destroy humans, and humans began to destroy nature and one another. Death in every possible form has ruined what God originally created good. Romans 8:22 analyzes the situation, *"all creation groans in its bondage to decay."* If you are looking to blame anybody for the evils of this world, look no further than our own human hearts.

On the other hand is the reality of a great and good God, who always has been, and always will be, great and good. Having—in his greatness and goodness—created man and woman as the crown of his cosmic design, he has responded to man's decision to rebel against him and mar his pristine creation with death, by first promising a Saviour, then entering into our dark night in the Person of Jesus as Saviour, who by his death on the cross died the consummate death we had inflicted on the cosmos, and through his bodily resurrection from the dead gained mastery over the final enemy, and turned back the clock (as C.S. Lewis has said), so that the hope we have, as we groan presently for liberation from the presence of death, is to *"wait eagerly for our adoption as sons, the redemption of our bodies"* (Romans 8:23). We have this hope within us, because we know that while evil is bad, God is good, and while evil is strong, God is stronger yet, and is, therefore, able to turn evil to good.

"Why does a good God allow good people to suffer?" I am quite aware that both realities I just summarized for you will not completely satisfy your longing for an answer. I am also aware that no theologian to date has satisfactorily solved the impenetrable mystery of why a great and good God could allow the entrance of evil. But the purpose of this chapter is to try to get to the bottom of a more specific question, namely, what meaning there might be in the suffering of those who follow after Jesus. What role do pain, sickness and death play in the life of a disciple of the Suffering Servant?

There are two things I would like to state:

- If you are a follower of Jesus, the Suffering Servant, you will more than likely be in for more suffering on this side of eternity than non-Christians.

- If you are a follower of Jesus, the Suffering Servant, there are numerous glorious and redemptive reasons why you suffer as much as you do.

- The fact that I have just referred to Jesus our Master as the "Suffering Servant" gives us a hint of where the answer to all our suffering lies: In Jesus himself! It is absolutely essential that we stop right here, and drop a mental anchor precisely at this location.

Jesus, the Suffering Servant, is the reason his followers suffer!

A true Christian spirituality listens to the disciple Peter: *"Beloved, do not be surprised at the fiery ordeal among you, which comes upon you for your testing...but to the degree that you share the sufferings of Christ, keep on rejoicing...but if anyone suffers as a Christian, let him not feel ashamed, but in that name let him glorify God...Let those who suffer according to the will of God entrust their souls to a faithful Creator in doing what is right."* (1 Peter 4:12-19 [NAS]).

A true Christian spirituality takes into account the example and words of the apostle Paul, who describes walking in the power of the Spirit on the way to great glory as the clop-clop-clop of four-legged creatures, bleating in frustration every time the farmer forces them closer to their bloody end: *"For God's sake we are being led to the slaughter all day long"* (Romans 8:36, quoting Psalm 44:22).

There is a mystery involved in following Jesus. Do you hear those slow steps of a sober funeral procession? It is the redeemed, those whom Jesus purchased for God at the cross. They are marching towards death. Their heads are bowed. Psalm 116:15 (we mentioned this verse under the cornerstone of God's pleasures) pictures God over this sad parade with a look of pleasure on his face: *"Precious in the sight of the Lord is the death of his godly ones."*(NAS) Mysterious!

Yet precisely here—standing with Jesus, the Lamb of God, at a cross-shaped butcher block—we sheep discover the meaning of our own dark moments of pain, suffering and frustration. Every form of righteous suffering into which every follower of Jesus enters, is a following after Jesus into his death. It is part of our union with Christ in his cross.

There you have it! That's the reason! Our union with Jesus.

While the sufferings of people outside of Christ are merely the prelude to their entry into an eternity of the worst kind of suffering, the follower of Jesus *"carries on his body all day long the death of Jesus, so that the life of Jesus might be revealed through our lives"* (2 Corinthians 4:10). United to Jesus by faith, *"the sufferings of Christ flow over into our lives"* (2 Corinthians 1:5).

Francis Schaeffer commented in TRUE SPIRITUALITY that the Christian life is a pattern of re-doing the stages of Christ's life: serving others...going down to death ...lying in the grave...rising up again...serving others...going down to death...lying in the grave...rising up again...serving others...going down to death... lying in the grave...rising up again...and again...and again...No wonder Paul prayed for himself that he would experience Christian spirituality the way it normally functions: *"That I may know him, the power of his resurrection, and the fellowship of his sufferings, being conformed to His death"* (Philippians 3:10 NAS).

For the Christian there is meaning in suffering. Every time!

Following Christ means taking up your cross

The profound French theologian Calvin, though controversial, was a gentle pastor who loved his people deeply, and felt for them in their harsh experience with life and religious persecution. There was generally much suffering in Europe at that time, and many who belonged to the movement of the Protestants, as did Calvin, suffered additionally under the fury of the Roman Catholic Church. Serious physical ailments, accompanied by horrible pain, sidelined him at times. Then there was the death of his 1-year-old son, Jacob, followed by the sudden death of his wife, Idelette. Life for the Genevan pastor was filled with the realities of insult, opposition, embarrassment, extended family tensions, fatigue and loneliness. Calvin worked himself to the bone, seeking to assist Protestants in prison, counselling multitudes of parishioners, preaching pastoral application from the Bible every day at St. Peter's, plus founding and teaching in a school whose academic reputation became a magnet to children from everywhere.

Maybe it is his own experience with life's deepest sorrows that is the reason he gave great focus to one of Jesus' more poignant sayings about Christian spirituality: *"If anyone wishes to come after Me, let him deny himself, and take up his cross, and follow Me"* (Matthew 16:24 [NAS]).

Whether it is sickness, abuse, poverty, loss or persecution for one's faith, there are reasons why the Holy Spirit baptizes us daily into Christ's crucifixion, by having us carry our own cross in Jesus' name. In his famous work, THE INSTITUTES OF THE CHRISTIAN RELIGION[1], John Calvin lists several reasons. We can learn from him:

1. When you carry a cross, you can personally realize how close God is to you and how strong his arms are under you

We very quickly develop pride in our own abilities. We overestimate ourselves. We become self-sufficient, forgetting that *"our greatest comfort in life and in death is that we are not our own but belong, both body and soul, to our faithful Lord and Saviour Jesus Christ"*[2]. Therefore, God shoulders us with burdens, through which he graciously holds before our eyes how fragile we are. Problems are like a needle in the balloon of our self-sufficiency. They take the air out of the lie that we can be self-made men and women who design our own destiny. Suddenly confronted with our inherent weakness

---

[1] Especially Book 3, section 8.
[2] HEIDELBERG CATECHISM #1.

and our inability to secure for ourselves a life without problems, conflict or illness, we are cast upon the grace of God. Only when we find ourselves in situations that show us our weakness, do we discover how insufficient our own strength is and how sufficient God's grace is (2 Corinthians 12:7).

Calvin saw Simon the Cyrene as an illustration of the Holy Spirit. That's the guy who stood with his sons in the crowd, watching Jesus lug that 2-ton cross and begin to stumble under its weight. In the spur of a compassionate moment, Simon lunged out of the crowd to Jesus, grabbed hold of the sacred wood and put his shoulder under it, giving Jesus needed relief. When we are feeling our fragility under the weight of suffering, the Holy Spirit comes to us as the Heavenly Comforter and helps us carry the load (John 14:16). You do not see his shoulder, nor do you hear his footsteps next to your own. But someday you will look back at that awful time of suffering and will realize that the only reason you were able to come through it is because the Spirit of God was there.

"God is faithful, who will not allow you to be tempted beyond what you are able, but with the temptation will provide the way of escape also, that you may be able to endure it" (1 Corinthians 10:13 NAS).

2. When you carry a cross, you can experience God's faithfulness

When you have been suffering for awhile and have stayed close to God, you come to realize better than if you had never suffered, that God has kept and is keeping all his promises. When you feel forsaken by others you learn that God has not forsaken you, that he has not stopped loving you. Even if you become angry at God and forsake him, even if you accuse Him of having forsaken you in your suffering, the holy character of God remains constant: *"When we are faithless, he remains faithful, for he cannot deny himself"* (2 Timothy 2:13 NAS). And so Jeremiah calls out in the middle of his lamentation, *"Great is Your faithfulness!"* (Lamentations 3:23).

Honestly, this is the only reason why I am still a follower of Jesus: not because I have been consistently faithful—I have been terribly unfaithful numerous times—but he has been consistently faithful to me, in that he has been faithful to his promise to let nothing separate me from his love (Romans 8:38) or snatch me from his loving hold on me (John 10:28).

Pastor Calvin comments that every time you come through a trial with the recognition of how faithful God has been to you, it strengthens your faith and prepares you for the next crisis in your life. The God who has proven himself faithful will always remain faithful at remaining faithful.

3. When you carry a cross, God tests your patience

God tests us to prove the authenticity of our faith. God tested Abraham, the father of our faith, by telling him to sacrifice his son, Isaac, on an altar on Mount Moriah (Genesis 22). Once it was clear that Abraham was willing to go to any lengths to remain faithful and obedient to God, God intervened and would not allow the knife in Abraham's hand to plunge into his son.

The apostle Peter teaches us, *"In this you greatly rejoice, even though now for a little while, if necessary, you have been distressed by various trials, that the proof of your faith, being more precious than gold which is perishable, even though tested by fire, may be found to result in praise and glory and honour at the revelation of Jesus Christ"* (1 Peter 1:6, 7 *NAS*). The pressures of life put the squeeze on us. What comes out shows the substance of what is inside. True and saving faith is a gift from God (Ephesians 2:8), and God has injected into saving faith patience and perseverance. They are ingredients of authentic faith. Only when we are carrying our crosses, does the beauty and reality of God's gracious gift of faith come to full expression.

4. When you carry a cross, you learn to obey God

When you have been turning in one particular direction every day for many years, you need something that will help you develop a new pattern and turn in the opposite direction. Suffering teaches us to give up our old ways and seek God's new direction for us. King David, who throughout his life had to live with the painful consequences of the adultery he committed (he had sex with Bathsheba and when she got pregnant, had her husband murdered and married her to make it all look right), wrote, *"Before I was afflicted*

239

I went astray, but now I keep your Word" (Psalm 119:67 ^{NAS}). If God only ever gave us easy days, only ever gave us what we wanted, only ever held frustrations away from us, we would become lazy, spoiled and presumptuous in our relationship to him, just like a child who always gets from his parents what he demands. It is no surprise, therefore, that God gives us trials which make us more disciplined soldiers in spiritual warfare, and more ready to obey the commands of our Leader. By putting a bridle in our mouth, our Owner transforms us wild horses into useful stallions, who obey by trotting in the direction he wants to steer us. Afflictions are the bridle in our mouth.

5. When you carry a cross, you learn to pray

Most of us are terrible at praying. The root of this is our self-sufficiency, our arrogant belief that in most situations of life we can do something in our own power. When God takes away your crutches of self-reliance by taking away your health or your money or a meaningful person, you are cast upon him alone. Instead of leaning on your flimsy crutches, you now cling to God. You recognize how very much you are dependent on him for everything. You begin to cry to him. You plead with him. Then, when you realize that his strength alone is what is carrying you through the hard time, you begin to thank him. When you see that something sweet is developing through the hard experience you have come through, you begin to praise him for his faithfulness, his sovereignty, his mysterious ways, his love, his salvation. Suddenly you realize: you have developed an intimate relationship with your heavenly Dad in prayer. These moments of deep communion in prayer become so precious to you, that you plan to enter into them even when life is going well. Prayer becomes a way of life.

6. When you carry a cross, you enter into Christ's "suffering for righteousness' sake"

Following after Jesus means turning the hateful deeds done to Jesus onto yourself. In this way, we are deeply united with him. It may be that you are defending God's truth against Satan's lies, or that you are seeking to protect the innocent or stand up for what is right. If in such situations people belittle you, curse or reject you, even threaten to take away your job, your family, your possessions, your freedom or your life, *"consider Him who endured such opposition from sinful men"* (Hebrews 12:3). Jesus told us that when we are persecuted for being his followers, we are *"blessed"* (Matthew 5:10). The blessing lies in this, that we are running on the very same track on which Jesus ran, toward the very same finish line that he crossed victoriously.

If you are "in Christ", then anything that is done against you is done against Christ. It has the opposite effect in heaven as it does on earth. Are you being persecuted in that your possessions are being taken from you? Christ is increasing the real and eternal treasure for you in heaven. Are you being chased from home and family? Christ is preparing a place for you in heaven. Are you being rejected? Your roots of security and belonging are growing deeper into Christ. Are you being physically tortured? The bloody stripes on your body are the marks with which God brands you as his very own sheep (Galatians 6:17).

Some 50 years after Calvin's death in 1564, Richard Sibbes made the same point in his sermon, "The Secret Presence of Christ." The London preacher and scholar pointed out how Jesus, being present with us in every trial, turns every suffering, in the very moment it occurs, into a treasure waiting for us in heaven. Here is how Sibbes put it: *"God's people are gainers by all their losses, stronger by all their weaknesses, and the better for all their crosses, whatsoever they are."*

Martyrdom is not something we seek. But it will in some form or another mark the person who faithfully follows Jesus. Those two young German ladies followed Jesus to Yemen out of love for the Muslims there. When they were ruthlessly shot to death, Jesus received them by placing a victor's crown on their heads (Hebrews 12:2). You couldn't see it because it happened in the other reality, the one that is unseen to earthly eyes but someday will be fully revealed. Then you will also see and receive all that your losses on earth will have gained you for eternity.

7. When you carry a cross,
God is preparing you for an eternity with him

Every person longs for happiness. In searching for it, we allow ourselves to be blinded by the empty glamour of riches, power, and the acknowledgment of others. God knows how quickly we settle for those things. We are easily deceived. Consequently, the Father allows his own children to experience wars and upheavals, theft and poverty, sickness and disease, the disappointment of a difficult spouse, the infliction of hurts by our children, and the death and loss of dearly loved ones. These crosses put this present life into perspective for us. They show us how temporary everything is. The best of goods and possessions in this world are like smoke that blows off into nothingness with the mere shifting of the wind. But who of us would ever be able to tear himself away from the world's offerings, and start for the place where our true citizenship lies, if in this exile in which we are, we experienced nothing but continuous bliss?

Suffering whets our appetite for heaven, where that bliss is to be had.

Years ago, I taught a class in Cuba. Every morning and afternoon, 140 Cubans would gather to study the Bible's teaching about God. Then late afternoons, 3 of us, another Bible teacher, a Cuban lady and I, went to the city's outskirts to visit the poor. That is when I met Ernesto. This 70-year-old man lived with his 40-year-old mentally challenged wife and 12-year-old daughter in a three-room wooden shack with mud flooring. There was one bedroom for all three, consisting of two single mattresses. The only other thing the 12-year-old girl had in the way of furniture was a carton next to her mattress, which she used as her dresser for the few clothes she had. The kitchen had a few sticks in the middle of the room that served for a fire. The bathroom was a bucket that was filled daily from the nearby creek, so that the three could pour water over themselves and take a shower.

Through the translator, I spoke with Ernesto. We talked about life, its hardships and disappointments, about his wife who could not speak, and his daughter who longed for a university education and had no hope of ever getting one. We talked about God, about Jesus who had become Ernesto's Saviour and about the church to which the family walked 7 kilometers every Sunday morning. While we talked, a smile was on Ernesto's worn face. I asked him how he could be happy in the midst of his misery. The old saint pointed to the sky and said, "Very soon it will all change. I am going to go to my real home, because God has promised it to me."

That's a wide-lens perspective*! "Therefore we do not lose heart. Though outwardly we are wasting away...our light and momentary troubles are achieving for us an eternal glory that far outweighs them all. So we fix our eyes not on what is seen, but on what is unseen. For what is seen is temporary, but what is unseen is eternal"* (2 Corinthians 4:16-18).

Suffering teaches us to smart build our lives and to ask smart questions

Remember Bonhoeffer saying that the *Christuswirklichkeit*—the reality that Christ has paid it all, has risen, and is currently Lord over all—is the only reality that really is real? When we suffer, God is taking us deeper into the *Christuswirklichkeit*. In uniting us to the sufferings of Christ, God is showing us things about ourselves, about himself, about this world and about eternity that we otherwise would not learn. Think about the person for whom everything always remains as desired, the person who can keep everything in a box, controlled and predictable. Would not that life be lived superficially?

Calvin's point is that sufferings take us into the challenges of reality. We learn to navigate through the debris of a fallen and ruined world. We even begin to see good things we would have missed if bad things had not happened to us. For example, a number of parents were interviewed recently by a magazine. All of them had been pregnant with special needs children, but although most had been counselled to abort, none did so, and all testified that their child, with all the challenges (even death in early infancy in a few cases), had opened the parents' eyes to beautiful things they otherwise would not have seen.

That is why God does not want us, in the face of suffering, to scream accusingly, "Why, God?" or arrogantly, "Why me, God?" When we react to suffering as if God were being unfair toward us, we blaspheme God by making us out to be his judge, instead of the other way around. We also prevent ourselves from learning lessons God wants us to take from the suffering he places on us. Suffering is a course in the school of discipleship, through which we learn lessons we otherwise would never learn. Instead of "Why me, God?" our inquiry should be, "What, God, do you want to teach me through this?"

- Do you want to teach me how small I am and how great and mighty and powerful you are? (the lesson Job had to learn).

- Do you want to show me that every decision I make and action I take has consequences, and you want me to learn to think twice next time, before doing what led to this painful experience? (the lesson David had to learn).

- Do you want me to learn that no matter how successful I am in what I do and how recognized I become by my peers, I can only do what you enable me to do and only be what you make me to be? (the lesson Elijah had to learn).

- Do you want me to learn to rely on your grace for the strength I need to take the next step? (the lesson Paul had to learn).

- Do you want to break me of my self-righteousness? Do you want me to learn humility and become the meekest person on earth? (the lesson Moses had to learn).

"It is good for me that I was afflicted, that I may learn your statutes" (Psalm 119:71 *NAS*).

Every moment of suffering is the opportunity to ask the right question, in order to grow in wisdom regarding God's ways with us.

Don't run and hide from suffering
Just as there are right ways to look at suffering, there are wrong perspectives and teachings:

- Suffering is not something the Christian seeks for himself. Suffering is not an end in itself. We do not suffer because there is virtue in suffering.

- Suffering is not a reason to develop a "martyr complex" or a "victim mentality." In our attitude, we are not to take on a defeatist mentality, but to live in the triumph of Christ's resurrection and the confidence it gives us for tomorrow.

- Suffering does not add to our salvation, nor is it a means whereby we can win God's favour. Every hermit's self-infliction of pain or monk's denial of pleasure for the sake of gaining the approval of God has had no saving value and is a denunciation of the doctrine of grace.

With these safeguards in place, it is essential to note that no Christian is exempt from the honour of entering into the fellowship of Christ's sufferings. *"For it has been granted to you on behalf of Christ not only to believe on him, but also to suffer for him"* (Philippians 1:29). When you decide to follow after Jesus, you decide to take up a cross daily.

Suffering calls for emotional expression and honesty

Stoicism is the philosophy that denies the reality of pain. It is the religion of pretending. But pretending is not a Christian response to suffering, not if suffering is part of the *Christuswirklichkeit*. Pretending that it does not hurt is pretending to be strong when God wants you to be weak. God created us with emotions, and feelings are the voice of the soul. They tell us what is going on deep within. When our emotions 'talk', we need to listen to them.

Many of us have been taught, directly or indirectly, to silence the voice of the soul. Everything from the parent's rebuke, "Oh, stop crying like a baby!" to a friend's advice to "just grin and bear it," teaches us to deny that we are in pain. Worse yet are the clichés, "It's not going well? Maybe there is sin in your life," or, "Honour your mother and father, so don't you ever criticise me again!" These kinds of statements encourage the person in pain to not admit his pain. They ingrain in us the unchristian idea that it is wrong to get angry, to feel frustrated, to be hurt, to sorrow, to weep.

Consequently, we learn to stuff away our emotions. We have to struggle daily with the drunken parent, the abusive father, the perfectionistic and unbearably strict mother, the unaffectionate and disappointing spouse, the suffocating and legalistic church community, the ridiculing peers, the tragic loss of someone or something special...and always the message sounds: Stuff away your emotions! So you put a stranglehold on your feelings. The pain just lies there, smothered and handcuffed in the corner of the soul, whimpering for you to acknowledge it. But you are afraid to feel pain, afraid to admit pain, afraid to express pain. You have been conditioned to think the pain will hurt you, judge you and destroy you. You try to dampen the pain through alcohol or drugs, shopping binges or overeating, anorexia or bulimia, or gambling, indecisiveness or control-freakishness, promiscuous or abnormal sex, seething bitterness and angry words or violent actions. Then you pass your unhealthy way of handling pain on to your children, who pass it on to their children. It's a downward spiral.

The beauty of our Redeemer is that he stepped into this downward spiral to bring to our whole person the liberation we long for (Romans 8:23). That includes setting free your emotions! Here is how to apply his redemption of your emotions:

- Ask the Holy Spirit to help you move into your emotions and understand what emotions are there (you could begin with praying Psalm 139:23, 24). Name the emotion. As you do so...

- Stop differentiating between positive and negative emotions, as if only positive emotions are godly and negative emotions ungodly. All emotions are valid, because all emotions find their holy and redemptive parallel in God. Both Old and New Testaments testify to the fact that God feels wrath and anger, joy and laughter, love and compassion, regret and sorrow and jealousy and hatred. Learn to see ALL emotions as having a godly origin (before the fall twisted them into self-centred, self-serving emotions). All are part of our original created selves.

Look at Jesus! Gentle, mild and patient, he angrily calls the self-righteous Pharisees by some very harsh names (Matthew 23). Then he manhandles the money changers out of the temple, hurling the tables and religious ornaments through the air behind them (John 2). Do you remember your Master in the Garden of

Gethsemane, how his soul was in the absolute deepest agony over the cross he was about to carry? Calvin says, *"If we condemn emotional expressions of sorrow or anger, hurt or frustration, what shall we do with the reports of the gospels, that our own Lord's body trembled, as he threw himself on the ground, wept before the Father at the sight of the cross, and wet the ground with his bloody sweat drops. He was in such agony! We are not called to be rocks that cannot be moved, but souls that follow Jesus into the tears of sadness, insult, rejection, pain, and abuse"*.[3]

So: freely and safely acknowledge every emotion you feel!

- Now analyze the elements that surround your emotion. Ask yourself what gave rise to this emotion. Ask yourself what in your past is associated with this emotion. What does the emotion tell you that you believe in? Does that emotion speak about justice, because injustice was done? Does that emotion speak about faithfulness, because betrayal toward you was committed? Does it speak about dignity, because someone was devalued or treated like an object?

- Take your emotion before God in prayer. Tell him your emotion and why you feel the way you do.

- Now do the God-centred thing: Look at the same emotion in God, be it compassion, hate, jealousy, regret, joy or sorrow. Compare—what kinds of things would give cause for the emotion in God's case, and how does that compare with what gave rise to the same emotion in your case? Are you angry for the same reason God gets angry? Are you rejoicing over something God would rejoice about? Are you weeping over the same kinds of things Jesus wept about? Do you feel hurt for the same reason God would feel insulted?

- Ask God to help you align your emotions with his emotions.

If God would have reacted differently than you did, ask God to forgive you for your selfish reaction. Ask him for help to express your feelings as he does.

If God would have reacted the same as you did, give vent to that emotion in a manner that is constructive to others, that is forgiving

---

[3] INSTITUTES, III.8.9.

toward the wrong-doer, and that exhibits the fruit of the Spirit. In this way, even your emotions—as a very important part of your being—become Christ-like.

Is there really a reason for carrying a cross?

In February 2007, an email arrived from our colleague, whose son had been deprived of oxygen at birth: *"Yesterday we brought our baby home. Finally, after 8 weeks in the hospital, we can begin to live a relatively 'normal' life...We continue to pray for healing, and trust God for what he will bring our way. We love our son, and are very blessed to have him as our son. This little guy has created so much joy for us, and in this short time we have learned more through this extraordinary trial than we could have in an entire life of ordinary happenings. God is so good."*

Honestly, I still do not understand why Joe Pinzka suffered so severely from cancer and died so young. Many of us were horrified. Joe's wife, Karen, was deeply distraught. However, the way Karen's grieving church community came around her and cared for her little daughter became a testimony to many in our town of the power of God's love. Then tall and handsome Donn decided that Karen and her baby needed some "special attention." The wedding that followed, a new dad for a kid who needed cuddling, the additional two children, the happy home life...all gave evidence that life with God has some painful seasons followed by times of great blessings, that carrying your cross leads to a resurrection of sorts, that weeping may last for the night, but joy comes in the morning. That is much better than going through painful seasons without God or hope!

It has been decades since Joni Eareckson Tada had the terrible diving accident that left her a quadriplegic. Her well-documented life has included seasons of wrestling with God. Recently she acknowledged in a book that things are not getting easier but harder for her, as her bones are beginning to crumble under the weight of quadriplegia for so many years, and cancer has added to her bodily woes. But she is keeping her focus on Jesus. In this way, her ministry to handicapped children, called Joni & Friends, and her multitudinous talks, seminars and books, have brought to a battered and bruised world of hurting people hope and comfort and love for God whose plan A for our lives, as Joni recently wrote, is always "good and loving."

Many years ago, Joni released an album of songs. The music expressed her emotion about living life in a wheelchair, with no part of her body able to move except her mouth and eyes. One song moved me so deeply in 1987 that I wrote down the words. I am glad I did and that I can share them with you now:

Joni's Waltz

"Though I spend my mortal lifetime in this chair,
I refuse to waste it living in despair,
And though others may receive gifts of healing,
I believe that he has given me a gift beyond compare:

For heaven is nearer to me, And at times it is all I can see
Sweet music I hear coming down to my ear,
And I know that it's playing for me.
For I am Christ the Saviour's own bride,
And redeemed I shall stand by His side.
He will say 'shall we dance', And our endless romance
Will be worth all the tears I have cried.

I rejoice with him whose pain my Saviour heals,
And I weep with him who still his anguish feels,
Earthly joy and earthly tears are confined to earthly years,
But a greater good the word of God reveals

For heaven is nearer to me…
In this life I have a cross that I must bear, A tiny part of Jesus' death I
can share,

When some day I lay it down, He has promised me a crown
To which my suffering can never compare.

For heaven is nearer to me…"

There are a lot of unanswered questions and plenty of mystery in our sufferings. But one thing is crystal clear: Every form of righteous suffering into which a follower of Jesus walks like a sheep, bleating in frustration and about to be slaughtered, is a following after Jesus into his death. It is part of our union with Christ, an aspect of our being identified with our Saviour, the Suffering Servant. We go through every cross down into a grave and back up to a resurrection...through a cross down into a grave and back up to a resurrection...through a cross down into a grave and back up to a resurrection...through a cross...

...until the final resurrection, and then it is all glory forever.

1.Memorize Matthew 16:24 and 2 Corinthians 4:10-11.

2. Is God's way with his children harsh? Sometimes it definitely feels that way. Read and meditate on Job 27:2; Psalm 38:1-3.

3. Read Psalm 66:8-12 and 68:18-20. What do you think, is the distinction many people make between God giving us bad experiences and God allowing (permitting) bad experiences a correct or false one?

4. In this chapter the basic premise we pursued was that Jesus is the reason his followers enter into (his) sufferings.

- **Read Psalm 69.** What indications in this Psalm are there, that king David's expressions of suffering are somehow tied in with the suffering Jesus underwent for us (and David)?

- **Read Acts 9:1-5.** How is the connection between the persecution of Jesus' followers and the persecution of (the ascended) Jesus expressed?

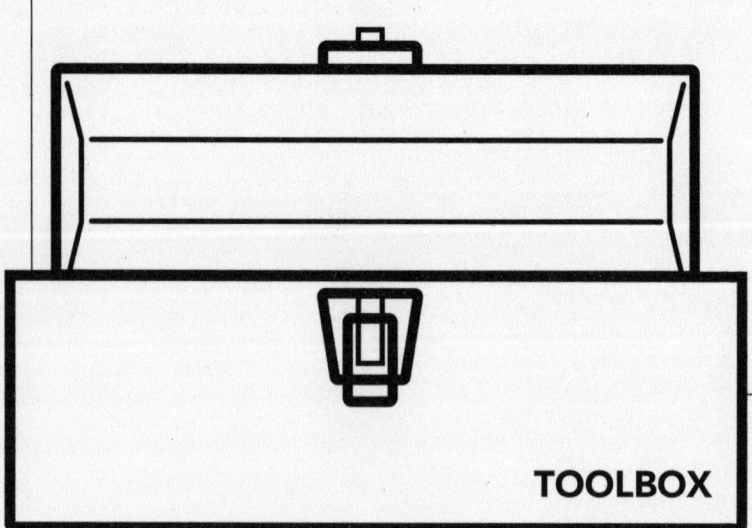

TOOLBOX

5. Meditate on Hebrews 4:14-16

6. Our own suffering prepares us for effective ministry: 2 Corinthians 1:3, 4. How?

7. For more reading:

- Nancy Guthrie, ed., Be Still My Soul: Embracing God's Purpose and Provision in Suffering. Wheaton, Illinois: Crossway, 2010. I highly recommend the book I referred to above as containing Joni Eareckson Tada's perspective, in that it also contains brief chapters on the topic of suffering by some of the most noteworthy authors in the history of Christian spirituality.

- Randy Alcorn, If God is Good: Faith in the Midst of Suffering and Evil. Portland, OR: Multnomah, 2009. Alcorn asks the questions many ask about God and suffering: Is God a sadist? Does the problem of evil and suffering really disprove the existence of God? Alcorn argues, that what we may have, is God already restraining 99% of evil and suffering that could happen and would happen if there were no good and sovereign God. If God were to eliminate any one evil, the result might be worse. Maybe the child's disability leads him and his parents to become servant-hearted rather than self-absorbed. I.e. pointless suffering may have a point we don't see. Example: abortion pandemic. Apparently useless, it does reveal the breadth of human selfishness and people have come to Christ because of aborting their baby. Alcorn writes: "It is all speculation. We will never know, at least in this life, why so many have died so young. At some point we need to return to two basics: the Old Testament teaching in Job and other books that God is much wiser than us, and the New Testament teaching that God did not watch from a distance but took on extreme suffering Himself two millennia ago.

SECTION 4

We are here to change the world

In the building project the roof is the last and final thing to go onto a new house. Years later, the roof is still there, that is, if a tornado has not blown it off.

When you sit in an airplane and—minutes before landing—look down directly below you, it is the roofs of homes which are most visible to you. In the same way, God looks down onto the spiritual house of your life. Your roof indicates to him, that your spiritual house has been built properly and to completion. In this final section it is time to build the roof onto your house.

Jesus stated that all the principles of spirituality and all the directives of godly living can be summarized by the way you orient your life in two directions: First, to love God with all your heart; secondly to love the next person with a need as much as you already love yourself.

These two sides of the same love-affair translate into a two-sided roof on your spiritual house. One side—the 'love your neighbor as yourself' side—is the Spirit's call to be missional, to be outward-looking, to be other-engaging. This is the side that says: Christian spirituality is incomplete until you bring the personal richness of Christ in you into the public arena of others. The other roof side—the 'love the Lord your God with all your heart' side—is the Spirit's motivating work in you, to direct every action to the honour and glory of your God and not yourself. This is the side that takes everything he has given you, produced in you, and enabled you to do, and carries it back to him with a smiling 'thank you'.

Have you noticed that every chapter in this book ends with what I like to call the "postmodern question", 'what's in it for me?' In this final section of the book we come to the amazing truth about that question: A God-centred spirituality in a Me-centred world is about a God taking the Me seriously. God, our creator and designer, takes our desires and longings seriously because he knows that the fulfillment of them lies in himself. When we build our spiritual house according to God's blue print, we build a roof that is oriented outward toward others (being missional) and upward toward God (glorifying God). No spiritual life is complete in design without this two-sided roof.

You will read why this roof—pointing to others and to God—ends up fulfilling yourself.

It will even endure and outlive all the storms and tornadoes that blow on it, precisely because it is not Me-centred.

12
The Ceiling
Doing the Mission of the Smart Builder God

The practice of a public spirituality

I walked into Starbucks for a late-afternoon jump start to my drained battery. As the young lady behind the counter asked how she might help me, I was totally oblivious to the clothes I had on.

"A tall Caramel Macchiato, please."

"So how are you going to change the world?" the lady with a long blond ponytail on the other side of the counter asked, while her eyes were glued to the cash register.

I was taken off-guard by her question, and for a second my brain went into overdrive, trying to figure out what she might mean. Then my head popped downward and I saw the white writing on my blue T-shirt. I had been given this shirt as an honorarium a few years earlier by one of the Christian campus organizations, for whom I frequently spoke at the University of Toronto.

"Oh, this...yeah...well, hmmm, I would like to change the world by letting as many people as possible know that in 33 AD, something happened that completely changed the world forever and changes it for each one of us today: the resurrection of Jesus. Like, if he really resurrected from the dead three days after he died on the cross, then he really is God and powerful and able to change anything in our lives that has died."

As I paid for my coffee, I asked in return, "So how are you going to change the world?"

Quick as lightning the lady responded with a smile, "I am going to change the world by serving coffee to people who are changing the world!"

I am sure that the Starbucks lady felt she wasn't in an ethical position to have a conversation about spirituality with me. She was being paid to serve people coffee, and there were other customers and co-workers standing around. Religion is not something a secular society deems publically discussable, and people with messages on their shirts like the one I had can be considered fanatical and dangerous to the public equilibrium.

But the reality is: we *are* here to change the world! The Latin words *missio Dei* were coined in 1952 at a world missions conference in Willingen, Germany. They mean 'the mission of God.' The intent of these words was to set a certain fuzzy and sometimes misrepresented reality into the clearest of lights: History, all of history, and every aspect of history, is His-story. It is God's story of seeking, saving, and rebuilding a creation that is lost and in ruins. That means that missions is not—or certainly should not be—an arrogant and imperialistic forcing of one's ideas and way of life on another culture. Instead, it is God—out of grace and in his holy love—pursuing people's hearts in the many various cultures he created, appreciates, respects and preserves.

You will notice that I said "rebuilding a *creation* that is lost and in ruins". The *missio Dei* cannot be confined to evangelizing the souls of men and women. It goes much further. Missio Dei has to do with all that has fallen under the curse of sin and groans for its liberation (Romans 8:22, 23). God is on a grace-crusade to liberate every aspect of creation, to engage with, even fight for Paradise Lost until it has fully become Paradise Regained. Everything that is still undergoing decay, whether men, women and children; masculinity and femininity; nations and races; the environment in all of its many facets; world economies; social issues, politics; education; medicine–, God has it all in view.

Missio Dei: God is on a mission to change the world

Hebrews 3:1-6 describes God's mission in the picture we painted at the outset of this book: He is building himself a house. Strictly speaking, the house of God is not bricks and mortar with a steeple on top, but a household, a family. To the Jewish recipients of the letter to the Hebrews, this would not be a new concept. Already in Numbers 12:6 in the Old Testament, we see Israel presented as the household of God. But with the New Testament house, God is building something even better, something much bigger and far more international. It is an enormous house, spanning the globe, filled with a tremendous diversity of people, a great variety of styles and the many languages, dialects and skin colours of the world. It is the unity of nations that the United Nations has wanted to create for years. Since God dwells in this house and this house is part of his story, it is the house that celebrates Jesus as its true Lord, orients itself to his Word, unites itself around his cross and experiences ongoing transformation through his Holy Spirit and his resurrection power.

The New Testament defines this household as a big family. There are 'brothers' and 'sisters,' the older people are called 'fathers' and 'mothers,' and when they usher people into this household of faith, those new entries are called 'sons' or 'daughters' of the 'fathers' and the 'mothers' who ushered them in. I have been in this family long enough that I am a 'brother' to many and a 'father' to a few. Like any family, including my own in which my older sister called me 'stupid' when I sat on a rock with a loaf of bread, there are spats in the family of God that have to be worked through and resolved. But we are a family. To many people, it is the only family they have.

Sandy Scott is a friend of mine. Susan and I were part of a home fellowship group that met regularly in Sandy and Melody Scott's condo in downtown Toronto. It was a wonderful group of people; some of us were very new to Christian spirituality, others of us long-time adherents. Two members of the group lived in a bad neighbourhood of the city in the simplicity of lifestyle that bordered on poverty. One woman was terribly sick with a life-threatening tumour on her spinal cord. One man could not see straight. Some of us were white, a few were brown and some were somewhere between white and brown. We met every Sunday evening for potluck supper, worship, laughter, serious Bible study and prayer for our city and one another. I was the pastor of the church, but Sandy was the pastor of this home fellowship group.

I will never forget a speech Sandy gave one evening. It was a spontaneous expression Sandy made at the end of yet another wonderful and harmonious evening. As usual, Sandy expressed his heart in tears. Here is how I remember it:

"Before you all go, Melody and I want to tell you how very important each one of you is to us. I am—what many would call—a loser. I was educated by one of the best universities in North America, had a decent marriage and family and a great career ahead of me, but as you all know, I became an alcoholic and lost everything. For years I lived and slept along the railroad tracks. My wife understandably divorced me, my children were embarrassed by me, and all of them hated me. I was a homeless man for so long and so completely lost in a world of booze, mindlessness and unconsciousness, that all connections to my family were severed. Some years ago God met me in a deep and profound way. Through a man, who sought me out at the railroad tracks, God overwhelmed me with his irresistible grace. He pulled me from my grave. Like a miracle he healed me from my addiction. He led me to Melody, who was equally broken from an abusive relationship. God brought us into a deep and personal relationship with Jesus and with each other. Maybe you have noticed that we can hardly keep our hands off of each other. We are at the age of 60 enjoying a passionate marriage, and that is the reason why by 9:30 tonight you will all have left our condo. But the truth is, I basically have no family. My ex-wife is remarried and wants nothing to do with me. My children think of me as an embarrassing moment in their lives, and ever since they heard that I am passionately in love with Jesus, they think of me as more than an embarrassment—they think of me as a fundamentalist idiot. I have no family. So here is what I want to say:

You are my family. You are my sons and daughters, my brothers and sisters. When we eat, talk and laugh together Sunday evenings, I think, 'This is like the happy meal time a Christian dad loves to have with his kids.' When we pray for each other I think, 'This is like kneeling with your sons and daughters at their beds and praying together before they go to sleep.' When we sit and discuss the harsh realities of our lives, like Joe's poverty or Martha's tumour, my heart leaps with the thrill that I—like a dad—am privileged to discuss in honesty and vulnerability with my children, how God would lead us and heal us and change us through our circumstances.

You are my family. You are the only family I have, and you are the best family I could have asked for, because we are so real and authentic with each other. When we are finished being family on this side of eternity, our family life together will go on and expand vastly on the other *side of eternity. I am absolutely thrilled and deeply thankful to God for you, my dear family."*

The guy who couldn't see straight had tears rolling down his cheeks, identifying with much in Sandy's story. We were all deeply touched by the reminder that our home fellowship group functioned as a 'home' to Melody and Sandy. Melody led us in a prayer of thanks to Jesus for this mystical expression of grace and truth he was building in the middle of urban skyscrapers. In fact, Jesus is the whole reason this family even exists and continues to be built. Hebrews 3:1 calls Jesus God's "apostle" and "high priest": *"Holy brothers, who share in the heavenly calling, fix your thoughts on Jesus, the apostle and high priest whom we confess."* The word *"apostle"* means "sent out", similar to the meaning of our word 'missionary'. Before there were Jesus' 12 apostles, and then a wider body of so-called 'apostles' (Romans 16:7), there was God's one great Apostle.

Let's look at a few important aspects of Jesus' apostleship:

Jesus was APPOINTED to be God's Apostle to us

Hebrews 3:2 describes him as having been *"appointed"* by God. This appointment takes us back into eternity past. There is a hint of this in Hebrews 2:11-13, but other passages in the Bible refer to an agreement between Father and Son as well, such as Psalm 2—to where a covenant of redemption is made within the Trinity. What was this unbreakable commitment they made to each other? It was that the Father would send the Son (John 8:16, 18)—as Jesus would describe it—to *"do the work of Him who sent me"* (John 9:4). This is crucial for understanding the *missio Dei*: Jesus' work was intricately and inseparably tied to the Father. He did not come with his own agenda. His task was to mirror the ongoing work of God. Jesus imaged on earth the very thing the Father was doing in the heavenlies. His words, while his own, were the words the Father was speaking at the same moment. His deeds, though completely the result of his movements, were the actions of the Father. His life and character was the exact replica of the Father's, so that if you wanted to know who God is, what he is like and how he functions you can look to Jesus and find it there (see John 14:7-11). Jesus carried out in the visible, earthly realm what the Father was securing and sealing forever in the heavenly realm.

Jesus TESTIFIED about God as God's Apostle to us

Jesus referred to his mission as "testifying" or "giving witness" to the work of the Father (e.g., John 3:11). He specifically said on numerous occasions, that his purpose was not to ultimately direct people to himself but to be the Father's revelation to us (cf. John 1:1, 14). Not only did his words echo truth and grace (John 1:17) as found in the Father, not only did his works point to the sovereignty, power and mercy of the Father, but his character of integrity, compassion and joy revealed the holiness, love and pleasures of the Father. To that end, Jesus was anointed and empowered by the Holy Spirit to enter into the work the Father had sent him to do.

Jesus OFFERED HIMSELF as God's Apostle for us

This aspect of his apostleship is described in Hebrews 3:1 with the second designation of Jesus: "high priest." The Old Testament understanding of a priest was someone who stood before God on behalf of the people and prayed for them. Even more—and I think this is the emphasis in Hebrews—he brought a sacrifice to God. A Hebrew high priest would slay a lamb, lay it on the altar and offer it up to God as a sin-offering, praying for the forgiveness of the nation's sins, and sprinkling the blood on the people standing by.

This is how Jesus accomplished his apostolic mission. As our priest he made a sacrifice of a perfect lamb to God, crying out, "Forgive them!" But the startling thing about Jesus was that he, the priest, carried *himself* as a lamb to the altar. He offered up himself, sprinkling his people with the blood that cleanses us from all unrighteousness.

God is on a mission! He sent Jesus as a priestly apostle into the world in order to build himself a beautiful house. Hebrews 3:6 celebrates this grand building project of God: *"And we are God's house, if we keep our courage and remain confident in our hope in Christ."*(NLT)

Missio Dei: We are partnering with God to change the world

Jesus is the head of the house which we are. As his life blood mystically flows from his headship to us, we, the occupants of the house, *"share in the heavenly calling"* (Hebrews 3:1). This is not an invitation to participate in the mission of God; it is an announcement that, as a matter of fact, we do. It is not an option given to those who follow Jesus and confess his name; it is the reality into which confessors of Jesus have been transferred. We see this specifically in that the very things that are said of Jesus' apostleship are said of ours. Due to our union with Jesus, his apostleship is shared with us and carried out by us.

You are APPOINTED to be God's apostle to the world

Like Jesus was the 'appointed' one of God (Hebrews 3:2), so God's children are referred to in the Bible as 'appointed' or 'elect' or 'called out.' We need to be careful and discerning at this juncture: being 'the called out ones' or 'the elect' does not make Christians the elite, nor does it mean some kind of removal from the world. It means we have been taken out of the world, fused into Jesus and sent back into the world to impact the world with the character, words and deeds of Jesus. Along these lines, a significant missiologist of the 20th century, Leslie Newbiggin, made the radical claim that mission has at its core the doctrine of election. This may startle you at first, but read what one of Newbiggin's students wrote in a magazine about his professor's understanding:

"I discovered that his entire missiology revolved around that idea. God's people are elected to join in God's mission to call others to God in keeping with the Abrahamic calling, 'blessed to be a blessing.' There is therefore a dual purpose: God wants to reconcile people to himself, but also to reconcile people to each other. The election of individuals cannot be separated from God's election of the church: we are elected to be God's missionary people. The church is, by its very nature, missional.

This has two major implications. First, the church, not the individual, is the basic unit of evangelism. A community that lives out the truth of the gospel is the best context in which to understand its proclamation... Second, the unity of the church matters to the mission of the church. Disunity undercuts the gospel of reconciliation that we claim to bring to the world... Whatever we need to do to help this generation to hear the gospel (John 8:16, 18), we need to do it together.

As Newbiggin wrote, 'I have been called and commissioned, through no merit of mine, to carry this message, to tell this story, to give this in-

vitation. It is not my story or my invitation. It has no coercive intent. It is an invitation from the one who loved you and gave himself up for you. That invitation will come with winsomeness if it comes from a community in which the grace of the Redeemer is at work.'[1]

The force of this is staggering. Let's consider several implications:

1. You are an apostle of God

If you have decided to be a follower of Jesus, you have no choice but to be a missionary.

This explains why Scripture not only describes Jesus, the appointed (elect) One, as God's mission-partner, but every follower of Jesus, as well. 1 Corinthians 3:9 calls us *'co-workers with God'*, who are being built into *'God's building.'* That means we are not only the object of God's mission, but we are simultaneously building partners with God in his home-expansion project. Just as Jesus did not come with his own agenda, neither do we carry out our own. We carry out his, mirroring—as Jesus did—God's character, words, and works wherever we are.

For that reason, we are identified as 'witnesses' of our Lord. Jesus said, *"You will receive power when the Holy Spirit has come upon you, and you will be my witnesses"* (Acts 1:8 *NLT*). Again, to witness of Christ is not an option for a follower of Jesus. It is our calling! It is our identity! Clear and simple! For this reason Jesus said. *"Whoever acknowledges me before men, I will also acknowledge him before my Father in heaven. 33 But whoever disowns me before men, I will disown him before my Father in heaven."* (Matthew 10:32, 33).

2. The unity of the household community matters

There are many who decry denominations. To be sure, I, too, am discouraged with denominations that have come about by church splits or hot-headed behaviour. But all in all, I think denominations are a good thing. They are—simply put—the manifold expressions by which this world-wide house of God seeks to stress the many sides of truth. If it takes four gospel accounts to stress the various sides of Jesus, why not many denominations to stress the multitudinous aspects of God?

---

[1] Krish Kandiah, in CHRISTIANITY TODAY, January 2010, p. 47.

What we desire is an end to the divisive spirit of denomination-alism! Otherwise, our apostolic witness of Jesus will continue to suffer badly.

Allow me to take the situation of the German church as an example of what shows the need for reformation within Christian spirituality everywhere. In Germany, as in other countries, we have various histories of 'various churches'. We have the history of the state church—both Protestant and Catholic—with its gradual decline since the late 19th century. There is a certain arrogance with which many pastors in the German state church operate, namely the attitude that the true church of Germany is the state church, and that all other expressions of church outside the German state church are of lesser quality or even illegitimate. Meanwhile, the free churches of Germany, with their own history, exhibit a similar arrogance, and for the most part have sought to distance themselves from anything liturgical that would remind one of the state church.

I know that similar sparring between church bodies goes on in other countries, as well. But I would ask the question: Is it possible that in God's mind there are many forms of church and worship, ALL of which are valid applications of biblical ecclesiology? If so, we are instructed in Scripture not to draw bold lines between the one and the other, while declaring our particular version of church as the one closest to the truth. Instead, we are called to enjoy our denomination's tradition and emphasis while being respectful and grateful for all other 'expressions of church.' More, we should join with other expressions in cooperative ministries that bless the city. Yet more, we should point people who wish to enter the household God is building to an expression of church we think will best fit their point of development, instead of unthinkingly bringing them to our own. And by all means, we should be praying for each other, Free Churches asking God to bless state churches that are holding true to his Word, state churches requesting of God to bless the city through the local free churches.

Such a show of unity is a vibrant *apostolic witness* before the unchurched world to the Trinity of God (John 17:20-23). When the world sees such diverse forms of worship yet one world-wide church, and such diversity of people, races, styles, emphases and historical traditions, but one unified household God, it can start to make sense of the Trinity, which is a diversity of three Persons in one Godhead.

Unity is the strategy the builder of the house had in mind for his missio Dei.

"And we are his house!" (Hebrews 3:6)

3. Only churches that are gospel-driven can fulfil the apostolic mandate

Those steeped in a legalistic sub-culture and a fundamentalist attitude may look good to their self-righteousness, but they are no good to the world. Quite the opposite!

Winsomeness toward the world does not come by compromise or accommodation. It arises out of a gospel-driven spirituality in the heart, which in brokenness recognizes that...

In and of myself I am more sinful
than I ever dared to believe,
but
in Christ I am more loved and accepted
than I ever dared to hope.

Gospel-driven churches will not see the lost and pagan person as a threat to the church's holiness, but will find a reflection of the sins of the lost and pagan person in his own heart. Church members will not see themselves as better than the lost and pagan people "out there", but as privileged to be *"sharers in the heavenly calling"* (Hebrews 3:1), honoured by the presence of non-Christians and welcoming toward all who wish to search out the unfathomable riches of Jesus. After all, it is only by grace that the Christian's poverty-stricken soul has received a filling of the Christ-treasure himself.

As the church engages with the unchurched in grace and love, while holding on to holiness and truth, it is fulfilling its mission to the world. Churches that are not gospel-driven need to stop playing church, because they have stopped participating with God in his mission, the *missio Dei.*

4. The church is by nature missional

One of the phrases of Bonhoeffer that has stuck with us is "Kirche für andere,"[2] the church for others. The point this 20th century church reformer was making bears even more weight when we remember that he was making the point while many in the church had capitulated to the Nazi pressure of its time and were turning a blind eye to the abuses and persecution heaped on people, instead of protecting them. Bonhoeffer actually found the inspiration for being the "church for others" in a late 19th century German theologian. He furthered the point by underlining that Jesus had come for 'others,' that he was for 'others.' He was, in fact, for everyone who felt a need for God out of recognition of his own spiritual bankruptcy.

That could be—and was—the poor and the rich, the housewife and the prostitute, the business man who uses the prostitute, the upstanding citizen and the convicted pervert, the alcoholic and the non-drinker, the homeless and the man who has two homes and a butler, and the soldier and the pacifist. The one group of people for whom Jesus had no time was the Pharisees who saw themselves as 'having arrived' spiritually, as spiritually healthy and as good enough for God. Jesus was not for such, he was 'for others.' The church that follows its Lord Jesus, is present for 'others' ("Für-andere-Dasein"). It is, therefore, by nature outward-looking. In representing the Jesus-for-others, it becomes the 'the church for others.' It becomes missional! It fulfils its biblical mandate, whether Old Testament or New, to take care of the poor, the orphans and the widows in distress, because *"this is pure and undefiled religion"* (James 1:27). The church is called to *"do good to all"* (Galatians 2:10).

This should not imply that the apostolic role of the church is merely doing good to society. The church, in fact, is called to evangelism and social responsibility without prioritizing the one over the other or dichotomizing between one and the other. We are missional in word-and-deed, in character, verbal testimony, and actions of justice and service. Bonhoeffer's warning to the church of his time and of ours was that if we turn our congregations into a

---

[2] Eberhard Bethge, „Was heißt Kirche für andere?" In PTH 58, 1969, pp. 94-105.

"huddle of the comfortable" instead of the church for others, we have ceased to be the church of Jesus Christ.

Missio Dei: We are priestly apostles who change the world

A new word has been coined in the past several decades, and I have made reference to it already: "missional". It emphasises the teaching of Christian spirituality, that neither select people nor especially spiritual people are called as missionaries, but that every follower of Jesus is called by God to be a missionary; and we are not merely called to be missionaries to a distant land—though such a calling may well come to anyone of us from God—but we are for sure called to be missionaries to our immediate surroundings. Wherever God has us living and breathing, we are his priestly apostles there with the mandate to change the world. Let us stress the point again, that God has not made being missional an option. Every follower of Jesus and every local church is, by nature a missional priestly apostle.

This has monumental implications for living out Christian spirituality in a pluralistic, secular culture.

The first is this: Christian spirituality is not a privatized religion. Instead, it must be, by its very nature, a personal spirituality gone public. Let's take up a matter that was already introduced in chapter 6. Since the Enlightenment, we have been differentiating between secular and sacred. Following Kant, we have placed in the so-called lower storey, "objective facts", things of the "public square", things that are to be taught in our schools, that are deemed scientific and empirically verifiable and need no "I believe" as a preface. In the upper storey, we have placed subjective values and beliefs of the private world of ethics and religion.

But thinkers like Francis Schaeffer, Leslie Newbiggin, Cornelius van Til, Dietrich Bonhoeffer and a host of others have exhorted us to challenge the 2-storey thinking as a wrong world-view. It is irrational and a false compartmentalization. Bonhoeffer's meditations in prison, that would end up becoming the manuscript for his ETHICS, sounded like this: *"All things appear as in a distorted mirror if they are not seen and recognized in God."*[3] God is not merely

---

[3]   Metaxas, p. 469.

a religious reality or religious concept. God invented reality, and reality can only be seen truly as it exists in God. Nothing exists outside his realm. Sound strange? The apostle Paul said the same thing to the agnostic philosophers of Athens: *"it is in him that we live and move and have our being"* (Acts 20:28).

Bonhoeffer goes on: *"In Jesus Christ the reality of God has entered into the reality of this world. The place where the questions about the reality of God and about the reality of the world are answered at the same time is characterized solely by the name: Jesus Christ (remember Bonhoeffer's concept of Christuswirklichkeit?). God and the world are enclosed in this name...we cannot speak rightly of either God or the world without speaking of Jesus Christ. All concepts of reality that ignore Jesus Christ are abstractions."*[4]

Excuse me, did a bomb just drop on your world view? Bonhoeffer is saying that the world and Jesus Christ are not two realms that bump up against each other. Instead, the world can only understand itself if it is sees itself in relation to Christ. Any different way of viewing its world is heinous rebellion and complete distortion. But God, in his missional grace, is *"bringing all things in heaven and on earth together under one head, even Christ"* (Ephesians 1:10). On the basis of this one and only reality, the so-called *Christuswirklichkeit*, Bonhoeffer called the Christian to a "this-worldliness." Not allowing for the distinction between sacred and secular, he wrote:

"The Christian is not a homo religiosus, but simply a man...I am still discovering right up to this moment, that it is only by living completely in this world that one learns to have faith... By this-worldliness I mean living unreservedly in life's duties, problems, successes and failures, experiences and perplexities. In so doing we throw ourselves completely into the arms of God, taking seriously not our own sufferings, but those of God in the world – watching with Christ in Gethsemane."[5]

I think with 'this-worldliness' Bonhoeffer was trying to catch Jesus' mandate to not be of the world (we are born of God) but in the world (we are ambassadors of God). The church needs to humbly, yet boldly, enter the public sphere with a persuasive retelling of the Christian story. The public sphere is part of the only reality that exists. It is also where God exists. In fact, it cannot exist outside

---

[4] Ibid.
[5] Letter to Bethge, July 21, 1944. Quoted from Metaxas, p. 484.

of God, though it is in rebellion against God. In this one reality is also where the church *is.* In reality she has never been anywhere else. The moment the church thinks she is on the fringe or removed, or pretends she should have nothing to do with the culture in which she dwells, she is disobedient and following the voice of our Enemy, the devil, instead of the voice of her true shepherd.

Since the only reality is God's reality in Christ, our persuasive retelling is not merely telling God's story as a spiritual option we have chosen, but as public truth. Just as a scientist does not present his findings as a personal preference, but as something that merits universal agreement, we present God's story as he revealed it in and through Jesus Christ. Its public and historical truthfulness is confirmed by the resurrection. We do not speak of it as a personal preference, but as truth that should gain universal acceptance. We commend the faith once given and passed on, with the humble admission that we might not have exhaustively grasped the truth, but that we have truth that needs to be investigated and seriously engaged.

The second radical implication is this: As witnesses to the truth of God in Jesus, the crucified and risen Lord of all, we must learn to take on suffering as part of our daily experience. We must write over our personal lives: *"What cost God everything, cannot be cheap for us...*

"...Cheap grace is the grace we bestow on ourselves. Cheap grace is the preaching without requiring repentance, baptism without church discipline, Communion without confession. Costly grace is the treasure hidden in the field; for the sake of it a man will gladly go and sell all that he has. It is the pearl of great price to buy for which the merchant will sell all his goods. It is the kingly rule of Christ, for whose sake a man will pluck out the eye which causes him to stumble...Such grace is costly because it calls us to follow, and it is grace because it calls us to follow Jesus Christ. It is costly because it cost a man his life, and it is grace because it gives a man the only true life. It is costly because it condemns sin, and grace because it justifies the sinner. Above all, it is costly because it cost God the life of his Son: 'you were bought at a price,'

and what has cost God much cannot be cheap for us...Costly grace is the incarnation of God."[6]

All of God's people—every single one of us—are called to 'incarnate the gospel' through our lives. This means all of us, no matter where we live, are called into persecution and suffering. In countries where the church of Jesus is growing fast or is under tremendous pressure from the state or other religions, followers of Jesus are experiencing ridicule and oppression or expulsion from their families or are being brutally assaulted and killed for their faith. But in the West, and under the subtle sway of secularism, a rich part of Christian spirituality has been lost in the privatization of faith and the silence of God's 'apostles'. We have moved into a survival mode, thinking that it is an option for us to believe the Christian faith without people around us knowing we are followers of Jesus. And many of us 'Christians' have swallowed unthinkingly the western consumer-mentality so deeply into ourselves—the mentality of always 'needing' to have a little more, a little better, a little faster with as little discomfort as possible—that we think it normal to approach the church community as one who owes us the satiation of our needs and wants.

This kind of Christian spirituality is impossible! It is *cheap grace, and what cost God everything cannot be cheap for us.* In the book of Revelation such spirituality is described as making Jesus so nauseated, he vomits us out. Instead, biblical descriptions of Christian spirituality sound like this:

"Trouble or hardship or persecution or famine or nakedness or danger...For your sake we face death all day long" (Romans 8:35, 36). "For Christ's sake I delight in weaknesses, in insults, in hardships, in persecutions, in difficulties. For when I am weak then I am strong" (2 Corinthians 12:10 *TNIV*).

The challenge of Christian spirituality is for followers of Jesus to take up the cross of public and priestly apostleship. The cost of our discipleship, work and ministry may translate into mental fatigue, physical exhaustion, economic duress, emotional stress, deep bouts of discouragement, personal sacrifice for others, sudden interruptions, opposition and criticism (sometimes even from your family).

---

[6] Dietrich Bonhoeffer, THE COST OF DISCIPLESHIP, New York: Macmillan Publishing, 1977, p. 46.

It may mean having to take a stand for which others ridicule you, saying "yes" to what all others say "no" to, and "no" to what all others say "yes" to. It may get you beat up, barred from a job, thrown off the team. It may get you killed. We must learn that this is the norm of Christian spirituality. Anything less is something other than true spirituality.

In no way should this be interpreted as a call to rabid fundamentalism, intentional martyrdom, a politicized version of Christianity, or obnoxious or strange behaviour on street corners. It is simply a challenge for a robust faith and authentic spirituality: What Jesus experienced as God's priestly apostle to us, cannot be different for Jesus' priestly apostles to the world.

Practically speaking, what does it look like to be missional?

1. You ARE a priestly apostle in the world

You testify to the beauty of Christ through your Christ-like character. Your integrity, ethical values and priorities mirror to the world who Jesus is in his grace and truth.

We used to have cultural exchange students live with us. It was a great way for our daughters to learn to appreciate other cultures, and for us to share with others the happiness of our family. Most of our visitors were Japanese or Korean. One Japanese girl, Yako, on the first evening of her stay with us was confused when we all took hands at the dinner table to give thanks to God for the food. Yako asked us in very broken English what it means to pray. Susan simply explained that prayer is when we talk to God.

"God? What is that?" That is how six delightful weeks with this 19-year-old girl began. She had never heard of God, and had no concept of what God is. Over the ensuing weeks we had a few conversations about God, but not many. Mostly she just watched us, listened to our prayers, and enjoyed our family life. And we laughed a lot together. At the end of her stay with us, we all drove in silence to the meeting place where the group of cultural exchange students was to be driven to the airport. As we stood in the parking lot waiting, Yako cried. Just before she turned to climb into the bus, she tapped my wife on the chest and said, "I believe there is a God. I saw him in there."

One way we testify to Jesus in the world is through our character.

2. You are WHERE you are as a priestly apostle

If God calls you to another country to serve him and the people there, go! But the fact is that every Christian is an apostle wherever he or she is.

We are apostles to our city. We live in the city to love the city, pray for the city, and do good in the city.

We are apostles to our neighbours. As we share with them through hospitality how good God has been in our lives, as we serve them in kindness and goodness, and treat them with a character that expresses the fruit of the Spirit, we let them know that God is calling them into the blessing of his love.

We are apostles to our growing network of non-Christian friends. We are intentional about being in places where we can move into the lives of people who do not know God, build relationships and naturally express through character, words, and deeds of compassion, the God who has inhabited our lifehouse.

3. You DO what you do as a priestly apostle

This applies to your occupation. In German we have a helpful distinction between *Beruf* and *Berufung*. The former word means 'career' or 'occupation', the latter word means 'calling'. In English we have the word 'vocation'—'career' as a derivative from the latin *vocare,* 'to call.' Your career is your calling. Your *Beruf* is not an end in itself, but the means God has given you to fulfil your *Berufung*. We are apostles to our workplaces. Where we work is the mission field to which we are called. We impact supervisors, fellow workers, customers, clients and patients through character, deeds, and conversations that point people to the holiness and love of God.

It also applies to Jesus' mandate to 'love your neighbour as yourself,' by serving people in need. As individuals and churches, we do deeds of mercy and compassion, as we move into people's lives and serve them at their point of need.

My father taught me this when I was a young boy. He regularly drove to the other side of town to pick up Herr Grünewald who lived on the outskirts of our city in a cardboard shack he had built for himself. Dad, an educated theologian, brought this smelly man home, personally bathed him, then had him eat at our table and enjoy our family. My dad was a priestly apostle to an utterly destitute man.

One of my daughters taught me this also. When she saw a homeless man lying on our front lawn taking a nap, she made a peanut butter and jelly sandwich and took it out to him. That was being a priestly apostle to the 'neighbour', the next person in need.

While our kids were growing up, it was our custom at Christmas time to ask ourselves, "What will we give Jesus for his birthday this year?" One year we purchased warm socks and filled them with many different necessities for teenagers who live on the street in the cold winter. On Christmas day we drove around the city and gave gifts to Jesus: *What you do unto the least of these, you do unto me,* he taught us, so we looked for those many considered *the least of these.* A 17 year old homeless teenager ended up driving home with us and eating a sumptuous Christmas dinner with us. That gave us the opportunity to allow the young man to experience a family where the children were not called demeaning names or beaten up. For me it was the only Christmas meal I have never forgotten!

Remember the nightmare of a house we purchased in Toronto? It was big enough that we eventually built a separate apartment in the basement. That is where our exchange students lived. That is also where we were able to house Cuban refugees. Many years ago, Susan and I were able to take a vacation in Cuba. It was God's way of placing his burden for the Cuban people and country on our hearts. When word got out about our love for Cubans, the telephone started ringing: would we take this or that Cuban couple that had just fled from the oppressiveness and poverty of the Communist rule there? It became a wonderful way to share our home and food, our love and family with delightful people who had lived in fear and poverty.

I have given you just a few small examples of how we, who have followed Jesus into the world he has come to save, can express our apostolic identity. But mercy, compassion and justice are equally the domain of the church. Whether it be trained church members ministering regularly to people dying of AIDS, giving shelter to refugees, visiting immigrants and caring for them, going weekly into poor neighbourhoods and doing an after-school-program for children, working at freeing prostitutes from the slave trade they are caught in, cleaning up trash in the neighbourhoods, or whatever it is, the church is God's elect bearer of hope and joy, peace and love to the city. Under the leadership of a team of deacons, who provide training, encouragement, prayer support and follow-up, church members move into and sacrifice themselves for their surroundings as God's priestly apostles.

4. You SAY what you say as a priestly apostle

What if we were to adopt a lifestyle in which talking about God-in-our-world was our normal, everyday way of conversation? Since God-in-our-world is the only reality that really exists, what would it be like if we turned our public conversation into conformity with that reality?

We would spontaneously remark about the greatness of God by giving him credit for good things that happen and we would do it as if the bystanders would view the content of our remarks as obvious.

We would point to the costly grace of his mission through the life, cross and resurrection of Jesus, wherever and whenever we find ourselves around people of a different outlook, and we would do it with no worry about the consequences we would have to bear.

We would enthusiastically share with a friend about the latest bit of transformation the Holy Spirit has caused in our lives, and we would do it with the attitude that we, *'the chief of sinners'* (1 Timothy 1:15 *NKJ*), need all the transformation we can possibly experience.

We would turn to the person in distress, and courteously ask, "Would you like me to pray for you right now?" and we would thank him for his honesty if he said "no!"

Missio Dei: a different way of measuring success

Years ago a campus organization asked me to lead a discovery group at the University of Toronto, much like the one I was to lead a few years later in Frankfurt. The organization appealed to Christian students at the university to come and bring their student friends. For six weeks in a row I showed up in a classroom on campus ready to discuss. The group was hardly a success, certainly nothing worth mentioning in a book! Only one Christian young man came to most of the meetings. The other 1-3 people who came were different people every time, so that any kind of continuity was lost. I wasn't sure if I needed to change to a different deodorant or if I had lost my ability to interact with people the age of my children or what precisely the cause of this discouraging development was. But I was discouraged!

Weeks after the discovery group had run its 6-week course I was sitting in one of the libraries at the university, when one of the student leaders of the campus organization spotted me.

"Hey, Dr. Beck, great to see you. I have been wanting to connect with you and tell you that I am really sorry that I could never make it to any of the discovery group sessions. How did it go?"

Something happened to me in that moment. Normally I would have lamented how poorly things had run on the basis that few had come and that nobody had shown interest in giving their life over to Jesus. Instead, the Holy Spirit reminded me of a passage from the Bible, and I came out with a response that even surprised me: "I think we could call it a success!"

"That's cool! Tell me about it!" he said with a wide smile.

I then referred to the Bible passage that had just registered in my head: *"Thanks be to God, who always leads us in triumphal procession in Christ and through us spreads everywhere the fragrance of the knowledge of him. For we are to God the aroma of Christ among those who are being saved and those who are perishing. To the one we are the smell of death; to the other, the fragrance of life"* (2 Corinthians 2:14-16). Then I said, "I think I successfully stank up the classroom to the glory of God every time."

The young man's smile had noticeably faded as I recited the verses, and with my last sentence it was completely gone. With a troubled look he asked, "But how is being a smell of death to people a success?"

"Well," I started thoughtfully, "I can see how it glorifies God if students attend the group and decide against him and with that decision seal their destiny of eternal death."

"What?" The student could not believe his ears.

I tried to explain my thoughts, "I think what Paul is driving at in this passage is that every person will stand before God on the Day of Judgment, including every student who came to our discovery group and decided against following Jesus, and who will eventually die without ever changing that decision. At the judgment seat, God will say: 'why did you not give your life to him who gave his life for you?' The student will answer something like, 'hey God, I did not know that I was supposed to.' God will answer, 'You are without excuse! In 2001 you sat in a classroom at U of T and heard that in Jesus I had made my way to you to bring you the way to me. You decided against my way. Since I am just, I must give you what you have decided for: an eternity without me!' No accusation can be made against God for giving the student for all eternity what the student freely decided for. In fact, the bystanders around the judgment seat will applaud God for being so fair with everyone, not forcing his ways on the student but giving the student what he always wanted. The justice of God at the judgment seat will be vindicated by the decision the student made in 2001. It means that my 'smell' glorifies God's justice in the end."

I admit, the student looked shocked. He said, "But how could the student know in the discovery group that Jesus was the only way God was enabling the student to come to God?"

"How much clearer can God speak than through a resurrection?" I reflected.

"Well, I guess if you see from the perspective of what it does for God," the startled student responded.

"But that is just the point," I went on. "Everything we do, we do from the perspective of what it does for God. Naturally, every person goes at something with the question: what will it do for me? I have lived my own life for many years this way, searching for my own significance in large and impressive numbers and results with which I could wow people. But if we start there, we will be quickly disillusioned. We will have to consider our lives as having brought us very little. But if we do everything from the perspective, 'whether smell of death or aroma of life, what is it doing for God... did it glorify God in some way or another,' then we always end up getting something out of our actions. We will end up feeling that somehow it was a rewarding experience."

I was as startled over my thoughts as the student from the campus group was. Maybe I surprised myself how thinking about my apostolic mission from the perspective of God's glory, allowed me to see what the world would call 'failure' as 'success.' The measure of success is in our own faithfulness in mission—whoever we are, wherever we are, whatever we are doing—as being unto the Lord. God is glorified by the results, even if the world would measure those results as failure.

■ **What's in it for me?**

- **The thrill of experiencing the power of the gospel when it changes people through YOUR life**: When your testimony through character, words, and deeds has been instrumental in pointing someone to God and to the experience of becoming a spiritual house inhabited by God, you feel absolutely elated. It is not pride, or getting all puffed up about an ability to impact others. Instead, it is the amazement over God's power to change lives through little you; it is a sharing in the dance that the angels do in heaven when God has once again brought someone into his house and enlarged the family.

- **The thrill of giving generously to others:** Giving comes in many forms. The reason the Bible says, *"It is more blessed to give than to receive"* (Acts 20:35) is because God's Word knows our hearts. We are wired by God in his image, and that means that we naturally love to give. We naturally love to share; we naturally love to sacrifice for the good of someone else. Our sinful me-centredness into which we have fallen has defaced all that naturalness and twisted it into self-consumption and selfish self-preservation. But as an archaeologist gently brushes away the dust from the colourful pieces and glues them together into a beautiful vase (whose lines of brokenness are always visible), God's supernatural salvation restores the naturalness of the self. That is why giving, sharing and sacrificing starts to feel so good! It is the real me expressing itself.

Since giving generously is so foreign to the me-centred self, God sought to give his people in the Old Testament a guideline for giving. He expected them to regularly give 10% of their belongings (called a 'tithe') to the priests to cover their daily needs. Since the new covenant is a bigger, better, more spiritual covenant, the New Testament sets the guideline for giving even higher. We are called to give freely and as we are able. That means, the more God gives us, the more we give to others. We give generously and liberally. We give to others in faith that God will give us every day our daily bread. We take pleasure in God the Giver by feeling the pleasure of giving.

When that happens, our lifestyle changes:

- **We are no longer driven by materialism,** the philosophy that the experience of things can satisfy our deepest longings. Instead we are driven by the vision expressed in the Lord's Prayer, "Your kingdom come." Our desire in life is that the benevolent rule of God find its clear expression through what we do with what we own. Our goal is no longer possessing a comfortable home but sharing the comfortable home we possess...no longer amassing wealth and things and a big bank account to live like kings and queens but to ask ourselves how our wealth and money could express to someone what a lavish Giver the King of kings is. The goal is not simply to give 10% of our income to our church community as a weekly offering but to increase our giving with every pay raise or unexpected income we receive.

- **We make modesty our standard of living but not of giving.** This is not to say that God frowns on wealth. He doesn't! But he does frown on self-consumption. The wealthy are just as important in the kingdom of God as the poor. In fact, the wealthy have a very special and envious opportunity. My wife calls it 'financial freedom,' and encouraged me years ago to set it as a goal in our marriage. 'Financial freedom' is not having so much that you can buy whatever you want. It is to have as much as you need to cover basic expenses plus enough over and above that to regularly help others have enough to cover their basic needs.

'Financial freedom' is what I see in my friend Igor, who lives with his wife Mary in Frankfurt and could be a wealthy banker, but who doesn't accept promotions, the accompanying pay raises and increased hours of work, so that he has more time to enjoy his wife, raise his three children and help his church community accomplish some vital ministries to the city.

'Financial freedom' is what I experience in my physician-friend Michael, who years ago was so deeply touched by the gospel of grace when his personal life was in ruins, that since then he has been volunteering his weekly day off at a shelter for street youth in Toronto, providing them with free medical care and counsel.

'Financial freedom' is what I witness in my sister, who with her husband moved into the financial and economic despair of Reykjavík, Iceland. They took on a huge financial risk in buying a house while many were losing theirs, in order to come alongside a country that was rocked heavily by the financial crisis, and to move into the lives of the people who feel helpless and hopeless.

If we were to look at the lifestyles of these people, we would characterize them as 'fairly modest'. They would also tell us that they are content with life and deeply gratified by the contribution they are making toward others.

- **We trust God for our daily needs.** A high-powered financial advisor in Toronto once encouraged a group of us Christians: "Give away a little more than what you can afford to give away, so that you are 'forced' to trust God for your daily bread." I don't think she was telling us to be reckless or irresponsible with our money. Her point was that many of us have so much that we do not need to trust God for things. Or at least we tell ourselves that we have no cause to be anxious about tomorrow and no cause to make requests to God (Philippians 4:6, 7), because the paycheque tomorrow is secured. But if you give away a little more than you can afford to give away, you will start praying to God daily to 'give us this day our daily bread.' It seems somehow Jesus envisioned that for us in the Lord's Prayer. The financial advisor's point was: "Giving more than you 'can' is the easiest way to learn faith."

Think about it: What would it look like if you started acting generously toward others by giving to people in need and to your church a little more than you can afford to give? What things could you give away? How much would you give?

- **The thrill of knowing that your life is leaving an eternal legacy for others:** You may never know on this side of eternity what your legacy is. But if you are living for Jesus as a priestly apostle in this world, you will most definitely leave one.

Watkin Roberts was born in 1886 in Caernarvon, Wales. As a young man, he studied law and medicine and could have had a great career in either. Against the advice of the Welsh mission board, he went to India in 1908 as a medical dispenser. His heart was overwhelmed with a burden for the vast unevangelized areas of India. After reaching Manipur, in northeastern India, and after several days of trekking over hills and steep mountain passes, he arrived at the Mizos people, located in southwestern Manipur. It was a dangerous region of 40 tribes, many of them headhunters. The religion of the region was spiritism.

A woman in Wales had sent Roberts 5£ to cover personal needs. Because he felt he had none, he purchased Gospels of John, translated by his Indian coworker, Dala, with the money. He sent the Gospels to chiefs in the northern parts of the Lushai hills. Most people in the region were illiterate, but many chiefs could either read or had personal readers. In each copy of the Gospel of John, Roberts attached a note that he was willing to come and serve the people as the chiefs saw fit.

Little did he know that he would be seen as the personification of a legend from the history of the Mizos: a man with an important book would arrive and he was to be received as a great teacher and the book was to be believed and followed. Another tradition of the Mizos prepared them for the gospel of Jesus. Civil war ruled among the savage tribes, and usually over the issue of territory. Whenever one tribe wished to make peace with the enemy, the chief would beat a drum three times loudly from the top of a mountain. If the neighbouring tribe was willing to enter into a state of peace, its chief would hit the tribal drum from its mountain top in response. Then the heads of the tribes would meet at the boundary line for a bloody ceremony: The chiefs would slay animals and spray the blood along the boundary line between the two tribes, establishing peace, peace at a cost.

As the chiefs read the Gospel of John, they learned about Jesus, sent from God to become our 'lamb of God' (John 1:29, 36), who was slain for our sins and whose blood, applied at the moment of personal faith in Jesus, cleanses us and forever demolishes the boundary line between two warring tribes, us and God. The chiefs saw in the gospel of Jesus the ultimate fulfilment of their tradition of peace making, and in the Gospel of John they saw the realization of the legend about the book that would show them the way to God.

Late in 1909 four persons from Senvawn carried the Gospel of John back to Watkin Roberts, with the following message: *"Sir, there is no one to teach the children; no one to help us. Will you come and tell us about God and establish work in our midst?"* Government officials strongly advised Roberts not to go. Those were dangerous jungle people, and their words could not be taken at face value. Roberts responded that he needed to go, "even at the risk of my own life."

Roberts, age 22, headed off with Dala and a third man, Dr. Peter Fraser, for whom Roberts worked. Roberts was warmly received by the headhunters, who affectionately called him 'Mr. Youngman'. For the next two years, the three men travelled through the region, explaining the gospel and organizing seminars to teach the other books of the Bible. A number of families committed themselves to Jesus.

In 1912, the three men returned to Wales, as Frasier needed special medical care. In 1915, Watkin married Gladys Dobson, who sailed to India with him. Their marriage started happily. Calcutta became their permanent residence, and soon the first child came into the world.

Life was hard for the family. Two children died in infancy. Discouragement set in for Gladys. Their fourth child, Paul, gave Gladys much stress due to his so-called 'energetic boyhood.' She was weakened through malaria and typhoid fever.

Roberts viewed Christian spirituality as a holistic faith that informs all of life. Consequently, he helped the former headhunters build schools, and trained people to become teachers. He brought in physicians who taught medicine, and the first hospitals were built. He brought in economists and nutritionists who helped people create a better infrastructure and healthy eating habits. He himself had good business skills and began to teach people how to start and run a business. Electricity came to the land. The first universities were built. Today this part of India has the highest number of Ph.D.s and engineers in the entire country.

In 1917, a great awakening swept the Senvawn region. Roberts and his mission agency were Presbyterian, a church denomination known for its emphasis on order and decorum over spontaneity and emotional expression. But he did not stand in the way of people being so filled with the Holy Spirit that they would travel from place to place singing, dancing, and sharing the good news about the Lamb of God. People became bold in turning against the evil spirits they had served for many generations, casting out demons in Jesus' name and denouncing the practice of sacrifices to appease the spirits. The gospel spread to numerous regions.

In 1929, however, darkness descended upon Roberts' ministry in the form of a man named H.H. Coleman. Funds were scarce, and missionaries, including the Roberts, were going without pay for long periods of time. Coleman and two others from the mission board came to India to investigate. Tensions had already been brewing between Roberts and the mission board's home council. Now Coleman spread a rumour among both church leaders in Senvawn and the mission board that Roberts had misappropriated funds for personal use and had lied when he reported that 9000 people in the region were now following Jesus. The church members in Senvawn believed Coleman and asked Roberts to leave India.

It was a dark day in November, 1929, when Watkin Roberts walked away from Senvawn, a banner behind him reading, "Go home, Youngman!"

Broken and broke, Roberts went to America to settle matters with the mission board and seek new support funds. Gladys and the children stayed in Calcutta, living in abject poverty until a business man gave her the money to travel to England. It would be another 2 years until she could pay for a trip to America. The mission board forced Roberts' resignation and Coleman took over as the new director. A defeated man, Roberts moved with his family to Toronto, Canada and did not return to India until 1957, allowing him to see some of the fruit of his hard labours before he died.[7]

Years went by. More years went by.

In February 2010, the Christians in Manitur celebrated 100 years of knowing Jesus. Ninety percent of the entire region—sons and daughters and grandchildren of headhunters—had embraced Christian spirituality and had been freed of generations of burdensome taboos and superstitions and the worship of demons, all associated with spiritism. A 5-day-long feast and celebration was planned.

But another development gave this party special meaning: the people of Senvawn had discovered several years after Watkin Roberts' death that they had been guilty of a terrible misinterpretation of Roberts. They had believed Coleman's distortion of the facts. So regretful were they of their actions against the man who had once been their hero and spiritual father, that they sought God for forgiveness. Their Christian understanding taught them that they needed to make things right with Roberts, or risk the loss of God's blessing. But Watkin Roberts was already dead. His son, Paul, who had served many years as a highly revered physician in Ecuador, was 88 years old and unable to make the 2-day flight to India. The only other Roberts in the family who was a Christian and could be invited to represent the Roberts family at the celebration was Watkin Roberts' grandson. This is how David Roberts and his wife were invited to come to India in February 2010.

After a long flight, David and Evelyn Roberts arrived at the airport in Calcutta exhausted. All they wanted was someone with a heavy foot on the gas pedal who could get them to their destination. When they passed through customs something strange happened. The man who had sat beside them quietly during the entire

---

[7] Information from the following sources: D. Ruolngul, THE ADVANCE OF THE GOSPEL, Part 1: History of the Coming of the Gospel in Manipur South with special reference to the Independent Church of India, Manitur: Smart tech Offset Printers, 2009; Jonathan Pudaite, THE LEGACY OF WATKIN R. ROBERTS: The Pioneer Missionary who advocated and empowered indigenous Christian leader. Meghalaya: Partnership Publication, 2009; n.a. Thukna Ropui: Amazing Deep, Hmar Christian Fellowship, Delhi, 2010.

flight came running back to them from the reception area in order to vigorously shake their hand. He kept bowing and saying, "Mr. Roberts, Mr. Roberts." The explanation of this curious moment lay on the other side of the doors, as David and Evelyn stepped into the receiving area. What greeted them was not a driver with a heavy foot, but a banner that read, "Welcome back, Mr. Roberts," and 1800 cheering people. Like heroes, the shocked Roberts were escorted out of the airport and into a motorcade, led by 12 police motorcycles, which ushered them to their destination (This is no lie, I am not making this up!).

The motorcade made a surprise stop in Senvawn. Here they were met with the next shock of their lives. Thousands of people gathered around their car, all with white sashes around their necks. They represented peace and forgiveness. As David and Evelyn stepped out of the limousine, everyone got on their knees in a plea to the grandson to receive forgiveness for their maltreatment of Watkin Roberts. The town mayor took the Roberts by the hand, and led them in a solemn ceremony up the steps of the town hall. In a room on a decorated table lay 7 copies of a document, describing the sin of Senvawn against Watkin Roberts and God, and outlining the repentance of the inhabitants. It was read by the mayor, and then David Roberts was asked to sign all 7 copies. After he had done so, the town got up off its knees. The people cheered and many wept. The days of a boundary line between the people of Senvawn and the Roberts was washed away by the blood of God. Now everyone longed to shake Watkin Roberts' grandson's hand and embrace him.

The next several days' celebration of 100 years of faith in Jesus was dizzying for David and Evelyn. With many having travelled for several days, 24,000 people gathered in praise of God and thanksgiving for Watkin Roberts. There were concerts, sermons, worship, pig roasts, more worship and thanksgiving, sermons, pig roasts, more worship and on and on. David Roberts, who had been asked to prepare one speech, had to give four. Evelyn Roberts was treated as if she were the wife of the apostle Peter. As she took in this joyous spectacle, overwhelmed that something of this historic magnitude could—of all people—be happening to her, she thought back one brief moment to a conference on a particular Saturday in

1995, when—confused by many years of new age occultism and convinced that she desperately needed the liberation of the God of the Bible—she had leaned over to the man who would become her pastor, and had asked, "what is a parasite?"

A few years after her conversion to Jesus she met and married David and became Evelyn Roberts. With that, she joined a family line that humbly and self-sacrificially walks the path of missio Dei: The legacy of Watkin Roberts has touched Evelyn's heart. What he did and modelled in India, she does today in the Dominican Republic. She resides in Toronto, but she has 300 poor children in the DR, whose spiritual mother she has become.

And the missio Dei goes on! Not just in the Roberts family but in and through God's entire family. We are the ever increasing household that lives its identity and understands its mandate to be priestly apostles of Jesus. Whether we are explaining the impact of the resurrection of Jesus to someone in Starbucks, or are serving coffee to someone who is explaining the impact of the resurrection, WE ARE HERE TO CHANGE THE WORLD, because the resurrection of Jesus changed everything!

1. Learn to tell God's story by learning to tell your story with God.
How did you come into a personal relationship to God? What prompted you to seek God? What has it changed? Write out your story and learn to tell it to someone in 4 minutes.

2. Memorize Matthew 28:18-20.

3. Recommended reading: John Piper, Let The Nations Be Glad: The Supremacy of God in Missions, Grand Rapids: Baker Books, 1993.

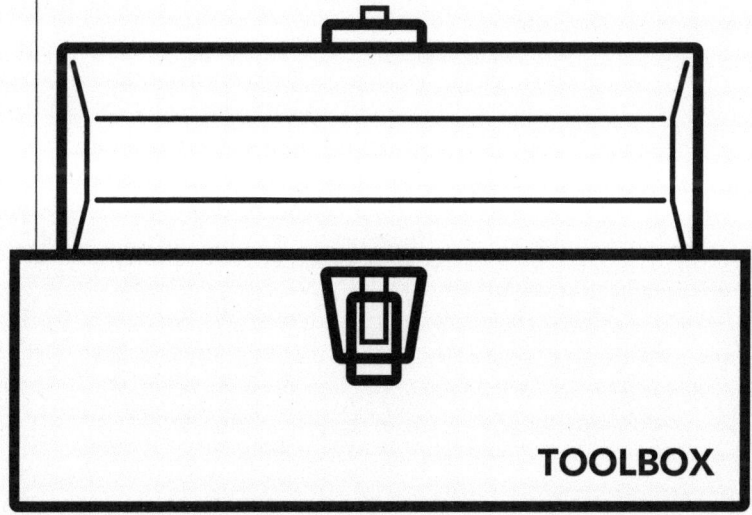

TOOLBOX

13
The Roof

Living Your Utmost for the Glory of God

The fulfilment of a God-centred me

Every person wants his life to be about the greatest thing there is. The question is: what do you think is the greatest thing to live for?

The great quest of philosophers for thousands of years has been the *Summum Bonum*, the highest good. This is a worthy quest. It is the 'holy grail' of all quests. If Christian spirituality is—as I defined it for Maria at the café several years ago—every person's attempt to attain righteousness, meaning an assurance that you are accepted, approved and appreciated by the highest standard of goodness there is, then the philosopher's quest is ultimately the search of every human heart: Everyone wants to know the *Summum Bonum* and longs to be found fully acceptable and appreciated by that highest standard of goodness.

What is the highest, most glorious good in life?

The first words of the Old Testament are, *"In the beginning God created..."* I love these words because of what they mean:

- They mean there actually was a beginning. There was a point at which time began, in which a big bang of some sort happened, and every original animate and inanimate thing began.

- They mean that before that beginning, there already was God. Eternally there, uncreated, self-existent, self-defined, self-generating, self-sufficient.

- They mean that this God made a big bang happen. He was real creative and brought into being what was not yet. He spoke, "Let there be," and—bang—it was.

The rest of the Bible describes what a glorious God our God is. Psalm 8:1 proclaims, *"O Lord, our Lord, how majestic is your name in all the earth."* The psalmist sees God's glory expressed through what he created (v.3): *"When I consider your heavens, the work of your fingers, the moon and the stars, which you have set in place,…"* Seeing how glorious our God is, the writer now shifts from viewing God to looking at the human being (v.4): *"What is man, that you are mindful of him?"* He is so enthralled with the majesty of our Creator that he cannot fathom that God would rate man as high as he does (v.5): *"Yet You have made him a little lower than God".* (NAS) What a position of dignity every human being holds in the universe, and all because God holds the highest position above him!

The psalmist has developed a cosmic hierarchy in this psalm: God created man to be *"a little lower"* than his Creator. Yet *"You made him ruler over the works of your hands; you put everything under his feet"* (v.6). That means over the breathtaking snow-capped mountain ranges, over the humongous whales in the sea, over the wild animals roaming the jungles, the cattle on the ranch and the sheep on the farm. Man rules over it all. But in the last verse, the singer-writer-composer returns to where he began: God! He ends with the refrain with which he began: *"O Lord, our Lord, how majestic is your name in all the earth."* (v.9).

In his work, GOD GLORIFIED, Jonathan Edwards answers the philosopher's quest for the *Summum Bonum*, the greatest Good:

"God Himself is the great Good to which they (by 'they' Edwards refers to people who have entered into a relationship with God) are brought to the possession and enjoyment by redemption. He is the highest good, and the sum of all that good which Christ purchased. God is the inheritance of the saints; he is the portion of their souls. God is their wealth and treasure, their food, their life, their dwelling place, their ornament and diadem, and their everlasting honour and glory. They have none in heaven but God; he is the great good which the redeemed receive at death, and which they rise to at the end of the world. The Lord God is the light of the heavenly Jerusalem; and is the 'river of the water of

life' that runs, and 'the tree of life that grows in the midst of the paradise of God.' The glorious excellencies and beauty of God will be what will for ever entertain the minds of the saints, and the love of God will be their everlasting feast. The redeemed will indeed enjoy other things; they will enjoy the angels, and will enjoy one another; but that which they shall enjoy in the angels, or each other, or in any thing else whatsoever that will yield them delight and happiness, will be what shall be seen of God in them."[1]

What is the most glorious, majestic, high-ranking being or thing or person or object there is? Our great God! He always has been the *Summum Bonum* and always will be. Postmodern thinking begins and ends with the 'me', claiming there is nothing outside 'me' that can give 'me' meaning in life. Christian spirituality, however, begins and ends with God. As in Psalm 8, the majesty of God is the first bookend and the majesty of God is the last bookend. And man has been placed in between the majesty, and in man God is writing his-story. It is when we esteem God as the beginning and end of all, that we are esteemed into the magnificence of God.

God's glory is the answer to the postmodern quest for the real me.

What is the most glorious meaning of life?

The answer the Bible gives is clear and logical: Since everything comes from a glorious God, and everything is made possible through a glorious God, and everything will return to the glorious God, then God is the only one for whom it is worthwhile to make your life count. Romans 11:36 says it like this: *"For from Him, and through Him, and to Him are all things. To Him be the glory forever."*

In this book we put it like this:

If you want to trust the most powerful good there is, then you will make the sovereignty of God the first cornerstone of your lifehouse.

If you want to become the most beautiful person there is, then you will make the holiness of God the second cornerstone of your lifehouse.

---

[1] Owen Strachan and Doug Sweeney, JONATHAN EDWARDS: LOVER OF GOD. Chicago: Moody Publishers, 2010, pp. 63-64.

If you want to love the loveliest thing there is, then you will make the love of God the third cornerstone of your lifehouse.

If you want to take pleasure in the most enjoyable thing there is, then you will make the pleasures of God the fourth cornerstone of your lifehouse.

It is all about God. Therefore, the Westminster Shorter Catechism's first question asks, "What is the chief end of man?" and answers with a phrase coined in 1647: "To glorify God and enjoy him forever."

But what does it mean to glorify God?

1. We glorify God by expressing his holy character in all we do

One of my early professors for New Testament studies explained to the class once that the Hebrew background for the word 'glory' in the Gospel of John brings with it the meaning of 'weight.' Which reminds me of my wife.

Ever since I married Susan over 34 years ago, I have had weight issues. I am not saying my weight problems are Susan's fault. It's just the way things are. Whenever I stand on the scale, and nervously await the results in the form of a number (which I would rather not mention here), it becomes clear to me that her cooking has had a deep internal impact on me. Someone may want to console me by saying, 'Don't worry, be happy, it's just a number!" But the fact is the number on the scale is not simply a number. It is the expression of what I am bodily. All of me. Every bit of me, expressed by a number on the scale.

That is how it is with glorifying God. Imagine you are the scale, and God stands with his great, sovereign, righteous, loving weight on top of your life and expresses himself through your life. What you do and how you do it is like the number on the scale: it reveals for all who see and experience you what the weight of God is. Through your actions, words, attitudes, thoughts and the integrity of your character, you are an expression of God's personhood: how gracious he is, how good he is, how forgiving he is, how joyful he is, how creative he is, how fair he is in his righteousness, how sad or angry he is about unrighteousness, how humble his attitude is and how self-controlled he is in his reactions.

To glorify God means to express his glorious personhood in all of life's situations, in every moment, in all deeds done and words spoken. That is the reason why God created us men and women, and why he created us in his image and according to his likeness: to glorify him. Even in the smallest things, "Whether we eat or drink or whatever we do, we do everything to glorify him" (1 Corinthians 10:31).

When anyone asks me what the meaning of life is, there's my answer. "I do my work in a manner...treat my spouse in a manner...drive my car in a manner...spend my money in a manner... enjoy my luxuries in a manner...love and raise my children in a manner...organize my time in a manner...I seek to do everything in a manner THAT GIVES FULL EXPRESSION TO WHAT GOD IS LIKE."

2. We glorify God by worshipping him with worship that is truly worthship

When we glorify God, we praise his character. We focus on his wonderful works and we celebrate his wonderful person. If the first meaning of 'glorify' is 'to express the full weight of God,' then the second meaning has to do with esteeming God, with throwing compliments at God. In English we are helped by the original word for 'worship', which was worthship. Worship is declaring to God his worth.

Let's see how biblical writers describe this aspect of glorifying. Psalm 115:1 exclaims, *"Not to us, O Lord, not to us but to your name be the glory, because of your love and faithfulness."*

Then there's Psalm 136. It takes us into a worship gathering about 1,000 years before Jesus. The leader faces the congregation and starts off: *"Give thanks to the Lord, for he is good,"* and the congregation responds, *"His love endures forever."*

Then the leader of worship calls out, *"Give thanks to the God of gods,"* and the congregation calls back, *"His love endures forever."*

The leader says, *"To him who alone does great wonders,"* and the congregation bellows, *"His love endures forever."* It just keeps going like this for quite a while.

Psalm 145 jubilantly resounds, *"I will exalt you, my God and King; I will praise your name for ever and ever. Every day I will praise you and extol your name for ever and ever. Great is the Lord and most worthy of praise; his greatness no one can fathom."*[NLT] In the Psalms the congregation focuses all its attention on the amazing qualities of our glorious *Summum Bonum*.

I love how this theme of glorifying God runs through the last book of the Bible, Revelation. Revelation 1:5,6 says: *"To him who loves us and has freed us from our sins by his blood, and has made us to be a kingdom and priests to serve his God and Father—to him be glory and power for ever and ever! Amen."*

Revelation 5:12 translates us into the heavenly realm. A great mass of enthusiastic people are gathered. All those who as God's household finished the journey here on earth have joined the triumphant community above. Together they euphorically raise their voices, *"Worthy is the Lamb, who was slain, to receive power and wealth and wisdom and strength and honour and glory and praise."*

In Revelation 19:1,2, we are at the end of history. Evil has been vanquished once and for all. All deceivers and deceptive systems that held people in their sway have been laid bare and condemned at the bench of Truth. The wrong has been righted. Righteousness reigns! *"After this I heard what sounded like the roar of a great multitude in heaven shouting: 'Hallelujah! Salvation and glory and power belong to our God, for true and just are his judgments'."*

Throughout all of history, both on earth and in the heavens, people have recognized that God is so staggeringly beautiful in his person and amazing in his ways that they feel the need to declare to him how worthy he is. That is worship! What strikes me is how the entire emphasis of glorifying God is on *God*. The instruments play a role, but only a supporting one. The composer of the liturgical piece and the leader of the chorale have an important role, but only a secondary one. The congregation plays a significant role but not the major one. The primary place in worship belongs to God. He is at centre stage.

This is a point where I must admit I need to change. I am so beguiled by the consumerism of our me-centred world that I tend to approach the worship of God from the perspective, 'is it worth it for me?'

From that perspective, what determines the quality of worship is the quality of the instrumentation, the style of the service, how interesting the preacher could make a dry topic and how warmly I was greeted. When someone asks me, "So how was worship?" I begin to speak about the things I liked and did not like including that it went 15 minutes too long.

But where is the perspective that this is about God? Where is the sense of having been smitten to the core with the beauty of God? Where is the experience of being so overwhelmed with his holiness that I feel small? Where is the brokenheartedness from being moved by his awful and terrifying hatred of my sin that moved him in wrath to rip his Son apart at the cross? Why am I not on my face before him in humility and gratitude?

We are so taken up with our own trivialities that we miss being awed and filled and thrilled by the sight of God's glory. However, we do the best for our little selves when we discipline ourselves to step into God's presence and declare to him his worth. It puts the whole universe with all its problems and challenges into proper perspective. It puts us in our place and helps us realize that since God is great, and my life belongs to him, my life has great value.

This is not true for Sunday worship services only. It's a lifestyle. Worshiping God by declaring to him his worth is something we do daily, all week long, 52 weeks a year. We praise and exalt him in our prayers, in our sudden thoughts about him, in our spontaneous thanks either audibly or inaudibly, in our songs, in our outbursts of joy or amazement of what we see, as well as in our silence and reverence. We can glorify his great name in the shower, at the table, at the workplace, in the car, in class, in the pub, in front of the TV and with our Bible study group.

If it is the greatest thing we can do, and we will do it forever, then the time to begin is now, and the place to declare to God his worth is wherever you happen to be.

3. We glorify God by finding our satisfaction in him

We dealt with this under the 4th cornerstone. As Piper is prone to say, *"God is most glorified by us when we are most satisfied in him."*

It glorifies God when you laugh your heart out over a great joke, because humour finds its origin in Him.

It glorifies God when you can walk away from an exam and know, regardless of the result, that you gave your best, because God gave you strength and wisdom.

It glorifies God when you work hard and with integrity, not extending breaks and lunchtime beyond company rules, because God gave you the job, and the way you reflect his righteousness at work exalts him.

It glorifies God when you enjoy a sumptuous steak (all vegetarians, please replace 'steak' with 'tomato'), because God is the giver of that good and perfect gift.

It glorifies God when you have sex with your spouse, because God created sexual euphoria to give marriage pleasurable moments to celebrate oneness, such as Christ enjoys with his bride, the church.

It glorifies God when you walk through the woods on a cold autumn day, breathe in the fresh air with delight and kick up the colourful leaves that lie on the path, because you are basking in the joys of nature's creator.

It glorifies God when you honestly and authentically tell him that you feel too tired to talk to him and that you feel too dry to lift your voice in enthusiastic praise to him.

It glorifies God when you thank him for the good things you have, and for what the bad things can teach you, because you are thereby declaring your complete dependence on him in good as well as bad times.

What is the most glorious grand finale you could imagine?

I have seen many great movies. Mr. Holland's Opus is definitely one of them. This 1996 award-winning movie stars Richard Dreyfuss as the reluctant teacher, Glenn Holland.

Glenn Holland is a passionate musician who wants to write one great piece of music in his life. He begins his career as a music teacher in a high school and gets hooked on teaching. For thirty years he invests himself in students, instilling in them a love for music, teaching them to play instruments, imparting to them an ability to keep in concert with other orchestral sections. The movie shows the setbacks Mr. Holland experiences throughout his career, the tensions at home with his deaf son, the temptation to throw it all away. The biggest disappointment, though, is when the decision is made to cut the school's music program due to lack of funds. Mr. Holland is forced into early retirement. Despondent, the 60-year-old man feels like a failure.

On his last day, his wife and grown son arrive at school to help Glenn Holland carry his belongings out of the building. To his surprise, his son and wife usher him instead into the assembly hall. He enters to a standing ovation of cheering students, alumni and parents. A banner in front of the closed stage curtain reads, "30 Years. Thank you, Mr. Holland." The music teacher is moved to tears as his wife escorts him to the front row. The governor of the state, a former student of Glenn Holland, arrives. She takes the stage and speaks of how everybody in the assembly hall over several generations of students has been impacted by Mr. Holland. "We are your symphony, we are your notes," she says. To Mr. Holland's utter surprise she announces the first performance of Mr. Holland's composition, "The American Symphony." The guest of honour slowly ascends the stage. The governor hands him a baton. The curtain rises. Seated on stage is a large orchestra of students who have been taught and impacted by Glenn Holland over three decades.

The performance begins. It is a rousing piece of music. The looks on the musicians' faces make it clear: this orchestra is not playing the conductor's symphony for the audience but for the conductor himself. They are playing his symphony to honour him. The last grand notes are sounded triumphantly to the standing ovation of the entire assembly hall. The orchestra rises to join in the applause for the man who sacrificed much and gave his all to make out of nothing beautiful music, out of undiscovered talent good musicians and out of a sad music class a highly respected music program.

I remember the vain thoughts I had as I was moved by the climactic ending of this movie. Our church in Toronto had experienced numerous people converting to Jesus. The numbers in our fledgling church plant had grown to the point that people in this Canadian city were talking about us. I would never admit it at the time, but I was proud of what was happening in 'my' church. Maybe my name would enter the hall of fame of successful church planters some day. Maybe now I would feel like a man of significance. As I watched the assembly hall stand to applaud Mr. Holland, I wondered if my opus might turn out the same way when I would enter the assembly hall of heaven. Would angels and saints rise to applaud me? Would Jesus escort me to the front row and then ask me up on stage? Would all my hard labour for Jesus gain me some appreciation in the end? I had longed for it all my life.

It was 1996. The gospel had not sunk from my head into my heart like it would 10 years later. In two years I would come under attack from other church leaders and in three years my soul would be so beat up that I would spiral into depression. In six years I would leave 'my' church and in nine years I would leave the city for Germany, feeling like a failure. When I left Toronto in 2005, I was nowhere near the assembly hall and there was no orchestra in sight.

Every one of us goes through times in life where it looks and feels like God is stripping us of the glory we sought for ourselves. Vain glory! Like fool's gold. It is part of our nature to desire security and significance. It is the deep quest of every soul for approval and appreciation from the highest standard of goodness, from the *Summum Bonum.* Until the gospel sinks into our hearts and begins deconstructing our self-righteousness and reconstructing Christ's righteousness, we can sit in front of movies and wish the orchestra and audience would be applauding us.

Years ago I was reading through one of the volumes of John Owen's Works, when a few sentences leaped off the page at me. Owen said that the church of Jesus is the main focus of history. It takes front and centre stage in His-story of cosmic restoration.[2] That was a new thought for me. It hit me like the brick falling onto my shoulder the day I, the mud boy, wished I would have stayed in bed.

Owen's point, written during a turbulent time in England's history, is that all of history has but one purpose. At centre stage is God's work of making all things new by bringing all things under the lordship of Jesus (Revelation 21:5). The church—by which I do not mean some powerful, rich, cathedral-building institution

---

[2] William Goold, ed., THE WORKS OF JOHN OWEN, Edinburgh: Banner of Truth, 1983, Vol. XV.

with red-robed men, but people who have taken up their cross to follow Jesus—this church is the main movement of God's symphony of cosmic restoration. In and through God's people, and by the power of God's Spirit, God is moving forward. All politics, wars, economic developments, technological advancements, environmental beautification programs, architectural improvements and educational progress, all are merely precursors to God's final restoration of all things.

One day—at the 2nd Coming of Christ—we will hear the final movement of his symphony. In fact, we will be the orchestra. Jesus will be escorted to the front row of the assembly hall. The seed of the woman promised in Genesis 3:15, the Messiah, the Lamb of God, King of kings and Lord of lords, our Redeemer, Conqueror and Victor: He will mount the stage, he will take the conductor's baton, and he will direct the symphony of restoration he has composed throughout history. We will play for him. We will stand with all angels and saints and applaud him.

Yet while we are playing the fabulous notes something will begin to dawn on us all. Jesus wrote the notes for which he is getting the glory, but (to quote the governor in *Mr. Holland's Opus*) we are his notes. We are his symphony. We the redeemed along with all our works done for Jesus as priestly apostles will be the melody and harmony, the rhythm and tempo of Jesus' composition. Every one of us will find ourselves somewhere in the grand symphony. All the deeds done for him, all the setbacks, disappointments and sacrifices because of him, all the people we led to Jesus and who now sit in the orchestra with us and for him, everything will show up and sound out in the symphony of praise. We are the reason his music is so beautiful.

When Jesus is done conducting, and the last triumphant note has been sounded, he will hand the pages of his composition with all of us notes in it over to God the Father. There will be a standing ovation and rousing applause in the great assembly. Then the hall will grow quiet. Everyone will sit down, except the Three-in-One. Jesus has taken his place at the side of the Father and the Spirit. In a surprise move, they will stand. The Father will tuck the symphony of restoration under his arm near his heart, and the Trinity will break into applause. They will applaud us, the orchestra, rewarding us for persevering through the journey of being transformed into Christ's image. The smile of the Trinity will fall on us for having become such a beautiful symphony of praise. The Son will form his fingers into a 'perfect-sign' and mouth to us, "you were great."

In that moment, all our longing for highest approval and appreciation will be satisfied forever. We will bow to the Trinity. We, the orchestra, will have found our significance in the conductor. We will have found our place in his symphony. We will feel forever honoured and esteemed, that our little lives and all our deeds for him have become his celebrated symphony.

Maybe the longing for significance I felt at the end of *Mr. Holland's Opus* wasn't so vain, after all. It's just that you and I are not the conductors. We are the magnificent music!

"Lord, you are their glory and strength, and by your favour you exalt our horn" Psalm 89:17.

"Pinocchio, come home!"

That is the bottom line: we were created to glorify God, to dance around him with adoration, to express his beautiful character through our character, to find our security and significance in him. That is what is natural to us. That is the real self. He is our real self.

But we became unnatural. In the moment we crowned ourselves 'in Adam' as the Supreme Being and fashioned our own *Summum Bonum* we crashed into the putrid cesspool of self-love, self-pride, self-absorption and self-indulgence. Humanism and secularism were born in our self-centred hearts. Sin gave birth to post-modernism, with its metarule that there is 'no metarule over this life–, baby!' What was from the start the most natural thing for a God-created being, namely glorifying God, became the most unnatural thing. Mankind created the me-world.

We are horribly self-centred and self-indulgent, and the deeper we reach into ourselves, the farther in we get sucked. For all the advances in technology, biology, psychology, anthropology, philosophy and theology, we have become imprisoned to our self-absorbed selves. We cannot get out of the problem, because we created the problem. We are the problem!

The dance in our self-made prison cell goes on and on. The wearier we get dancing around our golden selves the more we fall into exhaustion and despair. The gold we thought we might find in ourselves was only 'fool's gold' all along. We have come to the end of ourselves. Our only hope is that someone outside of ourselves reaches into our self-absorbed dance and pulls us out.

That is precisely what God did! God invented our humanity. We sinned, so he entered into our humanity through Jesus in order to redeem it. When you come humbly and repentantly to God through the God-man, Christ Jesus, you participate with God in his re-creation of your humanity. It is the reason why your heart feels a sense of fulfilment when it starts to dance around God, why you feel right when you act, live and become more and more like Jesus. You are becoming free. Free to be the authentic me, the me that does not need to cover up to preserve an image and pretend everything is okay. This is the paradox of Christian spirituality: life only makes sense when the self orbits not around the me but around his Highness, the true Supreme Being, the King of Hearts, the Restorer of Paradise Lost. God-glorification, not self-glorification, leads the self to a full heart, to joy and peace, because God's glory is the fullness, joy and peace for which the me was created. It's the real Me.

Like Pinocchio, the wooden creation of Geppetto, who rebelled and tried it his own me-centred way: When he returned to the workshop he became a real boy.

1. Memorize Psalm 19:1 and Romans 8:31.

2. Memorize Psalm 103 (either alone or as a family). It is a wonderful psalm of praise that summarizes so many things God has done and does, for which our lives should praise him and centre on him.

3. Add to your times in prayer a time of praise. Learn to frequently tell God what a wonderful God he is and what wonderful works he has done. Point out to him specifics of what makes him so great. This will do several things for you:

- It will lift your spirit. Self-pity drags down the human spirit, but praising God lifts it up, because it puts reality in perspective.
- It will develop in you a positive spirit.
- It will teach you how to compliment people. Compliments—pointing out to others things in them that are praiseworthy—are a way we encourage people. When we learn to compliment God, it carries over into noticing and pointing out positive things in others.

TOOLBOX

Maria's Journey #5
An Extraordinary Life
in an Ordinary World

Maria is 30 now, Monica 5. I met with Maria in a Starbucks not far from her small apartment north of Toronto. The young woman sitting in front of me on a sofa showed no signs of poor health. Her neatly kept blond hair, bright blue eyes and easy smile gave no evidence that she had been suffering from chronic fatigue for the last five years. Maria lives on disability today. She has—by her own admission—virtually destroyed her body through years of sniffing cocaine, chain-smoking cigarettes and binging on alcohol. Through the power of God she has come clean of it all. But all our decisions and actions have consequences. Some leave permanent scars. Maria is learning to carry the scars and to heal from the wounds.

The moment was right for me to ask a painful question: "What happened when you were 17, Maria, that you decided to throw away your religious upbringing?"

The young woman started in thoughtfully: "Remember how you once talked to me about Bonhoeffer's notes he wrote in jail about 'religionless Christianity'?" I nodded in the affirmative, but I had no idea where Maria was going with that thought.

"I look back now on my teenage years and I realize that what I was searching for was a religionless Christianity. A Christianity that had a living and powerful and righteous God at the centre, whose purpose with us was not to choke us with religious rules and rituals but to enjoy with us a relationship. Instead, what I saw and experienced in most Christians was a religion-full Christianity, full of dos and don'ts. I started feeling pretty beat up by this version of Christianity, by the whole

303

image-thing and the consumer mentality that surrounded me. Life was about getting, getting, getting; having more and more; having it better and better; having it faster and faster...It was all so fake."

"How do you mean that?" I jumped in.

"Well, what I was hearing from your sermons was that Christianity is about experiencing a relationship of grace with a holy and righteous God, and then turning to your world with the grace received from God and extending it by serving people. But I did not feel grace coming from my Christian friends, neither to me nor toward the world. Most of my friends' Christianity was moralistic, like always doing the right thing in order to be accepted as good Christians. What was missing was grace, compassion, the freedom to be real, to struggle, to fail, to forgive. Then when someone in our church hurt me badly, I had enough. Enough of church, enough of religious Christianity, enough of being nice and fitting in. I basically bolted!"

I responded: "What brought about the difference in your life?"

Without hesitation, Maria answered: "Monica! She was a turning point in my life."

"Really? How so?"

Maria looked down at the floor for a moment. "I was so lost in the me-hole I had dug for myself. I felt like I needed someone to save me by loving me out of my hole. I was desperate for someone to fill my needs. I poured my hopes into my boyfriend, that he could sort of save me, that he could give me the love I longed for. But he was just as lost and needy for deliverance out of his hole as I was. Then I got pregnant with Monica. At first that looked like disaster, especially when he left me."

"So how was it not a disaster?"

"Monica turned out to be a gift from God. With her, I began to realize that God is not one who wants to withhold good from us but loves to share his goodness with us. When I was pregnant, I viewed her as an interruption to my plans, as a bad result of my self-destructive ways. When I held

304

her, I thought, "How gracious of God to respond to my self-destructiveness with such a beautiful gift." Then I began to have such love for Monica that I started to put her needs in front of mine. I wanted to take care of myself, sure, but taking care of Monica became more important to me than my own wellbeing. My love for her felt so good to me. It felt good to be generous and self-sacrificing. I had never loved anyone like that before. Then this thought hit me: loving someone so lavishly is the way God must love us. The second thought I had was that to love someone so selflessly feels natural, as if to love others as God has loved me is somehow the real me."

As I listened to Maria, I realized that grace, relationships and forgiveness are themes that run through her entire story. Any spirituality that emphasises self-enhancement and self-actualization, or stresses moralism and religious performance to gain God's approval, would have had no power on Maria's existence. Worse, it would have driven her deeper into her sinkhole of despair. She needed Jesus' resurrection power to get her out of her self-consumption. She needed Christ's 'alien righteousness' instead of her self-righteousness to turn her upside-down-world right-side-up. She needed the intervention from God with his scandalous crucifixion love to absolve her of guilt and let her feel clean inside.

Andrew turned out to be the way she would have to learn the cost of forgiveness.

He seemed like a very nice Christian man at first. Maria felt delighted that he took interest in her and decided quickly to give him her heart. But Maria's pursuit of Andrew was driven by the motive to find herself a husband and Monica a father. The first few times together were very special. Andrew seemed like a Christian gentleman.

The downward spiral began with a punch on Maria's shoulder. She justified his action by accusing herself for having provoked him. A few weeks later it happened again. This time he was angry at her for being late to the movie theatre. When he told her that he was disappointed in her inconsiderateness toward him by keeping him waiting in front of the movie theatre, and she snapped at him that she could not help it, Monica had suddenly gotten sick just as Maria was intending to leave the house, Andrew suddenly gave Maria a push, causing her to career into the wall. Regaining her balance, she pointed her finger in his face and warned him, that if he would ever physically mistreat her again, she would register a complaint to the police. That sent Andrew over the top: He started hitting her alongside her face with both hands, yelling, "if you ever complain to the police, I will turn you into a cripple!"

Maria was frightened and immediately turned around and rushed home. At a loss, she wrote to me in Germany and asked for advice. I counseled her that she needed to stay away from Andrew, register to the elders of his church a complaint, and immediately call the police, if he started to harass or stalk her.

My email reached her about the time her 2 year old Monica told her one night that "that man always tells me I am bad and then touches me here," pointing between her legs. Maria was horrified, enraged, scared. Andrew had not only been physically abusive toward her, he had deeply scarred her little girl. That precious gift God had given her, and a sick person was ruining it! Maria started showing signs of deep anxiety and depression. She worried if Andrew might seek some form of revenge.

But the comfort of God met Maria in some unusual places.

One of those unusual places was in a book. "I was deeply wounded in 2008 from that horrible experience," Maria explains. "I heard William Paul Young speak at a conference and was absolutely spellbound. Here I was, a young mother of a little girl who had been molested by a man who was preparing for the priesthood, and the speaker was talking about the abuse he experienced in his childhood at the hands of his father who was a missionary. His talk was so raw. He talked about growing up and hating Christianity, just like I did. He spoke of his deep-seated rage, his falseness and pretence of who he was and his betrayal of his wife. God personally confronted him and brought him to a humbling recognition that God wanted to redeem him, forgive him and have a relationship with him. But to have a righteous relationship with God, Mr. Young needed to get clean about his father. He needed to forgive his abuser. For him that became an excruciating process. He wove it into a novel about a man whose child is murdered, and God appears to him and wants him to forgive the murderer, the now famous bestseller, THE SHACK."

"What a book, eh?" I erupted. "A lot of people have criticised it. How was your experience reading THE SHACK?" I asked her.

"It is such a helpful book! There are some spots in the book where the theology is a bit obscure. Nobody should take every line from the book as an outline of classical, biblical, orthodox theology..."

"Exactly my assessment," I jumped in. "But the way God is described in the book—well, I think I fell in love with God in a deeper way as I read how he approached this deeply wounded man and explains his own heart for him and about relationships and forgiveness."

Maria beamed, "That was my experience, too. I felt God's incredible love throughout this book," her smile faded, "until I came to the part on forgiveness. At that point I grew angry, threw the book in the corner and said, 'too simplistic!' I guess I was not yet ready to face my own need to forgive Andrew' Only several months later, after God met me in a very profound way during a worship service in my church, did I pick up THE SHACK again and continue to read the section on forgiveness. It just seems so unnatural, that God— who is a big, black woman called 'Papa' in the book —would want the father of the murdered girl to forgive the murderer. I think I had such a hard time with that, because I knew deep down inside that God wanted me to forgive those who have treated me unjustly. Including Andrew!"

"You mentioned there were several unusual places where God met you."

"I could not have worked through my need to forgive Andrew without my church community."

Maria went on to explain how after moving into her apartment and praying for God's direction regarding a church community, she felt a strong sense that she should visit the church her friend had suggested to her. The priest's warm-hearted reception of her and his relational way toward everyone; the way he preached from the Bible with theological depth, passionate conviction and heart-felt practicality; and the prayer-ministry the church offered to all spelled out to Maria that she had walked into what she called 'a hospital for the hurting.' When she returned the following Sunday, the priest began a preaching series from the Bible on forgiveness. His exhortation to the forgiven to be forgiving struck Maria's heart like an arrow.

"I knew I needed to forgive Andrew before my bitterness destroyed me. That does not mean that I do not desire justice. I do! Every human desires to see justice done. I had to let go of getting revenge. Andrew should go to jail for what he has done. But even if he did, it cannot pay back his debt to us. The damage is done. The first thing our pastor helped me understand in his sermon series on forgiveness was that nothing anybody does to me can take away the fact that in Christ I am—I think you used to say this to us, didn't you?—more loved, valued, accepted and appreciated than I ever dared to hope. Getting raped or beaten or having your child molested cannot take that away from me. That fact allowed me to put my trust in God by releasing Andrew from his debt to me and leaving that debt with God. God will see to justice; I no longer carry the burden to get even. That has given me a deep-seated freedom. It also made me aware that there are other people in my life I need to forgive. Every time I do, I feel more and more free."

"How do you forgive someone like Andrew?"

"In a dream I once saw Andrew as an abused child. That helped me understand that behind this abusive man is an abused person. He needs God's healing from the abuse he received, just like I need healing from the abuse he dealt me. He may never acknowledge that he needs help, may never come to terms with the monster he keeps hidden in the closet of his spiritual basement. But I can deal with the monster in the basement closet of my life, because of the assurance that regardless how this monster looks, I need not fear it. It will not destroy me because Christ's resurrection power protects me. With the security that in Christ I am more loved than I ever dared to hope, I can open the basement closet, let the monster growl at me with his threats and curses, laugh in his face and say, 'In Jesus' name, you are as good as dead to me.'"

"Do you feel like you have really forgiven Andrew?"

"Yes! Seeing Andrew as an abused child in that dream has filled me with compassion for him. I have communicated to him that I forgive him and exactly what that means. I pray for him every day, because I realize God wants to redeem Andrew from his shattered and abused image just like he wants to redeem me from my abusive rage toward others, like my parents."

Now I dug a little deeper. "Tell me, Maria; has this left noticeable psychological scars with Monica?"

The young mother looked down at the floor again in a moment of silence, then spoke slowly in a soft tone, "Through counselling we are trying to work through the damage. One of the main ways I notice the damage is in her difficulty to trust men, especially men who appear strong and authoritative. She basically ignores their presence, pretends they are not around. She also feels sudden panic attacks. Then she calls me and asks me to pray to God with her. The trauma will take years of counselling to reverse, a tragedy of so many children in this unjust world.

"But here, too, there is a positive flipside because I can tell God is not removed from Monica's life but involved in it at every step. The kid has become fascinated with the death of Jesus, as if she senses that here lies the mystery that, if unravelled, will unleash the power to live and heal. She asks me many detailed questions about what happened at the cross."

Maria shared how she once asked Monica, "What do you think Jesus did to the soldiers who killed him?" Monica didn't think long for the answer. "He's God, so he killed them!" Maria then asked Monica if she would like to look with mommy into the Bible to find out the answer. Together they read the account. Maria tells of Monica's reaction: "She was absolutely stunned that Jesus cried out to God on behalf of those who wronged and killed him, 'Father, forgive them!' Then Monica wanted to know, 'But mommy, how could he forgive them?'"

For the next half hour I tried to explain in childish terms what is indescribable for us adults: how God's 'scandalous love' and 'burning righteousness' kissed each other in Jesus at the cross."

Maria guessed, mother and daughter will have that conversation many times in the next several decades.

Much in Maria's life has gone wrong, but she does not view her life as a tragedy. The young woman not only believes in the sovereignty of a loving God in every bad circumstance, she knows she is wiser about life and all its difficulties as a result.

I asked Maria how she views her future. She was honest with me. She told me how much she would like to feel physical strength again. A house in the country with a big garden in which she could work for hours a day and live organically—this is her dream. A husband who loves her safely, and with whom she could have several more children—"they are such wonderful gifts"—and she could stay at home and be their mommy 24 hours a day. She does not want to get sucked into the me-hole again or the trap of a consumer-driven lifestyle. She values simplicity, a stable home, family and investing in relationships, in people, in her church community. She wants to delight in God's grace and extend it to as many people as possible.

"What if you never get a husband?" I asked the sensitive question.

Maria's face had a beautiful glow to it: "I have given my desires to God. He gave me my life back by instilling his life into me. I feel the pleasures of God in so many things daily. If I never have a husband and consequently never have more children, then I want to take in foster children. I feel a deep compassion for children. Maybe that came from the dream I had of Andrew being abused as a child. Maybe my life is supposed to be about caring for many little Andrews and helping them heal."

I let the power of Maria's last remark settle in. A Geppeto to many little Pinocchios…maybe that is the reason for all her misery.

It was time to go. I offered to pray for Maria and I began to speak to Papa about the girl I have known since she was 12. I am grateful for her, for the progress in spirituality, for the many ways God has dealt kindly with her. I said 'Amen' and her hand reached for mine: "And now I want to pray for you," and she started into a compassionate prayer, asking God to heal me after my surgery, and thanking God for the friendship we have enjoyed for 18 years.

As I watch her walk out of Starbucks I cannot help but think: There goes a real smart builder!

As the ruin falls by C. S. Lewis

All this is flashy rhetoric about loving you.
I never had a selfless thought since I was born.
I am mercenary and self-seeking through and through:
I want God, you, all friends, merely to serve my turn.

Peace, re-assurance, pleasure, are the goals I seek,
I cannot crawl one inch outside my proper skin:
I talk of love --a scholar's parrot may talk Greek--
But, self-imprisoned, always end where I begin.

Only that now you have taught me (but how late) my lack.
I see the chasm. And everything you are was making
My heart into a bridge by which I might get back
From exile, and grow man. And now the bridge is breaking.

For this I bless you as the ruin falls. The pains
You give me are more precious than all other gains.

Literature

1. Standard Works

Alexander, Archibald, Thoughts on Religious Experience, Edinburgh: Banner of Truth, 1998.

Augustine, Confessions, New York: Oxford University Press, 2009.

Bonhoeffer, Dietrich, The Cost of Discipleship (Dietrich Bonhoeffer Works, 4), Philadelphia: Fortress, 2003.

Calvin, John, Institutes of the Christian Religion, Peabody: Hendrickson, 2007.

Edwards, Jonathan, Religious Affections: A Christian's Character Before God, Vancouver: Regent College, 2003.

Lloyd-Jones, Martyn D., Spiritual Depression: Its Causes and Cures, Grand Rapids: Eerdmans, 1965.

Lovelace, Richard, Dynamics of Spiritual Life: An Evangelical Theology of Renewal, Downers Grove: InterVarsity, 1979.

Luther, Martin, The Freedom of a Christian, Philadelphia: Fortress, 2008.

Packer, James I., Knowing God, Downers Grove: InterVarsity, 1993.

Packer, James I., A Quest for Godliness: The Puritan Vision of the Christian Life, Wheaton: Crossway, 2010.

Piper, John, Desiring God: Meditations of a Christian Hedonist, Sisters: Multnomah, 2011.

Piper, John, The Pleasures of God: Meditations on God's Delight in Being God, Sisters: Multnomah, 2000.

Ryle, John C., Holiness: Its Nature, Hindrances, Difficulties, and Roots, Peabody: Hendrickson, 2007.

Schaeffer, Francis A., True Spirituality, Carol Stream: Tyndale House, 2001.

Sibbes, Richard, The Bruised Reed and Smoking Flax, Edinburgh: Banner of Truth, 1998.

Spurgeon, Charles, Lectures to My Students, Peabody: Hendrickson, 2010.

2. Highly Recommended Readings

Alexander, Donald L. (ed.), Christian Spirituality: Five Views of Sanctification, Downers Grove: InterVarsity, 1989.

Bridges, Jerry, The Practice of Godliness: Godliness has value for all things, Colorado Springs: NavPress, 1996.

313

Bridges, Jerry, THE PURSUIT OF HOLINESS, Colorado Springs: Nav-Press, 2006.

Bridges, Jerry, THE DISCIPLINE OF GRACE: GOD'S ROLE AND OUR ROLE IN THE PURSUIT OF HOLINESS, Colorado Springs: NavPress, 2006.

Erickson, Millard J., POSTMODERNIZING THE FAITH: EVANGELICAL RESPONSES TO THE CHALLENGE OF POSTMODERNISM, Grand Rapids: Baker, 1998.

Ferguson, Sinclair, A HEART FOR GOD, Edinburgh: Banner of Truth, 1987.

Lawrenz, Mel, THE DYNAMICS OF SPIRITUAL FORMATION, Grand Rapids: Baker, 2000.

MacDonald, Gordon, ORDERING YOUR PRIVATE WORLD, Nashville: Thomas Nelson, 2007.

MacDonald, Gordon, RENEWING YOUR SPIRITUAL PASSION, Nash-ville: Thomas Nelson, 1997.

McGrath, Alister E., SPIRITUALITY IN AN AGE OF CHANGE: REDIS-COVERING THE SPIRIT OF THE REFORMERS, Grand Rapids: Zondervan, 1994.

Murray, Andrew, IN SEARCH OF SPIRITUAL EXCELLENCE, New Kens-ington: Whitaker House, 1994.

Piper, John, A HUNGER FOR GOD: DESIRING GOD THROUGH FASTING AND PRAYER, Wheaton: Crossway, 1997.

Scorgie, Glen, A LITTLE GUIDE TO CHRISTIAN SPIRITUALITY: THREE DIMENSIONS OF LIFE WITH GOD, Grand Rapids: Zondervan, 2007.

Stott, John R.W., LIFE IN CHRIST: A GUIDE FOR DAILY LIVING, Grand Rapids: Baker, 2003.

Yancey, Philip, WHAT'S SO AMAZING ABOUT GRACE?, Grand Rapids: Zondervan, 2002.

Acknowledgements & Gratitude

This book was a team project. Many friends and family members in different countries read over the manuscript and offered valuable suggestions. Thanks, first and foremost, to my dear wife, Susan, for spending untold hours incisively cutting through the manuscript as well as desperately trying to shorten it.

In the *USA*, my brother and philosopher at Liberty University, Prof. Dr. W. David Beck, helped me especially with the chapter on the Bible. My good friend, David Heinaman, the first person in my life who made apologetics exciting to me, offered many helpful suggestions to my interaction with postmodern thinking. Drew Davis had particularly valuable suggestions to offer to several chapters.

In *Canada*, my English friend Dr. Bob Penhearow, president of Carey Outreach Ministries, read through portions of this manuscript with a particular eye on its usefulness in non-western countries. My dear friend, Dr. Gene Haas, professor of Systematic Theology at Redeemer University in Ontario, Canada, offered helpful insights to the contents of several chapters. My daughter, Sarah Fullerton, spent many hours of editorial work on the manuscript, improving the English and helping me express things in a manner that a European, whose native language is not English, can understand. Thank you.

In *Germany*, I thank Professor Dr. Armin Baum, a New Testament scholar and dear colleague of mine at the Freie Theologische Hochschule, who made sure that my biblical analyses were at a level of integrity. A former student of mine, Phillip Kriegeskotte, who was part of our team that planted Frankfurt CityChurch, gave sound feedback from the postmodern German perspective. Special thanks to my two assistants at the seminary, Anthony Fisher and Karyn Noll, for their feedback and contributions to the content.

In *England*, two young adults deserve special thanks from me for evaluating portions of this book from the young English scene. Both are living out Christian spirituality in the everything-goes culture of Camden, London: my daughter, Elizabeth Beck, and her co-worker, Ollie Smith.

Special thanks to Daniel Weninger, and his staff at pulsmedien. This young and growing publishing company in Germany was willing to publish klug_bauen in 2007, and now has taken the risk of branching out into a vastly expanded 2nd edition in English, with German and Russian editions to follow. Pulsmedien is open to the service of publishing this book in other languages as per request. I pray God will bless the faith and vision of the people at pulsmedien.

Thank you all! Thank you, God!
Stephen